**MARKETING FOR YOUR
GROWING BUSINESS**

Small Business Management Series
Rick Stephan Hayes, Editor

Simplified Accounting for Non-Accountants
 by Rick Stephan Hayes and C. Richard Baker

Accounting for Small Manufacturers
 by C. Richard Baker and Rick Stephan Hayes

Simplified Accounting for Engineering and Technical Consultants
 by Rick Stephan Hayes and C. Richard Baker

Simplified Accounting for the Computer Industry
 by Rick Stephan Hayes and C. Richard Baker

The Complete Legal Guide for Your Small Business
 by Paul Adams

Running Your Own Show: Mastering Basics of Small Business
 by Richard T. Curtin

Up Front Financing: The Entrepreneur's Guide
 by A. David Silver

How to Finance Your Small Business with Government Money: SBA and Other Loans, Second Edition
 by Rick Stephan Hayes and John Cotton Howell

The Entrepreneurial Life: How To Go For It and Get It
 by A. David Silver

The Complete Guide to Buying and Selling a Business
 by Arnold S. Goldstein

Getting Paid: Building Your Powerful Credit and Collection Strategy
 by Arnold S. Goldstein

Choosing Your Sources of Venture Capital
 by A. David Silver

Starting on a Shoestring: Building a Business Without a Bankroll
 by Arnold S. Goldstein

The Fundamentals of the Business Plan: A Step by Step Approach
 by Harold McLaughlin

Venture Capital: The Complete Guide for Investors
 by A. David Silver

Marketing for Your Growing Business
 by Rick Stephan Hayes and Gregory Brooks Elmore

MARKETING FOR YOUR GROWING BUSINESS

Rick Stephan Hayes
Gregory Brooks Elmore

A Ronald Press Publication
JOHN WILEY & SONS
New York   Chichester   Brisbane   Toronto   Singapore

Copyright © 1985 by John Wiley & Sons, Inc.

All rights reserved. Published simultaneously in Canada.

Reproduction or translation of any part of this work beyond that permitted by Section 107 or 108 of the 1976 United States Copyright Act without the permission of the copyright owner is unlawful. Requests for permission or further information should be addressed to the Permissions Department, John Wiley & Sons, Inc.

This publication is designed to provide accurate and authoritative information in regard to the subject matter covered. It is sold with the understanding that the publisher is not engaged in rendering legal, accounting, or other professional service. If legal advice or other expert assistance is required, the services of a competent professional person should be sought. *From a Declaration of Principles jointly adopted by a Committee of the American Bar Association and a Committee of Publishers.*

Library of Congress Cataloging in Publication Data:

Hayes, Rick Stephan, 1946-
   Marketing for your growing business.

   (Small business management series)
   "A Ronald Press publication."
   Includes index.
   1. Marketing.   I. Elmore, Gregory Brooks.   II. Title.
III. Series.

HF5415.H285   1985   658.8   84-25645

ISBN 0-471-09199-5

Printed in the United States of America

10 9 8 7 6 5 4 3 2 1

To all my students and clients,
who continue to teach me.

R.S.H.

To S.C.L. and S.L.S.
for their love and understanding;
and to my parents . . . for everything.

G.B.E.

PREFACE

There is a certain rogue, rascal, and vagabond—we never say his name lest he overhear us and pay us a visit—who travels from place to place, making his living (and a very good one it is) from the folly of others. Now there is the strangest thing about this fellow: nobody knows what he looks like, though he has been seen by nearly everyone in every village. Some say he's short, some tall, some lean, some fat. No one agrees with the others. Here's a story about him.

> One day, as the tradespeople began to gather in the marketplace, who should they find in the very center of the square but our rascally friend, sitting before a large pot, stirring it with a stick, and mumbling some strange words over it.
>
> This curious sight attracted the attention of several merchants, who gathered about him. Beside the pot was a sizable pile of golden coins. The pile grew every minute or so by the addition of one or more coins from the pot. Our vagabond would stir the pot, mumble something, reach into the pot, and pull from its recesses a golden coin.
>
> Naturally, such a sight as this raised a good deal of curiosity, and soon a large crowd gathered around. The affairs of the marketplace had gone to the devil. Finally, those who had been there longest could stand it no longer. They asked that rascal what he was doing.
>
> "Ah, but you can see plainly," he said. "I'm making my day's supply of gold out of the fine river mud that you have here."
>
> "Gold out of mud? You must be a madman."
>
> "Madman or not," replied the rogue, removing yet another piece of gold, "you can see the results."
>
> "But how is it done?"
>
> "Ah, that is a professional secret. After all, this is my living."
>
> A quick consultation took place among the merchants. With such an easy way of procuring wealth at hand, it behooved them to determine the secret.
>
> "Allow us to ease some of your labors," said the leader. "We will give you a thousand gold pieces for the secret—enough to last you for months."
>
> "Ah, no," said the rogue. "It is easy enough work, as you see," and he removed another piece of gold from the pot of mud.

Another consultation took place. "We will give you ten thousand pieces for the secret," said the merchants. But again the rascal demurred and added not one, but two pieces of gold to his pile.

"We will make you the richest man in these parts," said the merchants after yet another consultation. "If you tell us the secret, we will give you all the gold we have. With such wealth, you will never have to work again."

"Very well," said the rogue, with a great show of reluctance. "I will tell you. It's really very simple. This is no magical pot, nor is the mud special mud. The secret is in the words which you must recite continually as you stir the pot. When you have recited the magical formula three times, you may reach into the pot and retrieve the gold. Now I must not reveal the words of the formula publicly, so I will whisper them to your leader, and thus pass on in the traditional manner the secret of my craft."

Then, with much show of secrecy and pomp, the vagabond took the merchant aside and delivered the magic words. Then he handed over the pot and the stick and was given in exchange all the gold that the merchants had with them. There was so much gold that if he had not had a donkey with him, he could not have carried it 10 feet.

Immediately the merchant sat down in the village square and prepared to apply the secret knowledge imparted to him, and all the others gathered around to watch. Carefully he stirred, while our rogue loaded the donkey. "One moment!" cried the rogue, as he rushed back to the square. "I have forgotten to tell you the most important secret of all. When you have recited the formula three times and are reaching into the pot, you must not, under any circumstances whatever, think about the brown monkey!"

From a traditional folktale, thanks to Paul Jordan-Smith.

This story illustrates some important marketing concepts. The rogue knew his general market (greed) and his market segment (the merchants) very well. He knew how they thought and what they would do. You could say he understood who his customers were and how to get to them.

He offered a product (the pot and stick) and a service (the secret) that his customers desired and for which they would pay. His product and service seemed to be right for the market.

His timing was right, he had the image that the merchants would buy, and he was very persuasive.

But then there was the brown monkey. Was his a defective product? A poor service? Like I said, he knew the market.

The purpose of this book is to allow you to understand your market and your customers and how to increase sales by knowing this.

RICK STEPHAN HAYES
GREGORY BROOKS ELMORE

Topanga Canyon, California
Mt. Washington, California
March 1985

CONTENTS

1. **Introduction**   1

   Timing, Image, and Persuasion   2
   Market Planning   5
   Contents of This Book   6

2. **Defining Your Market**   11

   Profile of the Market   12
   Market Segmentation   27
   Target Markets   33
   Summary   36

3. **Market Research**   38

   Importance of Market Research   38
   Steps in a Research Project   39
   Primary or Secondary Information   43
   Secondary (Strategic) Research   43
   Industry Secondary (Strategic) Research   45
   Consumer Secondary Research   50
   Competitor/Industrial Customer Secondary Information Research   52
   Tactical (Primary) Research   55
   Preparing a Questionnaire   56
   How to Conduct Mailings and Interviews   57
   Processing and Analyzing the Data   59
   Summary   61

4. Customers: Your Best Source of Money — 62

    Your Customer — 62
    Locating Your Business — 63
    Secondary and Primary Research in Location Analysis — 67
    Methods for Building a Customer Base — 78
    Customer Referrals — 84
    Summary — 86

5. It's All in the Image—Well, Most of It, Anyway! — 87

    Choosing an Image — 88
    Your Company's Present Image — 97
    Creating an Image of Your Company — 99
    Public Relations — 101
    The Press Release — 104
    Articles for Trade Publications — 111
    The Press Kit — 111

6. Design Advertising: Brochures and Printed Material — 113

    Logo, Letterhead, and Business Forms — 114
    Brochures — 118
    Steps to Preparing a Brochure — 120
    Package Design — 127
    Summary — 128

7. Advertising Channels — 164

    Planning Your Advertising — 165
    Yellow Pages and Directories — 169
    Newspapers — 171
    Trade Publications and Magazines — 171
    Outdoor Advertising — 172
    Transit Advertising — 172
    Radio — 173
    Television — 174
    Displays — 174
    Point of Purchase — 175

Advertising Specialties	175
Special Promotions	175
Trade Shows	176
Seminars	180
Telephone Sales	181
Summary	184

8. Putting Your Program Together — **185**

Making a Marketing Plan	185
Paying for the Plan	197
Product Pricing	200
Distributors and Representatives	204
Summary	206

APPENDIXES

1.	**Sample Market Plan (The Country Garden)**	209
2.	**Reference Sources for Media Planning**	225
3.	**Marketing Sources of Information**	229
4.	**Press Release Information Forms**	241
5.	**Marketing Glossary**	247
6.	**Bank of America Small Business Reporter**	263
7.	**National Directories for Use in Marketing**	271

INDEX — **281**

1

INTRODUCTION

Hodj'a Eddin went to the bazaar to buy some cloth. To his dismay, he found that the booths of the cloth vendors were full of customers, bidding against each other and driving the prices up. After a moment's thought, the wily Hodj'a placed himself at the lower end of the bazaar and began to shout, "Oh people! You should see the bargains at this end of the bazaar! Oh, what bargains! They are giving things away down here!"

A few people moved away from the cloth vendors' booths to see what the noise was about. Someone began to walk faster and then someone else ran, and soon more and more people were flocking into the booths at the lower end of the bazaar, leaving those of the cloth vendors practically empty.

Hodj'a watched them running to the lower end of the bazaar first with glee and then with growing anxiety.

"I wonder," he thought. "What if . . .?" And he ran as fast as he could after the crowd.

Everyone seems to be confused about what happens in the marketplace. It is a place of mystery. How do you get people to buy? How do you find and influence the people who do buy? Why is a product hot one day and a disaster the next?

Understanding the market takes work. It is not easy to make the right decisions, to get the right product or service to the right people at the right time. One company can have a great product that dies; another company can have a mediocre product for which they can't meet the demand. Of course, some say market success is due to what people call luck. This may be true, but the difference between short-term and long-term success owes more to understanding the market and planning than to luck.

This book is designed to help you understand the marketplace. This is a *workbook*. That means two things: (1) it requires some work on your part, and (2) there are forms and illustrations to help you in the learning process. Filling in the forms in the book will not only help you discover your own market but will allow you to understand the process. The best way to understand is by doing.

Understanding marketing requires that you grasp the totality of what a market is. Understanding marketing also requires that you understand your immediate customer. All elements of marketing are interrelated and important. Understanding one requires understanding the other. The following story illustrates why you cannot isolate one area from the others.

Once upon a time—and this is a true story—there was a student. He used to go every day to sit at the feet of a great teacher to take down on paper what the master said.

Because he was so fully occupied with his studies, he was unable to follow any gainful occupation. One evening when he arrived home, his wife placed a bowl before him, covered with a napkin. He took the cloth and put it around his neck, and then he saw that the dish was full of—pens and paper. "Since this is what you do all day," she said, "just try to eat it."

The next morning the student went, as usual, to learn from his teacher. Although his wife's words had distressed him, he continued to follow the accustomed pattern of studies and did not go out looking for a job.

After a few minutes' writing, he found that his pen was not working well. "Never mind," said the master, "go into that corner and bring the box you will find there and put it in front of you." When he sat down with the box and opened its lid, he found that it was full of—food.

You need physical nourishment as well as mental nourishment. You need to know about your immediate customer as well as the general market. You need to get out and actually do the required market research as well as read this book.

This book will start with the basic knowledge and then assist you in putting your marketing efforts into action.

It is said that there are three secrets to business success—*cash*, *cash*, and *cash*! There are also three secrets to marketing: timing, image, and persuasion.

TIMING, IMAGE, AND PERSUASION

Your business success depends on three factors and three factors only: timing, image, and persuasion (T.I.P.).

Buckminster Fuller considered the equilateral triangle the strongest structure in the universe. The triangle is strong and stable. The three areas for success in marketing suggest the use of this triangle. Illustration 1.1 shows the concept of the marketing triangle. Each side of the triangle represents one of the three T.I.P. concepts.

One of the oldest symbols is the circle, which has been said to represent the closed family, the sun, the earth, or a dragon swallowing its tail. It is the sign of eternity. Around the triangle in Illustration 1.1 are two circles. The inner circle represents a target market. The outer circle represents the market segment. Outside the circle is the whole of the marketplace.

ILLUSTRATION 1.1 The T.I.P. Marketing Model.

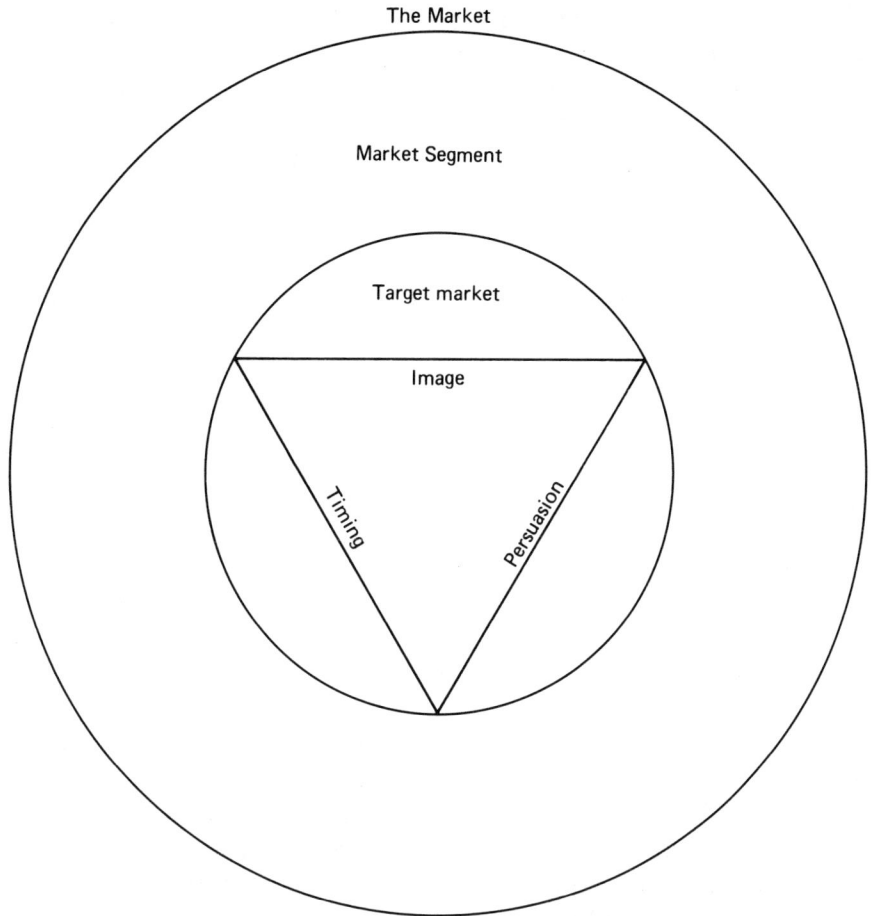

Timing

Timing is the most difficult of all the factors in your sales success. If you were a computer manufacturer in the late 1970s and early 1980s, when would you start manufacturing microcomputers? Apple started literally out of a garage in the mid-1970s. Their timing was right. IBM didn't get into the market until 1982. Their timing was also right. But only because they were a large, very experienced, and extremely profitable corporation. Other manufacturers who made more innovative computers at about the same time that the IBM-PC came onto the market (Osborne Computers) didn't do quite so well.

The company, like John Your's Yourcompany, that started in energy efficiency related businesses during the oil boycott also had the right timing. In the early 1900s a man came along with an idea of efficient manufacturing using a production line and a black car that he named after himself. His timing was right. In the 1970s a brilliant, experienced auto man started a manufacturing company that he also named after himself. His company manufactured a stainless steel–bodied car in Ireland. His timing was not as good.

Timing is a matter of understanding a marketplace very well, being ready to innovate, and having a bit of luck. There are markets in the next decade that still provide many opportunities. Industries like telecommunications, alternative energy, biological technologies, robotics, health products, and computers are expanding rapidly. In the upcoming years, the timing should be right for some component of these industries to be successful.

In the majority of cases good timing makes the difference between success and failure. To quote the fourth century B.C. Chinese philosopher Lao Tsu, good timing "anticipates things that are difficult while they are easy, and does things that would become great when they are small."

Image

Image is something that many small businesses ignore. But it is very important and the earlier a business creates an image it wishes to maintain, the better its success. A business creates an image whether it wants to or not. Whether that image is a good one that will help sales or a bad one that will hurt business is largely up to the business owner.

What image does your customer have of you? This is a basic question in determining your company's marketing and sales approach.

The way people think of your firm will be influenced by the way you conduct your business. If people come to your place of business, the premises must be clean and well designed with an atmosphere conducive to buying. If you take your service to the customer, the conduct of your employees (and your own, of course) will influence your image. Pleasant, prompt, and courteous service before and after the sale will help make satisfied customers.

Your company image is like a mirror. When people look into it, they see something they recognize. If you leave it to chance, your customers' image of the company may not be the one you want.

IBM, Texaco, and all the major corporations do advertising just to bolster their image. Even before Calculating Accounting Tabulating Machine Company changed their name to International Business Machine (IBM), they were concerned with image.

If your customer imagines your product or service to be high quality, well designed, innovative, or efficient even before they see you, do you think they will be more likely to buy? That is the benefit of a good image.

Persuasion

Persuasion is the art of convincing people to buy from you. Of the three components of sales success, persuasion techniques get the most play.

Persuasion takes many identifiable forms. A business persuades by its advertising, public relations, one-on-one discussion, group discussion, product quality, product packaging, pricing, distribution, and sales approach.

Persuasion is not a one-way street. You have to know what your customers want, who they are, and where they are before you can persuade them. This involves market research. You must get feedback not only from your customer, but from your industry itself.

Persuasion is making the mind of the people your mind.

The Market and Market Segments

Market means that group of individuals (customers) who will buy the product or service offered. The market for toothpaste is every man, woman, and child in the world who has teeth. The U.S. market for toothpaste is every man, woman, and child in the United States who has teeth.

Market segment means a part of a larger market. The market segment is an identifiable part of a larger whole market. A market segment of every man, woman, and child in the United States who has teeth would be children in the United States who have teeth, that is, a children's toothpaste market segment.

No small business can ever hope to get all the market for a product or service, but they can hope to control a segment of a large market. Apple Computer started their company to build a computer for a market segment of computer users—the computer hobbyist. At that time the computer hobbyist was a very small segment of the total number of computer users. Apple did not build a computer to replace the large defense and mathematical computers, the scientific computers, the mainframes, or the minicomputers.

As the market for microcomputer users grew, microcomputers became a large market (several billion dollars per year). When microcomputers became a large market it spawned many market segments: surge suppressors, software, peripherals, and so on.

A market is the overall customer base for a product or service; the market segment is a smaller, definable part of that larger customer base.

To find the best market segment for your company, you must first know the total market. Understanding the market segments will permit you to target your market. Techniques for doing both are discussed in Chapter 2.

MARKET PLANNING

In order to pursue increased sales, some planning is required. Planning helps minimize cost, give the company direction, and maximize effort.

Planning is a way to proceed efficiently. A market plan can provide the owner-manager with a pathway to profit. Unfortunately, the pathway to profit is lined with signposts bearing questions that require answers: What business am I in? What services do I provide? Where is my market? Who will buy? Who is the competition? What is my sales strategy? What merchandising methods will I use? How much money is needed? How will I price my product? How will I get the work done? . . .

This book is designed to help you answer these questions to clarify your own pathway.

It takes time, energy, and patience to draw up a satisfactory market plan. Use this book to get your ideas and the supporting facts down on paper. This book is designed as a participative plan for action covering all the major considerations in do-it-yourself marketing.

Market Plan

The market plan outline on page 7 will be explained and used in this book.

Your Answers

Throughout this book we will use a fill-in-the-blank participative approach to learning. There are a few questions you can start to answer right now using Form 1.1. *Note:* If you can't answer the questions, read Chapter 3.

CONTENTS OF THIS BOOK

Market research, market planning, pricing, advertising, and supervising the company image is a lot of work.

This book tries to make your workload a little lighter by guiding you through the marketing steps and allowing you at the same time to shape your own company's marketing, advertising, and sales programs. Workbooklike forms are included throughout this book so that you can begin to understand your own marketing programs.

The book is filled with charts, examples, and illustrations to render complicated ideas more simply.

Chapter 2 helps you define what your market is. The chapter also describes identifying market segments and target markets and the implementation of market mix.

Chapter 3 is on how to research the market. Research scares many entrepreneurs because it seems complicated. In this book the research process is simplified. This chapter describes the best business resources published. It also describes how to do "primary" research with questionnaires, including what types of questions to ask and how.

The title of Chapter 4, Customers: Your Best Source of Money, is a fairly accurate description of its contents. This chapter discusses your relationship with your customer, including how to create customer goodwill, how to get customer referrals, and how to increase the percentage of sales. The chapter also shows how to pick the right location. Location is so important, especially to a retailer, that the chapter takes you step by step from locating the best area for your type of customer to how to select a good store site.

Marketing Plan for Company

Profile and Products
- Profile of company
- Objectives of company
- Product or service description
- Advantages of these products over competition

Industry and Competition
- Historical growth of industry
- Government and industry interaction
- Technological and competitive factors
- List and description of five top competitors

Market Size
- Industry total market size in dollar volume and units
- Specific segment market size in dollars and units
- Your sales as a percentage of total market segment

Sales Objectives
- Results to be produced
- Objectives for next and future years

Customers
- Definition of who your customer is
- Company location and customers
- Customer money available for product purchases
- Media that reach these customers
- Lists of customers

Market Strategy
- Product
- Promotion
- Pricing
- Place (distribution)

Plan Implementation
- Who does what, where, how and when? A time and milestone schedule of implementation of market plan and a budget.

FORM 1.1 Profile and Products

Profile of Company

What business are you in?
___
___

What products or services do you offer and why?
___
___
___

Objectives of Company

Where do you want your company to be in 5 years?
___
___

Where do you want the company to be in 1 year?
___
___
___

Product or Service Description

How would you describe your product or service?
___
___
___
___

Advantages of Your Product or Service Over Competition

List the products or service your competitors offer customers.
___
___

List the products or services you offer customers.
___
___

Why is your product or service better?
___
___
___

Industry and Competition

Historical Growth of Industry

Has the industry you are in grown quickly? slowly? by what percentage?
___
___

FORM 1.1 Continued

Government and Industry Interaction

What are the government requirements in your industry?
_____
_____
_____

Technological and Competitive Factors

What is the most important technological factor in your industry?
_____
_____

How will you take advantage of this technology?
_____
_____
_____

List and Description of Five Top Competitors

Who are your top five competitors?
1. _____ 4. _____
2. _____ 5. _____
3. _____

How is your company better than them?
_____
_____
_____

Industry Total Market Size?

What is the total dollar volume of your industry nationwide?
_____

What is the dollar volume of your industry locally?
_____

What are your sales as a percentage of total local market?
_____
_____

Chapter 5 is about that ever so important factor in a business success: image. The chapter gives you techniques for creating the right company image. The chapter shows you how to get free advertising for your business. The chapter shows you how to prepare a press kit, how to write a good press release for publication, and how to get columns and articles into trade magazines.

Chapter 6 discusses advertising design. It discusses package design, logo, and letterhead design. The chapter shows you how to minimize cost when you do advertising design.

Chapter 7 discusses all the advertising channels available to sell your product or service:

Print media—newspapers, trades, Yellow Pages, brochures, flyers, billboards, and catalogs.

Broadcast media—radio, film, and television.

Promotions—displays, attractions, attention getters.

Person-to-person—telephone sales, seminars, trade shows, and in-house salespeople.

The last chapter, Chapter 8, takes all the components of your marketing program and shows you how to put them together into a marketing plan. It also explains how to put your plan into action, how to pick distributors and representatives, how to budget, and how to price your product.

The appendixes contain a sample market plan, a glossary, lists of resources, and other pertinent materials.

The object of this book is to give the small business person all the necessary techniques and procedures for shaping a marketing program in a manner that is easy to understand. This book is, above all, a practical guide. Each chapter will give you something that you can use the next day to strengthen your sales.

There are many more techniques than we cover in this book. There are more comprehensive guides to resources available at the bookstore. There are more detailed guides to everything discussed herein. To make your job of understanding marketing and getting a program going, we have only included the best, easiest, and most popular techniques. When we had a choice between the theoretical and the practical aspects of marketing, we chose the ones we knew would work.

Your primary job as a business owner or manager is to generate more sales; our job is to help you with your job.

2

DEFINING YOUR MARKET

What leads a small business person to discover marketing?

1. Decline in the sales volume.
2. Lack of growth in an industry.
3. Changes in the buying patterns due to changes in customer wants.
4. Increased competition.
5. Increased costs for sales expenditures.

You've identified a problem with your business, and you know it's marketing related. The next step is to begin to solve the problem by understanding the market.

To simplify the complexity of the marketplace, the authors use a model (see Illustration 2.1) that reduces marketing to six basic concepts:

The market.
Market segments.
Target markets.
Timing.
Image.
Persuasion.

The T.I.P. model consists of an equilateral triangle enclosed within two concentric circles. The area outside the largest circle is the market, which includes all those who can benefit from the producer's product or service and who can afford to buy it.

The inner circle represents the market segments or segmentation. Market segments are groups of consumers who share common characteristics. Inside the inner circle are the target markets. A market segment that you decide to serve becomes your target market.

The three remaining concepts are elements of a single equilateral triangle. Think of the triangle in the center as the place where the most focused and important marketing decisions will be made.

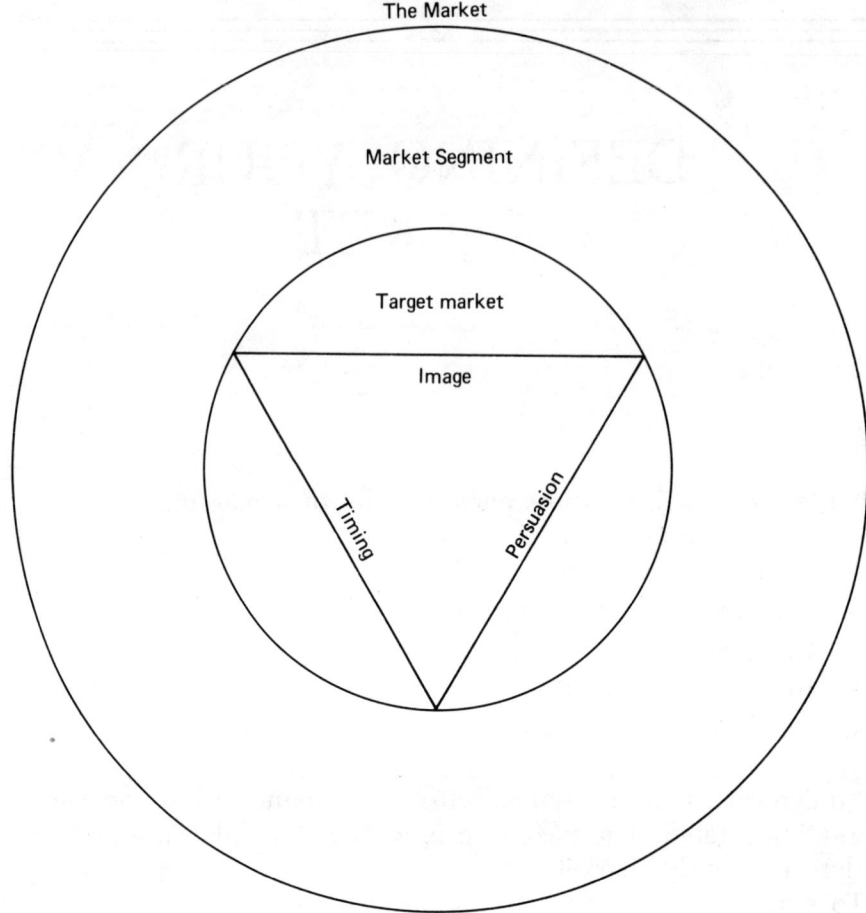

ILLUSTRATION 2.1 The T.I.P. Marketing Model.

Timing, in the marketing sense, is being at the right place, at the right time, with the right product. Timing is a variable of the outside marketplace that can change with little or no advance notice. *Image*, on the other hand, is a long-term concept that should be contemplated and cultivated. It permeates every aspect of the business as your customer views it. The short-term element is *persuasion*. It must be applied continuously. Persuasion closes the sale and reinforces the entire marketing effort.

This is a simple and nontheoretical view of the components of your market. The T.I.P. triangle will allow you to relate any aspect of marketing to timing, image, or persuasion. Some exhibit the influence of all three!

PROFILE OF THE MARKET

A market can be defined as the set of all actual and potential users of a product or service. For most small businesses, the shear magnitude of the total market can be somewhat overwhelming. Take, for example, the fact that the total U.S. consumer market is made up of more than 230 million people! This bit of market data is meaningless to a small business.

Using the information from Chapter 1, Profile and Products (Form 1.1), you can begin to characterize the overall market you want to examine. The size of a market will depend on the number of consumers who:

1. Have an interest in the product or service.
2. Have the necessary resources to obtain the product or service.
3. Have a willingness to relinquish those resources to obtain the product or service.

Implied in our definition of a market is what an economist would refer to as demand. This is a demand for products, goods, and services that satisfy needs. The ability of the customer to vote with his or her checkbook, especially in the consumer market, is a fundamental of the marketing system. That is, the customer decides which products to buy and from which firms to buy them.

If you are unsure of the market you are in or wish to enter, an excellent source for an overview is the *U.S. Industrial Outlook*, published annually by the U.S. Department of Commerce/Industry and Trade Administration. It comes out at the beginning of each calendar year. Industry forecasts, profiles, trends, and statistical information highlight this valuable source. This publication is for sale by the U.S. Government Printing Office; a copy may also be found in the reference section of most libraries. See Illustration 2.2 for a sample industry outlook.

In addition to this material, industry trade associations can be contacted for more specific information. This source will be explored in more depth in the chapters dealing with market research and your customer.

ILLUSTRATION 2.2 U.S. Industrial Outlook: Sample Chapter.

Household Consumer Durables

In 1982, combined product shipments by those household durable industries this chapter covers—household furniture (SIC 251), household appliances (SIC 363), and consumer electronics (SIC 3651)—are expected to increase about 3.5 percent from 1981 levels and to total $20.7 billion, after adjusting for inflation. In 1981, the combined value of product shipments declined 2.7 percent from 1980 levels.

Reflecting the Nation's economic slowdown, manufacturing activity in the furniture, household appliance, and consumer electronics industries was sluggish in 1980 and 1981. In 1982, moderating inflationary pressures together with increased levels of personal income resulting from mid-1982 income tax reductions and an expected upturn in residential construction, are expected to improve manufacturers' sales of household durables in the second half of the year. In the years beyond 1982, shipments of these household goods are expected to rise significantly in order to accommodate the needs of the Nation's fast-growing population group—the high-spending 25- to 34-year olds.

Buoyed by spending on consumer electronics, personal consumption expenditures for household durables covered in this chapter rose at a faster rate annually than total personal consumption expenditures in constant dollars from 1972 to 1980. As a proportion of all consumer spending, expenditures for these household durables rose from 4.4 percent in 1972 to 4.6 percent since 1977, solely because of large increases in spending on consumer electronic products. During the 8-year period, expenditures on consumer electronic products rose at a 6.7 percent compound annual rate while spending on appliances and household furniture increased at annual rates of 0.8 percent and 2.0 percent, respectively.

Shipments of automobile radios should increase about 8.8

Because of rapidly rising consumer purchases of imported televisions, video cassette recorders, and radios during the

Household Consumer Durables—1980–82
(value of product shipments, in millions of 1972 dollars)

SIC Code		1980[1]	Percent change 1979–80	1981[1]	Percent change 1980–81	1982[1]	Percent change 1981–82
	Total	20,550	−4.5	20,005	−2.7	20,695	3.5
251	Household furniture	7,200	−9.5	7,250	0.6	7,325	1.0
363	Household appliances	7,960	−1.7	7,720	−3.1	7,955.0	3.6
3651	Consumer electronics	5,390	0.8	5,035	−6.6	5,375	6.7

[1] Estimated by Bureau of Industrial Economics (BIE).

Selected Household Durables: Personal Consumption Expenditures
(billions of dollars)

Expenditure	1972	1977	1978	1979	1980	Compound annual rate of growth 1972–80
Total personal consumption expenditures:						
Current dollars	733.0	1,205.0	1,348.7	1,510.9	1,672.8	10.9
Constant dollars (1972)	733.0	823.7	863.9	930.9	935.1	3.1
Personal consumption expenditures on:						
Furniture, including mattresses and bedsprings						
Current dollars	9.9	14.6	16.2	18.3	18.4	8.1
Constant dollars (1972)	9.9	11.2	11.8	12.5	11.6	2.0
Kitchen and other household appliances						
Current dollars	11.1	13.5	14.9	16.8	17.7	5.3
Constant dollars (1972)	11.1	10.6	11.1	11.8	11.9	0.8
Radio and television receivers, records, and musical instruments						
Current dollars	11.4	17.0	18.7	20.3	21.6	8.3
Constant dollars (1972)	11.4	15.9	17.2	18.3	19.1	6.7
Total personal consumption expenditures on selected household durables:						
Current dollars	32.4	45.1	49.8	55.4	57.7	7.5
Constant dollars (1972)	32.4	37.7	40.1	42.6	42.6	3.5

Source: *Survey of Current Business*, Bureau of Economic Analysis.

U.S. Industrial Outlook 1982

ILLUSTRATION 2.2 Continued

1970's, the increase in manufacturers' shipments of consumer electronics products from 1972 to 1980 was about half the rate of increase in consumer spending on these products. Imports of consumer electronics accounted for more than 50 percent of apparent consumption of these products in 1980. In contrast, imports of major household appliances and furniture account for an insignificant share of domestic consumption, reflecting high transportation costs for these bulky products.
—*Renee L. Gallop, Office of Consumer Goods and Service Industries.*

CONSUMER ELECTRONICS

The U.S. consumer electronics industry (SIC 3651) produces television receivers, video disc players, automobile radios, phonographs, radio-phonograph combinations, stereo compact systems, high-fidelity system components, autosound systems, loud speakers, microphones, and related products.

According to the most recent Census of Manufactures (1977), 575 establishments were classified as belonging in this industry. Of these, 189 had 20 or more employees. Total employment and the number of production workers in the industry have been declining over the past decade and numbered approximately 68,000 and 50,000, respectively, in 1981.

During the past two decades, the composition and product orientation of the industry have changed substantially. Color television receivers have become the principal product, currently accounting for about 58 percent of the industry's shipments. Video disc players, which have only recently entered the market, are expected to become an important consumer electronics product.

Conspicuous by their absence from this list are consumer radios, audio tape recorder-players, and video cassette recorders (VCR's). Production of radios and audio tape recorders began to shift to Japan and elsewhere in the Far East in the 1950's, and it no longer exists in the United States. Volume production of consumer VCR's originated in Japan, with some parallel development by Philips in Europe. The United States does not produce any VCR's at this time.

As the U.S. market for color television receivers grew during the 1970's, imports also increased, particularly from Japan. From 1971 to 1974, U.S. imports of color TV receivers from Japan averaged approximately 1 million units a year, and then increased to a peak of more than 2 million units in 1976. An orderly marketing agreement (OMA) reached with Japan in 1977 resulted in a 25-percent drop in imports from Japan in that year and a continuing drop through 1980, when the OMA lapsed. In 1981, imports of complete receivers increased an estimated 52 percent. In 1979, additional orderly marketing agreements were concluded with Taiwan and Korea.

The consumer electronics industry has always been extremely competitive; imports from the Far East made it more so in the 1970's. In the face of this competition, U.S. manufacturers began to withdraw from the color TV receiver market, either discontinuing their operations or selling them.

With concern increasing in the United States over the rise in imports of TV sets from Japan, culminating in the OMA, Japanese producers began to acquire or build production facilities in the United States. The number of U.S.-owned firms declined from 18 in 1968 to 5 in 1981, while the number of foreign-owned companies increased from none to 9. U.S. plants with Far East ownership now supply 30 percent of U.S. industry shipments of TV color receivers.

Current Situation

Shipments by the consumer electronics industry grew at an

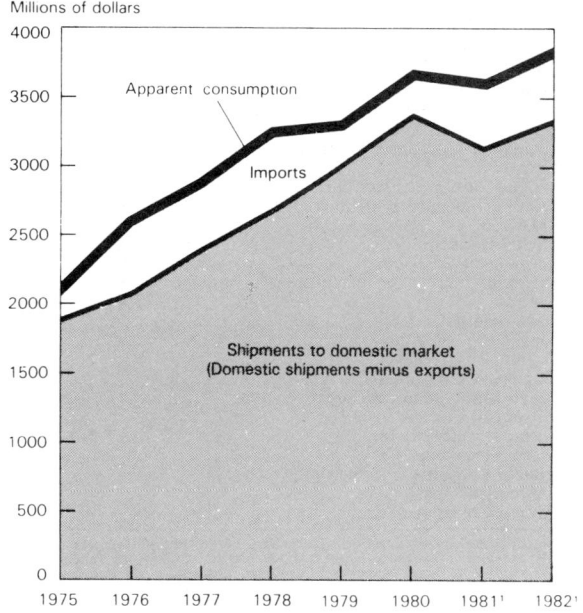

Color Television Receivers: Shipments, Imports, and Apparent Consumption

[1] Estimated by Bureau of Industrial Economics
Sources: Bureau of the Census, U.S. International Trade Commission

annual compound rate of 3.7 percent from 1972 to 1981. In 1981, however, they declined 7.4 percent, from a high of $6.6 billion (current dollars) to $6.1 billion. Already depressed by the slowing of the economy, and high interest rates, the market for domestic U.S. consumer electronic products suffered an additional blow in 1981 from a sharp increase in imports, principally video cassette recorders, up an estimated $550 million, and television receivers, up about $200 million. The total U.S. market for consumer electronic products in 1981, supplied by domestic industry shipments and imports, increased an estimated 6.8 percent to $9.8 billion in current dollars.

Imports

Imports of consumer electronic products, 85 percent of which come from the Far East, amounted to $4.9 billion in 1980, and rose an estimated 20 percent, to $5.9 billion, in 1981. A further increase of 10 percent, to $6.5 billion, is projected for 1982. During the past 9 years, imports have increased at a compound annual rate of 12.8 percent in current dollars.

The majority of consumer electronic products imported into the United States are in finished form. These include television receivers, audio and video tape recorders, radios, high fidelity components, and loudspeakers. A significant portion of imports, however, are color receiver printed circuit boards with mounted components and tuners for final assembly with cabinets and picture tubes in the United States. Japan produces these boards and tuners in Japan for Japanese plants in the United States, and U.S. manufacturers produce them on the Mexican border for their U.S. plants. Imports from Mexico during the first half of 1981 were at an annual rate of about

U.S. Industrial Outlook 1982

ILLUSTRATION 2.2 Continued
U.S. Producers of Television Receivers, 1968–81

Firm	1968	1969	1970	1971	1972	1973	1974	1975	1976	1977	1978	1979	1980	1981
U.S.-owned:														
Curtis Mathes Manufacturing Co.	X	X	X	X	X	X	X	X	X	X	X	X	X	X
General Electric Co.	X	X	X	X	X	X	X	X	X	X	X	X	X	X
RCA Corp.	X	X	X	X	X	X	X	X	X	X	X	X	X	X
Wells-Gardner Electronics Corp.	X	X	X	X	X	X	X	X	X	X	X	X	X	X
Zenith Radio Corp.	X	X	X	X	X	X	X	X	X	X	X	X	X	X
GTE Sylvania Inc.[1]	X	X	X	X	X	X	X	X	X	X	X	X	X	
Admiral Group[2]	X	X	X	X	X	X	X	X	X	X	X			
Andrea Radio Corp.	X	X	X	X	X	X	X	X	X					
Warwick Electronics Inc.[3]	X	X	X	X	X	X	X	X	X	X				
Magnavox Consumer Electronics Co.[4]	X	X	X	X	X	X								
Motorola, Inc.[5]	X	X	X	X	X	X								
Philco Consumer Electronics Co.	X	X	X	X	X	X	X							
Teledyne Packard Bell Co.	X	X	X	X	X	X								
TMA Co.	X	X	X	X	X									
Setchel-Carlson	X	X	X	X	X									
Arvin	X	X	X											
Emerson	X	X	X											
Cortron[7]	X	X												
Foreign-owned:														
Sony Corp. of America						X	X	X	X	X	X	X	X	X
Quasar Electronics Corp.[5]								X	X	X	X	X	X	X
Magnavox Consumer Electronics Co.[4]							X	X	X	X	X	X	X	X
Sanyo Manufacturing Corp.[3]									X	X	X	X	X	X
Mitsubishi Electric Sales[8]										X	X	X	X	X
Toshiba America, Inc.											X	X	X	X
Sharp Electronics Corp.												X	X	X
Hitachi Consumer Products of America, Inc.												X	X	X
Tatung Co. of America, Inc.													X	X

[1] North American Philips Corp. (subsidiary of the Philips Trust) purchased GTE's consumer electronics business (Sylvania and Philco) in January 1981 and merged it with its Magnavox Consumer Electronics Company to form NAP Consumer Electronics.
[2] Rockwell International Corp. purchased Admiral Corp. (now Admiral Group) in 1974.
[3] Sanyo Electric, Inc. (Japan) purchased the television-manufacturing facilities of Warwick Electronics Inc., effective December 31, 1976.
[4] North American Philips Corp. purchased the Magnavox Consumer Electronics Co. in 1974.
[5] Matsushita Electric Industrial Co., Ltd. (Japan), purchased the television receiver business of Motorola, Inc. in 1974 and renamed the business Quasar Electronics Co.
[6] GTE Sylvania purchased the "Philco" trademark in 1974; Philco discontinued television production in 1974.
[7] Admiral Corp. (now Admiral Group), purchased Cortron in 1969.
[8] Wholly owned by Mitsubishi (Japan); markets under the label "MGA."

Source: USITC Publication 1153, United States International Trade Commission 1981.

$450 million, and from Japan at a rate of $210 million. Imports of these assemblies from Taiwan, Singapore, and Korea, combined, were at a rate of $200 million a year.

Exports

Exports of consumer electronic products amounted to $1.1 billion in 1980. They did not increase during 1981 because of the economic slowdown abroad and the strength of the dollar vis-a-vis foreign currencies. Exports of color receivers to Latin America ran high in 1980 to meet the initial demand resulting from the recent start of color broadcasting in some Latin American countries. In 1981, exports of these receivers to Latin America declined to $165 million from approximately $205 million in 1980.

Outlook for 1982

Shipments of the consumer electronics industry are expected to rise 6.7 percent in 1982, to $6.55 billion in 1972 dollars. Product shipments should reach $5.4 billion. Employment in the industry is expected to increase to 70,000. The sale of color television receivers will provide the major impetus for this growth; the number of receivers shipped should rise from 9.0 million in 1981 to about 9.6 million in 1982. A large share of the demand for new television receivers is for replacement of aging sets with those incorporating today's technology and features such as solid state circuitry, electronic tuning, remote control, and a comb filter to increase picture resolution. Also, the widening choice of alternative video programing sources—cable, pay cable, subscription TV, video discs, and video cassettes—and alternative uses of the TV set for home computer and video game displays provide a stimulus for the ownership of more than one TV receiver per home.

Shipments of automobile radios should increase about 8.8 percent in 1982 to accompany the expected rise in automobile sales. In addition, the demand for supplementary, higher powered autosound equipment should continue to rise. The market for high-fidelity equipment, speakers, and accessory items should continue at or slightly above 1981 levels.

Although exports of consumer electronic products—princi-

1981 Profile
Radio and Television Receiving Sets

SIC Code: 3651

Industry data

Value of industry shipments (mil $)	6,200
Value added (mil $)	2,575
Total employment (000)	68
Total number of establishments (1977)	581
Number of establishments with less than 20 employees (1977)	389
Percent of industry shipments accounted for by 4 largest companies (1977)	51

Product data

Value of product shipments (mil $)	5,030
Value of exports (mil $)	1,110
Value of imports (mil $)	5,900
Exports as a % of shipments	22
Imports as a % of new supply[1]	54
Imports as a % of apparent consumption[2]	60

[1] New supply is the sum of product shipments plus imports.
[2] Apparent consumption is the sum of product shipments plus imports less exports.

Source: Bureau of the Census, Bureau of Labor Statistics, and Bureau of Industrial Economics. Estimates by Bureau of Industrial Economics.

ILLUSTRATION 2.2 Continued
Radio and Television Receiving Set Industry (SIC 3651): Trends and Projections 1972–82

(in millions of dollars except as noted)

Item	1972	1977	1978	1979	1980[1]	1981[2]	Compound annual rate of growth 1972–81	1982[3]	Percent change 1981–82[3]
Industry data									
Value of shipments[4]	4,440	5,732	6,442	6,573	6,625	6,200	—	—	—
Value of shipments (1972 $)[4]	4,440	6,046	6,703	6,707	6,632	6,140	3.7	6,550	6.7
Total employment (000)	86.5	74.6	76.7	68.4	71.0	68.0	−2.6	70.0	2.9
Production workers (000)	69.8	57.6	57.5	51.2	51.0	50.0	−3.6	51.0	2.0
Average hourly earnings of production workers	3.43	5.35	5.82	6.43	7.10	8.06	10.0	—	—
Capital expenditures	58.6	105.8	118.5	165.2	—	—	—	—	—
Product data									
Value of shipments[5]	3,610	4,731	5,467	5,344	5,385	5,030	—	—	—
Value of shipments (1972 $)[5]	3,610	4,990	5,689	5,453	5,390	5,035	3.8	5,375	6.7
Product price index (1972=100)	100.0	95.7	98.1	99.5	101.3	103	—	—	—
Quantity shipped (000):									
Television receivers, color	6,353	6,700	7,716	8,716	9,703	9,000	3.9	9,600	6.7
Television receivers, monochrome	3,150	1,215	1,015	712	585	—	—	—	—
Automobile radios	11,200	9,499	9,190	8,749	6,829	6,800	−5.4	7,400	8.8
Trade									
Value of exports	216	467	756	801	1,107	1,110	—	1,175	5.8
Value of imports	1,993	3,599	5,039	4,864	4,919	5,900	—	6,500	10.2
Export/shipments ratio	0.060	0.099	0.138	0.150	0.206	0.221	15.6	0.219	−0.9
Import/new supply ratio[6]	0.356	0.432	0.480	0.476	0.477	0.540	4.74	0.547	1.3

[1] Estimated except for product price index, exports, and imports.
[2] Estimated.
[3] Forecast.
[4] Value of all products and services sold by industry SIC 3651, Radio and Television Receiving Sets.
[5] Value of shipments of consumer electronic products produced by all industries.
[6] New supply is the sum of product shipments plus imports.

Source: Bureau of the Census, Bureau of Industrial Economics, and United States International Trade Commission. Estimates and forecasts by the Bureau of Industrial Economics.

pally television receivers, assembled and unassembled; automobile radios; loudspeakers; amplifiers; and sound recorders and players—increased at a compound annual rate of 19.9 percent between 1972 and 1981, they are projected to increase only 6 percent in 1982, to $1.175 billion. This diminished rate of growth in 1982 is expected to result from the continuing economic slowdown abroad and increasing competitive pressure from the Far East in terms of price and new products.

Imports, led by continued increases in TV receivers, chassis, and assembled printed circuit boards and by video cassette recorders, are expected to rise 10 percent in 1982, to a value of $6.5 billion. Major suppliers of the completed receivers are Japan, Taiwan, Canada, and Korea. Imports of color receivers are projected to rise 8 percent, to $508 million. Chassis and assembled printed circuit boards imported from Mexico, Japan, Singapore, and Taiwan are expected to increase 20 percent to $840 million. Japan is virtually the sole source for video cassette recorders, imports of which are projected to be up almost 50 percent, to $1.34 billion.

Long-Term Prospects

For the period 1981 to 1986, industry shipments in constant dollars are expected to rise at a compound annual rate of 5 percent, to $7.9 billion in 1986. This continued growth will follow from replacement sales and the increasing use of new video products and systems for home entertainment and information. Among these new products are video disc players, video cassette recorders, home computers, video games, and receivers equipped for receiving teletext broadcasts. The new services that will stimulate new product sales include cable television and pay cable, subscription television, prerecorded video cassettes and video discs, interactive cable communication, teletext, videotext, and TV services from direct broadcast satellites.

One of the major forces that will expand the demand for and use of TV receivers is the sharply increased number of video program sources available to the public. Cable television service, which began by bringing conventional broadcast television to areas where reception was poor or nonexistent, has now moved to suburban and urban areas, where it provides a variety of program services exclusive to cable. Of the total of approximately 84 million television homes expected in 1986, an estimated 31 million will subscribe to basic cable service, and 18 to 20 million of these, to premium, or pay cable, TV service. Other media for the delivery of pay programing to the home include subscription TV provided by a conventional TV station or a multiple distribution service (MDS) station, video discs and video cassettes, and direct broadcast satellites.

Access to the home TV receiver will no longer be limited to the presently available broadcast channels. Specialized and nonentertainment video programs, including video games, will be readily accessible. Nonentertainment uses of the TV receiver that are in prospect include the reception of teletext broadcasts, and as a display device for games, home computers, and interactive wired videotext services.

This expansion in channels for the delivery of video to the home, coupled with the low cost of satellite distribution to cable systems, will make special-interest programing available to the public and create demand for more than one receiver in the home. It will also stimulate demand for video disc players and video cassette recorder players.

The introduction of new and more versatile receivers will also contribute to the continued growth of the home video entertainment and information center. Current top-of-the-line TV receivers already incorporate digital tuning, remote control, and a comb filter. Large screen projection receivers are also available. Other innovations in prospect for the home receiver include provision for the reception of teletext broadcasts of textual information, stereo and bilingual sound, and digital signal processing. Individual TV entertainment-center components for assembly into a complete customized system are just entering the marketplace.

Further in the future of product innovation is equipment for high-definition, wide-screen television, as well as TV reception in the home from direct broadcast satellites. High-definition television will require wider video channels than are presently

U.S. Industrial Outlook 1982

ILLUSTRATION 2.2 Continued

allocated to conventional television broadcasting. These can best be realized through the use of satellites or fiber optic cables for distribution to the home.

The prospective increase in the importance and versatility of the home entertainment and information center promises to provide a steadily growing market for those manufacturers who are able to bring appropriately innovative products to the market in timely fashion.—*E. MacDonald Nyhen, Science and Electronics Division.*

Additional References

1981 Electronic Market Data Book, Electronic Industries Association, 2001 Eye St., NW, Washington, DC 20006.

Radio and Television Receivers, Phonographs, and Related Equipment, Current Industrial Reports, Series MA 36-M (annual), Industry Division, Bureau of the Census, Washington, DC 20233.

Television Digest with Consumer Electronics (weekly), Television Digest, Inc., 1836 Jefferson Place, NW, Washington, DC 20036.

The U.S. Consumer Electronics Industry and Foreign Competition. Prepared for the U.S. Department of Commerce, Economic Development Administration, by the Center for the Interdisciplinary Study of Science and Technology, Northwestern University, May 1980. Washington, DC 20230.

Television Receiving Sets from Japan, Determination of the Commission in Investigation No. 751-TA-2 under the Tariff Act of 1930, Together with the Information Obtained in the Investigation; USITC Publication 1153, June 1981, United States International Trade Commission, Washington, DC 20436.

Color Television Receivers and Subassemblies Thereof. Report to the President on Investigation No. TA-203-6 under Section 203 of the Trade Act of 1974 by the United States International Trade Commission. USITC Publication 1068, May 1980. Washington, DC 20436.

The U.S. Consumer Electronics Industry, September 1975, Bureau of Domestic Commerce, Washington, DC 20230.

Quarterly audio and video product import data and quarterly color TV import and production data releases are published by and available from the Sectoral Trade Monitoring Division, ITA, U.S. Department of Commerce, Washington, DC 20230.

HOUSEHOLD APPLIANCES

Current Situation

In 1981, high interest rates, weak housing starts and sluggish disposable income curtailed demand for household appliances. New housing starts, which account for about 20 to 30 percent of manufacturers' sales of appliances, were seriously affected by high mortgage rates. In 1981, new housing starts totaled about 1.1 million units, down from 1.3 million starts in 1980, which was one of the Nations' lowest housing production years since World War II.

Replacement purchases account for the largest share of the consumer appliance market. In 1981, personal disposable income, measured in constant dollars, increased only about 1.5 percent, interest rates on consumer loans fluctuated near 20 percent for most of the year, and some lenders restricted consumer credit. Under these circumstances, many consumers deferred making new outlays for appliances, some by repairing their old ones.

In 1981, shipments of household appliances decreased 3.0 percent, moving from $8.0 billion to $7.7 billion, in 1972 dollars. Current-dollar product shipments rose an estimated 3.4

1981 Profile

Household Appliances

SIC Code: 363

Industry data

Value of industry shipments (mil $)	14,007
Value added (mil $)	6,790
Total employment (000)	153.8
Total number of establishments	668
Number of establishments with less than 20 employees	325

Major producing states accounting for largest percent of industry shipments: OH, IL, KY, TE, IN

Product data

Value of product shipments (mil $)	13,200
Value of exports (mil $)	1,435
Value of imports (mil $)	1,110
Exports as a % of shipments	10.9
Imports as a % of new supply [1]	7.8
Imports as a % of apparent consumption [2]	8.6

[1] New supply is the sum of product shipments plus imports.
[2] Apparent consumption is the sum of product shipments plus imports less exports.
Source: Bureau of the Census and Bureau of Industrial Economics. Estimates by Bureau of Industrial Economics.

---

percent and amounted to $13.2 billion. Unit shipments of most appliances declined from 1980. Among major appliances, only shipments of portable microwave ovens increased significantly. Unit shipments of small appliances, such as coffee makers, fans, and disposals, were up slightly in 1981.

Growing Markets and Saturation

Future demand for household appliances will vary significantly among different types of equipment, depending on the degree of their market saturation. Most American homes already have refrigerators, kitchen stoves, irons, and vacuum cleaners, so demand is heavily dependent upon replacement markets.

In sharp contrast, microwave ovens, as a relatively new product, have penetrated only 25 percent of the market. They should experience high and continued growth in the future. Dishwashers, disposals, and food blenders should also experience continued growth, because these markets are only about half penetrated.

Productivity and Prices

In 1980, productivity in many manufacturing industries showed sharp declines. The major household appliance industries were no exception, although the overall decline was a modest 0.7 percent from 1979. This decline was in sharp contrast to the productivity gains for the appliance industries from 1976–79, when output per employee hour grew 2.7 percent annually.

Output per employee hour in 1980 registered healthy increases in the household refrigerator and freezer industry and the laundry equipment industry. Productivity gains in these two industries were 3.4 percent and 4.8 percent; from 1976–79, their annual productivity gains were 7.8 percent and 1.9 percent, respectively. The cooking equipment industry, which has had consistently sluggish productivity in recent years, showed a substantial 6.4-percent decline in 1980.

In recent years, productivity gains have kept price increases for household appliances moderate relative to prices for all producer goods. From 1976–80, producer prices for household appliances increased 5.8 percent annually, while prices

ILLUSTRATION 2.2 Continued

for all producer goods increased 10 percent a year. During the 5-year period, prices for household refrigeration equipment rose only 4.8 percent annually, and prices for laundry equipment and for cooking equipment moved up 5.5 percent and 6.2 percent, respectively.

Foreign Trade

Many export markets in 1981 experienced slowing economic activity, but exports of appliances increased 16 percent, reaching an estimated $1.4 billion. This occurred at the same time that appliance imports increased about 10 percent to an estimated $1.1 billion.

Since 1972, appliance exports have increased at a compound annual rate of 20.1 percent, almost twice the annual rate of increase of imports. Significant export increases in 1981 were large refrigerators and laundry equipment. U.S. manufacturers of these larger appliances compete well in foreign markets. Foreign production of large-sized appliances is limited because of the relatively low local demand for them and the large capital investments necessary to manufacture them. Foreign markets for such appliances will continue to grow as the standard of living of other countries continues to rise. Major export markets for household appliances are Canada, Saudi Arabia, Venezuela, the United Kingdom, and West Germany.

During 1981, imported microwave ovens, food mixers, and vacuum cleaners showed substantial gains. U.S. consumer demand for such appliances as microwave ovens and food mixers, which save consumers substantial time in the kitchen, is increasing. Major foreign suppliers of household appliances include Japan, Hong Kong, Taiwan, and Singapore.

Import penetration, or the value of imports as a percent of apparent domestic consumption, varies substantially by type of appliance. As might be expected, the rate in 1980 was low for major appliances, ranging from less than half a percent for laundry equipment to 5 percent for refrigerators. The rate for both microwave ovens and small electric housewares was 18 percent during that year. The range of import penetration rates for electric housewares is surprisingly wide. In 1980, the penetration rates ranged from 3 percent or less for automatic coffee makers and toasters to 43 percent for a category that included hair dryers, electric knives, and portable humidifiers. Imports are not likely to become a major factor for the large appliances because the cost of ocean freight is rising and these appliances have low value to bulk ratios.

Product Development

Increasingly, energy-saving features have played a dominate role in the improvements in household appliances. With higher energy costs, appliance manufacturers are emphasizing product features that enable consumers to save energy. For example, some dishwashers and clothes washers now contain their own waterheaters, so consumers can maintain household hot water temperatures at moderate levels but use hotter water in their cleaning appliances. Some types of appliances today use 30 percent less energy than those produced only 5 years ago. Many of the changes, such as improved condensors or the use of more and better insulation in refrigerators and freezers, were relatively simple and have short payback periods.

Another area of product development is the inclusion of microcomputers and microprocessors in appliances. Today, these devices set various controls in cooking equipment, refrigerators, dishwashers, and laundry equipment. Some appliances include automatic control devices such as special sensors that measure processing progress and regulate power levels and duration. Advantages of electronic adaptations are energy savings, increased quality and versatility, and faster servicing of the appliance.

A third area of manufacturing improvement relates to materials. For example, a special plastic used in the body of an electric kettle offers such advantages as low heat loss, high impact strength, resistance to denting, and more freedom in styling. Some refrigerators now use plastic for the outer parts of the door. Advantages are dent, scratch, and stain resistance and improved appearance. Although the use of plastic saves labor in assembling, the saving is nearly all offset by higher material costs.

Industry Concentration

As in many other industries, market dominance by larger producers of appliances is increasing. The market share of each of the four largest companies producing refrigerators and freezers, laundry equipment, and miscellaneous household appliances increased between 1958 and 1977. The market share of the four largest producers of refrigerators increased from 65 percent to 82 percent; for laundry equipment, from 76 percent to 83 percent; and for miscellaneous household appliances, from 32 percent to 46 percent. In other appliance sectors, the growth in concentration proceeded at a much slower pace. In no sector, however, did the four largest producers lose market share during this period.

In recent years, appliance companies have in many instances acquired other appliance producers, and have thus expanded their product lines. This merger trend continued in 1981. In January, Maytag acquired Hardwick Stove Company; in mid-1981, Magic Chef acquired the Revco consumer freezer division of City Investing Company; and near the end of the year, Allegheny International, Inc. entered the household appliance industry by acquiring Sunbeam Corporation.

Foreign-Owned Plants

Recognizing that most major appliances will continue to be produced domestically due to transportation costs, foreign producers who want to participate in the U.S. market are establishing plants here. In recent years, nearly a dozen foreign appliance manufacturers, including producers from Japan, Korea, and Italy, have established factories in this country. Many of these factories produce microwave ovens or compact refrigerators, but they are capable of expanding their production to include other major appliance lines. Some foreign companies now making portable microwave ovens in this country can be expected eventually to produce combination microwave and conventional ranges, and companies now producing compact refrigerators can be expected to offer mid-sized refrigerators. In the future, foreign companies are also likely to manufacture laundry equipment in the United States.

This infusion of foreign producers into the domestic market will increase competition among producers of appliances and give consumers a wider choice among appliances. Appliances manufactured domestically by foreign companies are likely to be similar to those manufactured in the companies' home country and to be energy and space efficient.

Microwave Oven Investigation Terminated

In December 1980, the Department of Commerce reached a final determination in its antidumping investigation of Japanese microwave ovens. It decided that the Japanese were selling some countertop models in the United States at less than fair value. The case was referred to the International Trade Commission for a determination concerning possible material injury to the domestic industry. If that agency found that sales at less-than-fair value had caused material injury, increased duties would be levied in the amount of the undervaluation. Before the ITC completed its investigation, however, the in-

U.S. Industrial Outlook 1982

ILLUSTRATION 2.2 Continued
Household Appliances: SIC 363; Trends and Projections—1972–82
(in millions of dollars except as noted)

Item	1972	1977	1978	1979	1980[1]	1981[2]	Compound annual rate of growth 1972–81	1982[3]	Percent change 1981–82[3]
Industry data									
Value of industry shipments (SIC 363)[4]	6,940.2	10,736.6	11,487.6	12,740.9	13,534.4	14,007.0	—	—	—
Cooking equipment (3631)	939.8	1,707.2	1,912.4	2,353.5	2,444.9	2,640.0	—	—	—
Refrigerators-freezers (3632)	1,719.7	2,576.6	2,773.0	2,683.8	2,638.9	2,737.0	—	—	—
Laundry equipment (3633)	1,356.5	1,792.8	1,946.1	2,214.7	2,201.2	2,281.0	—	—	—
Electric housewares (3634)	1,615.0	2,531.2	2,581.1	2,868.9	3,698.0	3,812.0	—	—	—
Vacuum cleaners (3635)	467.7	639.9	683.0	796.1	850.0	855.0	—	—	—
Sewing machines (3636)	159.6	304.9	324.3	399.0	380.0	370.0	—	—	—
Household appliances, n.e.c. (3639)	681.9	1,184.0	1,267.7	1,424.9	1,321.4	1,312.0	—	—	—
Value of industry shipments (1972 $) (SIC 363)	6,940.2	8,013.8	8,128.7	8,556.6	8,420.1	8,173.0	1.8	8,464.0	3.6
Cooking equipment (1972 $) (3631)	939.8	1,209.1	1,298.3	1,520.3	1,451.0	1,458.0	5.0	1,530.0	4.9
Refrigerators-freezers (1972 $) (3632)	1,719.7	1,848.4	1,896.7	1,772.7	1,641.1	1,577.0	−1.0	1,625.0	3.0
Laundry equipment (1972 $) (3633)	1,356.5	1,279.7	1,332.0	1,434.4	1,312.6	1,270.0	−.7	1,300.0	2.4
Electric housewares (1972 $) (3634)	1,615.0	2,088.4	1,983.9	2,068.4	2,428.1	2,365.0	4.3	2,470.0	4.4
Vacuum cleaners (1972 $) (3635)	467.7	516.5	523.0	585.8	580.6	564.0	2.1	578.0	2.5
Sewing machines (1972 $) (3636)	159.6	201.1	197.6	222.5	199.5	186.0	1.7	186.0	—
Household appliances, n.e.c. (1972 $) (3639)	681.9	870.6	897.2	952.5	807.2	753.0	1.1	775.0	2.9
Total employment (000)	163.0	162.2	168.0	161.4	152.3	153.8	−.6	156.9	2.0
Production workers (000)	131.1	128.6	133.0	127.0	121.5	122.7	−.7	125.1	2.0
Average hourly earnings of production workers	3.85	5.57	6.12	6.56	7.37	8.18	8.7	—	—
Capital expenditures	151.9	207.0	256.8	236.1	—	—	—	—	—
Product data									
Value of product shipments (SIC 363)[5]	6,592.1	10,167.2	10,807.6	12,025.9	12,770.7	13,200.0	—	—	—
Cooking equipment (3631)	1,027.0	1,806.5	2,089.2	2,212.1	2,298.0	2,480.0	—	—	—
Refrigerators-freezers (3632)	1,419.4	2,005.6	2,044.8	2,314.4	2,275.7	2,360.0	—	—	—
Laundry equipment (3633)	1,289.9	1,697.3	1,782.4	1,883.4	1,871.9	1,940.0	—	—	—
Electric houseware (3634)	1,448.0	2,304.0	2,371.7	2,730.4	3,519.5	3,629.0	—	—	—
Vacuum cleaners (3635)	439.2	710.4	758.1	860.2	920.0	925.0	—	—	—
Sewing machines (3636)	152.1	260.4	271.6	323.2	307.0	298.0	—	—	—
Household appliances n.e.c. (3639)	816.5	1,383.0	1,489.8	1,702.2	1,578.6	1,568.0	—	—	—
Value of product shipments (1972 $) (SIC 363)	6,592.1	7,592.7	7,660.3	8,097.2	7,960.0	7,720.0	1.8	7,995.0	3.6
Cooking equipment (1972 $) (3631)	1,027.0	1,279.4	1,418.3	1,429.0	1,363.8	1,370.0	3.2	1,440.0	5.1
Refrigerators-freezers (1972 $) (3632)	1,419.4	1,438.7	1,398.6	1,528.7	1,415.2	1,360.0	−.5	1,400.0	2.9
Laundry equipment (1972 $) (3633)	1,289.9	1,211.5	1,220.0	1,219.8	1,116.2	1,080.0	−2.0	1,105.0	2.3
Electric housewares (1972 $) (3634)	1,448.0	1,901.0	1,823.0	1,968.6	2,310.9	2,250.0	5.0	2,350.0	4.4
Vacuum cleaners (1972 $) (3635)	439.2	573.4	580.5	633.0	628.4	610.0	3.7	625.0	2.4
Sewing machines (1972 $) (3636)	152.1	171.8	165.5	180.3	161.2	150.0	−.2	150.0	—
Household appliances, n.e.c. (1972 $) (3639)	816.5	1,016.9	1,054.4	1,137.8	964.3	900.0	1.1	925.0	2.8
Quantity shipped, selected appliances (000 units):									
Ranges/surface cook tops	6,530	5,760	5,845	5,706	5,045	4,650	−3.7	—	—
Portable microwave ovens	NA	1,284	1,475	1,586	2,111	2,540	NA	—	—
Refrigerators	6,068	5,674	5,586	5,752	5,334	5,200	−1.7	—	—
Freezers	1,355	1,548	1,419	1,933	1,742	1,600	1.9	—	—
Washing machines	5,143	4,972	5,024	5,018	4,644	4,525	−1.4	—	—
Dryers (including combination)	3,919	3,588	3,638	3,572	3,234	3,100	−2.6	—	—
Dishwashers	2,922	3,200	3,370	3,395	2,701	2,500	−1.7	—	—
Trash compactors	NA	260	296	282	243	195	NA	—	—
Fans	10,927	15,270	19,032	21,906	23,772	24,500	9.4	—	—
Coffee machines	8,188	9,788	13,329	16,188	15,865	16,000	7.7	—	—
Disposers	2,541	2,823	3,212	3,186	2,789	3,100	2.2	—	—
Product price index (1972=100)	100.0	134.8	142.2	149.5	161.9	173.5	6.3	—	—
Trade									
Value of exports	275.8	778.7	964.4	1,060.5	1,237.5	1,435.0	20.1	1,650.0	15.0
Value of imports	439.2	829.3	991.9	957.5	1,003.8	1,110.0	10.9	1,220.0	10.0
Export/shipments ratio	.042	.076	.089	.088	.097	.109	—	—	—
Import/new supply ratio[6]	.062	.075	.084	.074	.073	.078	—	—	—

n.e.c. = Not elsewhere classified.
NA = Not available or insignificant.
[1] Estimated except for product price change, exports and imports.
[2] Estimated.
[3] Forecast.
[4] Value of all products and services sold by industry SIC 363.
[5] Value of shipments of household appliances produced by all industries.
[6] New supply is the sum of product shipments plus imports.

dustry withdrew its petition because it believed ITC was unlikely to reach a finding of material injury.

Energy Efficiency

In June 1980, the Department of Energy (DOE), pursuant to the Energy Policy and Conservation Act, proposed energy-efficiency standards for eight major household appliances. The act provides that DOE shall not promulgate a rule establishing appliance-efficiency standards if the rule would not result in significant conservation of energy or would not be techno-

ILLUSTRATION 2.2 Continued

logically feasible or economically justified. After receiving comments on the proposed rule, DOE officials decided to prepare a new notice of proposed rulemaking regarding the standards. This essentially started the rulemaking procedure over again. It is possible that the list of appliances the proposed rule covers will be reduced or that the proposed standards will be changed. Public comments will again be requested, and formal hearings held. The earliest that any standards are expected to take effect is January 1983.

Appliances have become much more efficient in recent years in large part because of the 1980 Federal Trade Commission regulation requiring efficiency labels. Also, manufacturers have made changes in anticipation of possible federal efficiency standards. The efficiency labels, required on seven categories of appliances, must contain an estimate of yearly energy costs for models of similar size and features, as well as a chart illustrating energy costs of the appliance based on a range of utility rates. Efficiency labels, together with increased energy costs, have stimulated consumer interest in energy efficiency.

Outlook for 1982

Manufacturers' product shipments of household appliances in 1982 are expected to continue the slow recovery from the slump experienced in 1980. The recovery, however, will be restricted by the continuing depressed conditions in the residential construction industry, as well as by high interest rates. Growth is not expected to accelerate before the second half of 1982. Product shipments, adjusted for inflation, are expected to increase 3.6 percent in 1982.

Long-Term Prospects

For the next 5 years, the outlook for the appliance industry is favorable. Interest rates are expected to decline and residential housing construction to improve. The number of households headed by people aged 25 to 44, the principal appliance buyers, will increase 20 percent in the next 5 years. In addition, the appliances now in use will continue to wear out and need to be replaced. Increased market penetration can be expected for appliances such as microwave ovens and dishwashers. These factors are expected to result in household appliance shipments, in 1972 dollars, rising at a compound growth rate of 4.4 percent between 1981 and 1986.—*John Harris, Office of Consumer Goods and Service Industries.*

HOUSEHOLD FURNITURE

Household furniture industry (SIC 251) activity is closely related to new residential construction, sales of existing homes, size of homes, new household formation, and real disposable income. During 1980 and 1981, furniture orders and shipments reflected the slowdown in new home building, slow sales of existing homes, and the high cost of borrowed money for manufacturers and consumers.

Current Situation

New orders and shipments by household furniture manufacturers improved in 1981 compared with the very low level of activity a year earlier. Household furniture product shipments totaled an estimated $12.4 billion in 1981, in current dollars, about 8 percent more than a year earlier, but adjusted for price changes, the increase was less than 1 percent. New orders increased an estimated 9 percent in 1981 over year earlier levels. Modest gains in retail furniture sales in 1981 mostly reflected replacement purchases as consumer incomes increased in the last quarter of the year.

1981 Profile

Household Furniture

SIC Code: 251

Industry data

Value of industry shipments (mil $)	12,905
Total employment (000)	315
Total number of establishments (1977)	6,161
Number of establishments with less than 20 employees (1977)	3,937
Percent of industry shipments accounted for by 4 largest companies (1977):	
SIC 2511—Wood furniture	14
SIC 2512—Upholstered furniture	15
SIC 2514—Metal furniture	13
SIC 2515—Bedding	21
SIC 2517—Wood, tv, and radio cabinets	45
SIC 2519—Household furniture, n.e.c.	39

Major producing states accounting for largest percent of industry shipments: NC, CA, VA, TE, MS, NY, PA

Product data

Value of product shipments (mil $)	12,400
Value of exports (mil $)	290
Value of imports (mil $)	945
Exports as a % of shipments	2.3
Imports as a % of new supply [1]	7.1
Imports as a % of apparent consumption [2]	7.2

[1] New supply is the sum of product shipments plus imports.
[2] Apparent consumption is the sum of product shipments plus imports less exports.
Source: Bureau of the Census, Bureau of Labor Statistics, and Bureau of Industrial Economics. Estimates by Bureau of Industrial Economics.

Historically, furniture output declines during recessions. Output fell 3.9 percent in 1970, 5.9 percent in 1974, and 12.8 percent in 1975, as measured by the Federal Reserve Board's Industrial Production Index. Paralleling the 10.9-percent decline in household furniture production in 1980, manufacturers' median after-tax profits on sales were 2.3 percent in 1980, down from 2.6 percent in 1979 and 2.9 percent in 1978, according to an annual survey conducted by the National Association of Furniture Manufacturers. The median return on net profit before taxes was about 6.8 percent to 7 percent, down from 8 percent in 1979 and 9.7 percent in 1978.

Reflecting lower furniture production, industry employment dropped 7.3 percent in 1980 to 305,100, and then increased modestly to an estimated 315,000 in 1981 as manufacturing activity improved. In 1978 and 1979, employment totaled around 330,000.

Diverse Furniture Markets

Manufacturers produce furniture for varied consumer markets which represent consumer groups with different income levels, lifestyles, and furniture preferences. These include the growing number of young adult and elderly single households and two-earner families as well as apartment dwellers and home owners.

High quality traditional and contemporary furniture pieces account for the major share of furniture shipment dollars. In recent years, demand for these products has been changing as consumers have tended to purchase individual, nonmatching furniture items instead of living room and bedroom "sets."

In response to the needs of consumers with limited furniture budgets, manufacturers are producing more functional and durable furniture that will fit into smaller living spaces. Increasingly, they are using easy-to-clean, vinyl-coated fabrics in a range of colors for upholstered living and dining room furniture. More knock-down (KD) or self-assembly furniture

ILLUSTRATION 2.2 Continued

is being sold for wall systems and entertainment centers. Also, moderately priced unfinished furniture has become increasingly popular. Unfinished furniture is no longer made exclusively of pine but has become available in more expensive hardwoods such as oak and mahogany.

Today's very large 25- to 35-year-old age group seem to prefer room space for such items as plants and pillows, and often they buy only a few furniture pieces—a colorful upholstered chair or a dramatic coffee table—that become the focal point of a room. In the past year, retailers were purchasing more higher-end summer/casual furniture made of wrought iron, wicker, and rattan, items that can be used indoors, as well as outside.

Furniture Production Methods

The U.S. household furniture industry is characterized by a large number of small establishments with a high degree of product specialization. About one-third of the 4,900 establishments engaged in the manufacture of wood, upholstered, and metal household furniture in 1977 employed 20 or more persons. Compared with other manufacturing industries, furniture production, especially of wood and upholstered furniture, is labor intensive. Most production is planned in response to new orders because of the wide range of different models, rapid style changes, and the bulky nature of furniture.

Over the past decade, composite board or particle board and medium-density fiberboard have been used increasingly in furniture manufacturing as substitutes for higher priced furniture hardwood. There has been considerable penetration of solid wood furniture markets with the growing use of these versatile, man-made materials to produce low-cost wall systems, tables, desks, and similar items at affordable prices. In the late 1970's, a large southern furniture manufacturer developed a new wood-filled, polyester material that can be screwed, cut, sanded, shaped, nailed, and finished like wood. Named Vestwood, this product weighs the same as wood and can be finished with wood materials. Many furniture products, including desks, chairs, dressers, and canopy beds, are now being made of Vestwood.

Other recent furniture production innovations include energy-efficient, airflow ovens and spray booths, as well as new air-dry systems that reduce drying time and furniture finishing costs. Increasingly, firms are using computer systems for more efficient order scheduling, inventory control, credit checking, and legal tag printing. Automated machinery is also being increasingly used in furniture factories.

Regulatory Trends

The Consumer Product Safety Commission (CPSC), instead of issuing mandatory rules on furniture flammability, recently approved an indefinite continuation of the 2-year trial voluntary furniture flammability program that the Upholstered Furniture Action Council (UFAC) developed in 1979. The UFAC is a trade organization consisting of five large furniture associations which represent firms that account for about 80 percent of the upholstered furniture industry's annual sales volume. Designed to encourage production of upholstered furniture that is resistant to cigarette ignition, the UFAC program includes a fabric rating system, criteria for construction, a labeling plan, and compliance procedures. Both the UFAC and the CPSC are monitoring program compliance.

In January 1981, the Federal Trade Commission proposed regulations on care labeling of finished upholstered furniture that is mainly used indoors. The proposed rule would require manufacturers and importers to attach to upholstered furniture legible care labels that describe the regular care needed, assuming ordinary use. The label would also carry warnings against harmful cleaning agents. A final rule will probably be issued in early 1982, subject to disapproval by Congress for a 90-day period.

Bedding Industry Trends

Like other household furniture sectors, manufacturers' shipments of mattresses, foundations, and sleep furniture were sluggish in 1981. In 1980, shipments of adult-sized mattresses—the major bedding category—declined about 15 percent in current-dollar value and about 12 percent in units. In contrast, shipments of dual-purpose sleep furniture increased compared with 1980, both in value and in units shipped.

Although interspring mattresses with matching foundations account for the bulk of bedding sales, markets have expanded in recent years for foam mattresses, air mattresses, heated waterbeds, and hybrid flotation systems. Hybrid flotation units feature water mattresses but look like conventional beds and use conventional sheets. Also, demand for electrically operated adjustable beds is growing. Convertible sofas, love seats, and chairs are also popular among consumers for extra sleeping space in today's smaller living quarters.

In response to production innovations in the manufacture of all types of bedding in recent years, the National Association of Bedding Manufacturers and the American National Standards Institute in 1981 adopted a revised and expanded "Voluntary Product Standard on Bedding Components." This revision of the 1962 standards will serve as an industry guide on the size relationship of bedding components, ranging from the frame and headboards to the mattress and foundation. The revised standards should result in greater uniformity among bedding products and resolve problems between bedding manufacturers and their suppliers. The new standards recognize such currently popular size terms as queen, king, and extra-long twin.

Foreign Trade Activity

Although imports continue to dominate furniture foreign trade activity, exports have risen significantly during the past decade, to an estimated $290 million in 1981. Exports continue to account for an insignificant share—only 2 percent—of domestic production, however. Principally because of its proximity and its similar consumer market, Canada is the largest U.S. export market. Canada has accounted for 35 to 40 percent of the value of U.S. furniture exports since 1975. About 20 percent of U.S. furniture exports are shipped to Saudi Arabia.

U.S. imports of furniture have more than quadrupled since 1972 and totaled an estimated $945 million in 1981. Major foreign suppliers include Taiwan, Yugoslavia, Denmark, and Canada. Some U.S. manufacturers are importing increased quantities of knock-down furniture and parts from Taiwan and Yugoslavia for assembly into finished furniture products in their U.S. plants.

Outlook for 1982

An upturn in residential construction together with moderating interest rates and higher personal income, are expected to stimulate demand for furniture by the last quarter of 1982. Because of the usual 12-month lag between a housing upturn and rising consumer furniture purchases, the value of furniture product shipments, adjusted for inflation, is expected to be about the same in 1982 as in 1981, reflecting sluggish activity during the first 9 months of the year. A strong pick-up in furniture production and shipments is expected in 1983.

U.S. Industrial Outlook 1982

ILLUSTRATION 2.2 Continued

Household Furniture (SIC 251): Trends and Projections 1972–82

(in millions of dollars except as noted)

Item	1972	1977	1978	1979	1980[1]	1981[2]	Compound annual rate of growth 1972–81	1982[3]	Percent change 1981–82
Industry data									
Value of shipments[4]	7,409.6	10,392.1	11,916.3	12,466.4	11,960.0	12,905.0	6.3	—	—
Value of shipments (1972 $)[4]	7,409.6	7,538.5	8,085.8	8,299.5	7,500.0	7,560.0	0.5	7,650.0	1
Total employment (000)	336.8	315.1	331.8	329.2	305.1	315.0	−0.8	—	—
Production workers (000)	287.2	268.4	282.4	278.2	255.8	264.0	−0.9	—	—
Average hourly earnings of production workers ($)	2.89	4.05	4.39	4.76	5.12	5.45	7.3	—	—
Capital expenditures	202.6	211.1	278.2	290.9	—	—	—	—	—
Product data									
Value of shipments[5]	7,129.5	9,933.7	11,493.0	11,961.1	11,500.0	12,400.0	6.3	—	—
Value of shipments (1972 $)[5]	7,129.5	7,211.7	7,803.2	7,957.9	7,200.0	7,250.0	0.2	7,325.0	1
Wood furniture (SIC 2511) (1972 $)	2,716.8	2,775.1	3,076.9	3,150.7	2,690.0	2,685.0	−0.2	—	—
Upholstered furniture (SIC 2512) (1972 $)	1,990.5	2,026.4	2,257.1	2,294.7	2,135.0	2,160.0	0.9	—	—
Metal furniture (SIC 2514) (1972 $)	859.3	852.0	854.5	817.9	810.0	815.0	1.4	—	—
Bedding (SIC 2515) (1972 $)	1,079.6	1,131.8	1,158.9	1,279.6	1,170.0	1,185.0	1.1	—	—
Wood-TV-radio cabinets (SIC 2517) (1972 $)	293.0	222.6	233.8	205.0	200.0	205.0	−4.8	—	—
Household furniture, n.e.c. (SIC 2519) (1972 $)	190.3	203.8	222.0	210.0	195.0	200.0	0.5	—	—
Product price index (1972=100)	100.0	138.3	147.9	158.8	174.6	187.9	7.3	—	—
Industrial production index (1967=100)	135.0	149.3	159.7	161.9	144.4	—	—	—	—
Trade									
Value of exports	32	136	156	176	218	290	65.1	—	—
Value of imports	204	464	638	783	847	945	18.6	—	—
Export/shipments ratio	.004	.014	.014	.015	.019	.023	—	—	—
Import/new supply ratio[6]	.004	.045	.053	.061	.069	.071	—	—	—

[1] Estimated except for product price index, exports, and imports.
[2] Estimated.
[3] Forecast.
[4] Value of all products and services sold by industry SIC 251.
[5] Value of shipments of household furniture produced by all industries.
[6] New supply is the sum of product shipments plus imports.

Source: Bureau of the Census, Bureau of Labor Statistics, and Bureau of Industrial Economics. Estimates and forecasts by the Bureau of Industrial Economics.

Long-Term Prospects

Continued increases in the formation of households and families among the Nation's fast-growing young adult population together with increased availability of affordable homes, will provide expanding markets for furniture in the years ahead. The number of Americans that will reach the prime homebuying age of 30 during this decade will rise to 42 million, up from 30 million in the 1970's and 22 million in the 1960's. In addition, the long-term upward trend in real average personal income is expected to resume in the next several years as today's young adult population moves into more affluent earning brackets and the number of two-income families continues to rise.

By 1983, household furniture shipments are expected to rise sharply, and they will continue on an upward trend for several years. As smaller sized homes are built in the 1980's, manufacturers will probably produce more modular wall systems and dual- or multi-purpose furniture such as table desks and ottoman-beds. During the 5 years ending in 1986, the value of shipments of household furniture, adjusted for inflation, is expected to increase at a 3.5 percent compound annual rate.—*Renee Gallop, Office of Consumer Goods aand Service Industries.*

Additional References

The Competitive Edge, various issues, the National Home Furnishings Association.

Furniture Design and Manufacturing, various issues, Delta Communications, Inc., Chicago, IL.

Bedding Magazine, various issues, National Association of Bedding Manufacturers.

"Monthly Statistical Report," National Association of Furniture Manufacturers, Washington, DC.

"Monthly Survey of Current Business," Southern Furniture Manufacturers Association, High Point, NC.

It is evident that the market is large and extremely complex. To begin to grasp the market into which you are going to sell your products or services, it is important to answer some questions about its operating characteristics. Use Form 2.1 for this purpose. The six questions are explained in the following sections.

Who Are the Occupants?

Consider who the individuals and/or households are and their characteristics, such as age, income, and sex. These elements will play an important role in the segmentation and target markets.

What Are the Objects Sold?

Look at the particular type of good or service to be purchased and decide in which of the following categories it belongs:

1. Nondurable goods—tangible goods that are consumed (e.g., soap and meat). They are consumed fast and purchased often; they have a small profit margin and brand identity.
2. Durable goods—tangible goods that survive being used (e.g., clothing and appliances). They are more profitable than nondurables, requiring more selling effort, service, and guarantees.
3. Services—activities, benefits, or assistance offered for sale. They are usually intangible and personal, requiring credibility.

or

1. Convenience goods—consumer goods purchased quickly, without much comparison. These may be either impulse or staple goods (e.g., cigarettes or soap).
2. Shopping goods—consumer goods that are compared for price, quality, size, and so on (e.g., furniture).
3. Specialty goods—consumer goods with unique characteristics, brand identification, and so on (e.g., stereo equipment and designer jeans).

What Are the Occasions of Usage?

Buying patterns reflect seasonal factors, religious factors, and often time of day and day of the week or month. Economic conditions can also slow or enhance the patterns of buying.

What Is the Organization?

Simply determine who the decision maker for the purchase of the product or service is. All you have to worry about is who will say "Yes, I'll

FORM 2.1 Market Operating Characteristics

Occupants of the Market

Who is in the market?

___

Objects of the Market

What does the market buy?

___

Occasions of the Market

When does the market buy?

___

Organization of the Market

Who is involved in the buying?

___

Objectives of the Market

Why does the market buy?

___

Operations of the Market

How does the market buy?

___

FORM 2.1 Continued

Outposts of the Market

Where is the market?

_____
_____
_____
_____
_____

Outlets of the Market

Where does the market buy?

_____
_____
_____
_____
_____
_____

buy." Then make sure you do what is necessary to make that happen. Sometimes there may be layers of decisions to be made before you get a yes. Be patient, and don't let the different personalities frustrate you.

What Are the Customer's Objectives?

The buyer of a product or service is making the purchase due to the lack of a useful object or service. Marketing tries to make the customer aware of his or her needs. People have three distinct groups of needs:

1. Physical: survival, hunger, thirst, and safety.
2. Social acceptance and self-esteem.
3. Self-actualization, which develops a system of values and self-realization.

What Are the Buying Operations?

To best answer this extremely complex question, use the following questions:

1. What are the major factors influencing the buyer?
2. What is the buying situation?
3. What decisions are involved?
4. What is the buying process?

Outposts and outlets are basic questions that can be answered with little explanation. These are status quo questions that should be considered.

MARKET SEGMENTATION

Attempting to sell to the entire market is foolish, unless you have a product or service that is absolutely unique. To provide a more cost efficient and direct marketing effort, different groups can be identified within the market audience. This is called market segmentation. Market segmentation is defined as a process of dividing a market into subgroups or segments with similar characteristics. For example, a total market may be divided into male/female or according to ethnic makeup. Any market with more than one consumer can be segmented. The more potential consumers, the more segments that can be identified.

Market segmentation is an important consideration to all business owners in that it affects all the other marketing activities. For example, if you were a retail store that wanted to serve the northwest side of Atlanta with stylish sports clothes priced at a moderate level, such a decision would affect where the store is located, what suppliers to use, what advertising media to consider, price levels, and numerous other marketing decisions. It is the basis on which all marketing and advertising strategies will be established.

Usually markets are segmented in the following ways:

1. By demographics—the oldest and most popular way. Statistical variables such as age, sex, and level of income are used to help you pick broad classes of people.
2. By geography—boundaries by region, city or county; population, density, and climate will affect patterns.
3. By psychographics. Consumers are grouped according to life-style or personality differences, including their activities, values, interests, and opinions.
4. By benefits. Consumers are grouped according to the kinds of perceived benefits they seek from the product or service.
5. By behavior or usage, that is, by differentiating users from non-users and further characterizing user groups (e.g., heavy vs light usage).
6. By situation—changes based on exposure to various groups or changes in the demands of the situation. Example, buying habits might be different, such as being on vacation or as a result of a special occasion.

Chart 2.1 outlines the major segmentation variables for the marketplace. You can use any number of combinations of these to identify your market segments. Once you are familiar with these variables, use Form 2.2 to give you a profile of the segmentation that exists for your product or service. *Note:* You may find it necessary to use Form 2.2 more than once. There will probably be more than one segment of consumers that you want to reach.

CHART 2.1 Market Segmentation Showing Common Breakdowns

Variables	Breakdown Factors
1. *Geographic*	
Region	Pacific, Mountain, West North Central, West South Central, East North Central, East South Central, South Atlantic, Middle Atlantic, New England
County size	A,B,C,D
City or SMSA size	Under 5,000, 5,000–19,999, 20,000–49,999, 50,000–99,999, 100,000–249,999, 250,000–499,999, 500,000–999,999, 1,000,000–3,999,999, 4,000,000 and over.
Density	Urban, suburban, rural
Climate	Northern, southern, arid, seasonal, temperate, eastern, western, subtropical, tropical
2. *Demographic*	
Age	Under 6, 6–11, 12–19, 20–34, 35–49, 50–64, 65+
Sex	Male, female
Social class	Lower-lower, upper-lower, lower-middle, upper-middle, lower-upper, upper-upper
Marital status	Single, engaged, married, separated, divorced, widowed
Family size	1–2, 3–4, 5+
Family life cycle	Young, single; young, married, no children; young, married, youngest child under six; young, married, youngest child six or over; older, married, with children; older, married, no children under 18; older, single; other
Education	Grade school or less; some high school; high school graduate; some college; technical degree; graduated college; advanced college degree
Religion	Catholic, Protestant, Jewish, other
Race	White, Black, Asian, Hispanic, native American, other
Nativity	Foreign born, native of foreign parents, native
Nationality	American, British, French, German, Scandinavian, Italian, Latin American, Middle Eastern, Japanese, Chinese, Portuguese, other
Native language	English, German, Spanish, French, others
3. *Psychographic*	(Note: There are no common breakdowns in psychographic analysis because the technique is still developing.)
Life-style	Gays, straights, others
Personality	Authoritarian, ambitious, gregarious, others
Factors	Cohabitation, single living, family unit living, others
Attitudes	Pro-nuclear energy, anti-nuclear energy, others

MARKET SEGMENTATION

CHART 2.1 Continued

Variables	Breakdown Factors
Self-image	Conservative, liberal, sophisticated, intelligent, others
Values	Views on ethics and/or morality (honesty, material goods, others)
Interests	Hobbies, modes of entertainment, other
Behavior patterns	Compulsiveness, shyness, others
4. *Usage*	
Occasion of purchase	Routine, special circumstance
Usage rate (staple items)	Use seldom, use sometimes, use often
User status	Nonuser, ex-user, potential user, first-time user, regular user
User loyalty	None, moderate, strong, absolute
User's product perception	Unaware, aware, informed, interested, desirous, intending to buy
Marketing factors	Perceived quality, price, service, advertising, sales promotion
User benefits	Comfort, convenience, durability, economy, health, luxury, safety, status, others

This not only tells you something about who the potential consumers are, but also something about where to find them. It should also suggest ways to promote the product or service. Form 2.2, when completed, is designed to let the market and its description identify more precisely the customer's wants and needs.

Form 2.3 will allow you to see potential consumer needs and how they relate to the market segments. Use this form to assist you in locating the appropriate marketing needs that you may hope to fulfill once you finalize the marketing plan. List all the potential consumers identified in the segmentation. Then list the benefits and characteristics of your product or service (e.g., design, economy, and variety).

If the consumer is interested in the characteristic listed, mark an X in that box. When Form 2.3 is complete you will have an idea of the importance of the segments based on specific product/service related characteristics. This provides the foundation for assigning each segment a value.

Another work sheet that can be utilized reviews your market segment(s) based on the dimensions you used to segment them initially. Since buyers' motivations are multiple, this exercise can be important for helping to identify all of them. Illustration 2.3 shows the major dimensions of market segmentation for toothpaste.

FORM 2.2 Market Segment Profile

Age	
Sex	
Income	
Occupation	
Education	
Marital status	
Income group	
Social class	
Region	
Climate	
Location	
Residential status	
Cultural origin	
Religion	
Political philosophy	
Personal interests	
Comments:	

FORM 2.3 Market Segment/Characteristic Matrix

Potential Consumers (Market Segments)	Product/Service Characteristics					

ILLUSTRATION 2.3 Major Dimensions of Market Segments for Toothpaste. (Source. Russell I. Haley, Benefit Segmentation: A Decision-Oriented Tool, *Journal of Marketing*, XXXII, July 1968, p. 33.)

Segment Dimensions \ Market Segments	Sensory Segment	Sociables	Worriers	Independent Segment
Principal benefit	Flavor, product appearance	Brightness of teeth	Decay prevention	Price
Demographic	Children	Teens, young people	Large families	Men
Behavioral	Users of spearmint flavored toothpaste	Smokers	Heavy users	Heavy users
Brands disproportionately favored	Colgate, Stripe	Macleans, Plus White, and Ultra-Brite	Crest	Brands on sale
Personality	High self-involvement	High sociability	High hypochondriasis	High autonomy
Life-style	Hedonistic	Active	Conservative	Value-oriented

Form 2.4 can be used to model your own market segment dimension analysis.

With these three work sheets you have a good sampling of where your segments are, some of their characteristics, and their relative potential. These work sheets will be useful in determining the target market(s) and in formulating the strategies (market mix) for them.

There are many ways in which to segment a given market, and numerous segments will be identified. Each of these will have unique characteristics, some meaningful, some not. To be useful in the market planning process, market segments must have:

1. Measurability—a way in which to measure the size and potential purchasing power. Some segments have variables that are hard to calculate.
2. Accessibility—the degree to which a segment can be reached and served effectively.
3. Substantiality—the degree to which a segment can be profitable enough to sustain a marketing program.

Since markets are not equally attractive, it is important that the company determine the segments that can best be marketed by the given

FORM 2.4 Market Segment Dimension Work Sheet

Market Segments / Market Dimensions				

resources of the firm. The process of segmentation offers certain benefits to a small business.

First, the seller has the opportunity to see the needs and relative competition for each potential segment. Second, segmentation study allows a company to fine-tune its product/services to the needs of the segments. Finally, segmentation is an activity that can assist the seller in patterning the program and budget based on the response characteristics of the specific market segments.

Market segmentation permits you to narrow the market down so that target(s) can be chosen. With this information, you can improve the decision making in such areas as promotion and advertising.

Analysis of market segments is not a one-time cut-and-dried event. The nature of all market segments is that they are constantly changing. American consumers are mobile, dynamic people exposed to multitudes of new ideas and stimuli.

TARGET MARKETS

The ultimate goal of your marketing efforts is the development and implementation of market strategy and tactics through:

1. Identification of target market(s).
2. Development of a marketing mix:
   (a) Product.
   (b) Price.
   (c) Place.
   (d) Promotion.

Identification of Target Market(s)

With the understanding that the market is a collection of market segments, we are now ready to identify the segments to which the business wishes to sell. If you have more than one market segment, which you probably do, a decision needs to be made regarding the most valuable segment(s).

Through an evaluation, which includes decisions on whom to serve, where, when, how, and with what return to the seller, you will be able to identify the target market(s). The evaluation will allow a relative value or priority to be placed on each segment.

Each market segment that is determined to be viable and worth pursuing becomes a target market. Some firms will have only one target. Others will have two or more. In the case of more than one target, multiple strategies may be needed to market the target markets properly.

How do you choose your target market(s)? Begin by asking the following questions to understand the viability of the segment.

1. *How Does It Differ?* Is the target distinguished from other segments? If there is more than one target, is there enough isolation to make the target receptive to your marketing efforts?
2. *Is It Viable?* Are the purchasing criteria of this target relevant to the purchase situation? (Is there sufficient demand?)
3. *What Resources Are Needed?* Is the target of sufficient size to ensure that any marketing investment can result in an adequate return?
4. *Can I Reach It?* The target market can only be used if you can reach it. It must be possible to direct a marketing strategy to each target. Each target may have different responses to things such as price, type of media used, and so forth.

The following example will give you an idea of multiple target markets. A trail-bike manufacturer might have the following targets:

Adult males who are outdoor enthusiasts.
Male teenagers without drivers' licenses.
Ranchers who use their bikes in their work.

As you can see, there is some overlap. To maximize sales, three different messages through three different media may be needed to reach all three targets.

Marketing Mix

The marketing mix is a set of four controllable variables that the firm uses in the form of a market strategy to influence the target market. Any variable under the control of the firm that can influence the level of consumer response is a part of the marketing mix.

E. Jerome McCarthy popularized the four-factor classification called the 4 Ps, although it was Neil Borden who named the classification scheme "marketing mix." It consists of:

Product.
Place.
Promotion.
Price.

Illustration 2.4 lists some of the marketing variables for each of the 4 Ps.

Some scholars have spent much time breaking the 4 Ps down (into submixes, etc). In this book we will only outline the basics of each. The important concept to understand is the relationship of the four elements to each other. They form the foundation for the strategy and implementation of the marketing plan. An example of a marketing mix will be presented also.

ILLUSTRATION 2.4   Four Ps Marketing Variables

Product	Place	Promotion	Price
Quality	Channels	Advertising	List price
Features	Coverage	Personal setting	Discounts
Options	Locations	Sales promotion	Allowances
Style	Inventory	Publicity	Payment period
Brand name	Transport		Credit terms
Packaging			
Sizes			
Services			
Warranties			
Returns			

Product. The right one for the target. It is the nature of the item or service itself as it is designed to satisfy a predetermined group of customers or segment. Included in this element are decisions related to selecting new products or services, branding, packaging, and adding or dropping items from the product line. It all comes down to developing the right *product* (or service) for the target market.

Place. Reaching the target; implies not only a geographic area, but all the channels and marketing intermediaries through which the product moves. You must consider where, when, and by whom the goods and services are to be offered for sale. Also look at transportation, storage, and distribution.

Promotion. Telling and selling the customer. Communicating to the target market about the right product in the right place at the right price includes advertising, selling, sales promotion, and any other communication means.

Price. Make it fair—you want to make it as attractive as possible. An equitable price goes along with the image you want to portray. You must consider competitors' prices, market size, and demand as well as discounts, markups, and terms of sale. Don't forget to check any legal restrictions affecting price.

Think of the 4 Ps (marketing mix) as a part of the inside of the T.I.P. marketing triangle. Underscoring all four of the mix elements are the three basic concepts of *timing, image,* and *persuasion*.

Marketing Mix Example

Source Perrier is a French company that sells soft drinks and bottled, naturally carbonated mineral waters. In the early 1970s, its sales were stagnated in its major market segment, Western Europe. Its efforts to expand sales began first by identifying the U.S. market (characterized by both low sales and demand in the past).

The company used segmentation to identify the affluent, health-conscious adult market as the target. The target market had 26 locations that were known to be receptive to higher-priced imported beverages and health foods. This target was the one of initial concentration. Within it, they identified key pockets that fit the segment profile.

The market strategy used involved the following:

Product. Repositioning the product from a gourmet specialty item to a readily available chic and "in"-drink alternative to both alcoholic and other soft-drink beverages.

Promotion. Perrier used snob appeal by advertising in high fashion magazines read by a more affluent reader. They also used Orson Welles as a personality for Perrier television commercials.

Price. Perrier was priced over 50% higher than the average soft drink. This only added to the already established aura of class and its snob appeal.

Place. Channels of distribution were modified. Over 75% of the distributors were replaced. This was done in conjunction with the change in emphasis from specialty gourmet shops to supermarkets and convenience stores.

The results of this strategy were tremendous. Their growth in sales was the genesis of a new and dynamic niche that continues to expand and intensify competition. Sales increased over 20% in one year. After only two years, sales of Perrier water represented half the company's total revenues of over $500 million.

Well over two dozen water bottlers have attempted to compete for the market segment created, including giants like Cadbury Schweppes, Ltd. and the Nestlé Company.

SUMMARY

The process of defining your market can be somewhat overwhelming since it is full of many difficult questions and concepts. The T.I.P. marketing model will help simplify the focus that a small business should have when looking at their marketing arena.

The concepts of segment and target market are hard to differentiate. Most authors regard them as interchangeable since the difference is actually negligible. The segment that you choose to go for becomes your target market. There is a great variation in size of segments; consequently, there is a range in size for the target market, too.

Use the work sheets to become familiar with your segments (eventually, your target markets). Keep these work sheets handy when you

ILLUSTRATION 2.5 Defining Your Market. (Adapted from Forrest H. Frantz, Successful Small Business Management. Reprinted by permission of Prentice-Hall, Inc., Englewood Cliffs, NJ.)

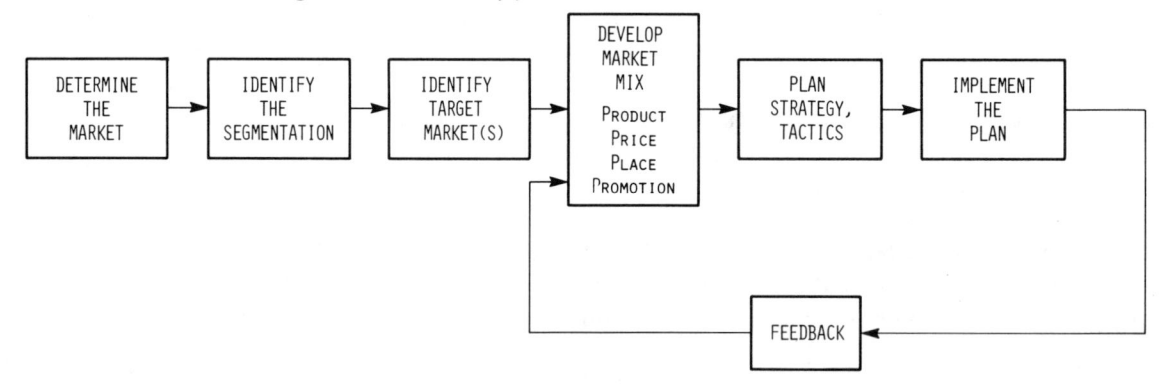

plan your promotion and media strategy. The characteristics of the potential consumers are invaluable as a source of ideas or approaches.

The decisions you make will depend on company resources, competitive market strategies, and many other product-, price-, place-, and promotion-related questions. Take these questions seriously. Do not be afraid to rework them in the planning process (Chapter 8).

Illustration 2.5 depicts the process of defining your market in a flow-chart format. This process was covered in the Marketing Mix section and will be further developed throughout the remainder of the book.

3

MARKET RESEARCH

Who wants to buy your product or service? If several groups of people want to buy, which is the easiest and cheapest to reach? Which will pay the most for your product? How much will it buy? Where are these customers located? How do you get to them?

The answer to these questions are found by market research.

People have been doing market research for some time. The children of Israel sent interviewers to sample the market and produce of Canaan. Marketing research as we know it today began around 1900 and grew as companies became more interested in regional and then national markets. Sampling techniques, as well as the use of the psychological interview, were developed in the 1930s.

IMPORTANCE OF MARKET RESEARCH

Market research helps the company recognize and seize profitable opportunities, identify the problems and results of current marketing programs, and develop alternative solutions to the problems. In other words, market research identifies the risks and consequences of sales strategies.

Strategic or Tactical Research Needs

There are two types of decisions: strategic decisions have long-range implications and effects; tactical decisions are short term and usually they are altered on a regular basis.

A company looking into entering a new industry or market needs strategic information because they are making a *strategic* move. They need information on competitors—strength, weaknesses, and market penetration. A company needs to know its market growth potential. What are the financial, production, and marketing requirements for success in that industry? This is strategic information.

When the company *does* enter the new industry they need certain short-term information. They need to know the prices charged by competitors, current product packaging, and the means of product distribution. This is short-term, *tactical* information.

People who are just starting a business need *both* strategic and tactical information. Strategic information answers the questions: What is the best location? What is the best customer to go after? How much is all this going to cost me? Tactical information answers the questions: How do I package my product or present my services? How do I get to the customer? What are my competitors doing?

The kind of information you need—tactical or strategic—will determine what publications or sources of information you need to consult. The following typical business information needs are ordered according to whether they are tactical or strategic needs.

Strategic	Tactical
Long-term forecasting	Short-term forecasting
Acquisition studies	Motivational research
Business premises location studies	Attitude surveys
Market potential	Customer acceptance of product
Market share . . . (customer characteristics)	. . . or service (packaging or presentation)
Analysis of channels of distribution	Price research
Identification of target markets	Competition's strengths and weaknesses

STEPS IN A RESEARCH PROJECT

The five basic steps in putting together marketing research are:

1. Define whether the need is tactical or strategic.
2. Develop the methodology you will use to do your research.
3. Collect the data.
4. Analyze and interpret the data.
5. Summarize your findings.

Define the Problem

Nothing in the research process is as important as defining the problem into which you hope to gain insight by your research. Be very specific when you formulate the problem. Instead of defining the problem as "getting into a new industry," you should be more specific and say the problem is "getting into a new industry at the lowest price level." The problem should not be to determine the best new packaging design, but to determine the best new packaging design among five alternatives.

To help you define the problem, you should ask yourself:

1. Is the need *strategic*, for entering a new market, or *tactical*, for bettering yourself in the present industry?
2. What area in your business do you think research will help?
3. Where do you want the company to be in one year? Three years?
4. How do you think research can increase your sales?
5. To increase your sales and go toward your one- and three-year goals, what information do you absolutely need?
    (a) Can you be more specific?
    (b) What objectives do you wish to accomplish?

To write down your answers to these questions, use Form 3.1.

Develop the Methodology You Will Use to Do Your Research

Once you know your problem and some of the objectives you wish to accomplish, you need a plan of attack. A methodology is a way of accomplishing your objectives to solve your problem.

If your objective in research is to find out tactical information about customers, product appearance, or pricing, your methodology would be to design a survey.

To research *tactical* problems, the following steps are recommended:

1. Determine sample size and makeup.
2. Determine sampling technique (e.g., telephone, person-to-person, mail).
3. Prepare questionnaire.
4. Conduct interviews.
5. Process and analyze data.

To research *strategic* problems, the recommended steps are:

1. Determine what published resources are needed.
2. Research and document your resources.
3. Process and analyze the data.

Collect the Data

Collecting data is the action stage of the research project. It requires discipline and considerable time. This is the stage of research that shows whether you are committed or not.

FORM 3.1 What Is the Market Problem?

Is the need *strategic*, for entering a new market, or *tactical*, for bettering yourself in the present industry? Why?
_____
_____
_____

What area in your business do you think research will help?
_____
_____
_____

Where do you want the company to be in one year? Three years?
_____
_____
_____

How do you think this research can increase your sales?
_____
_____
_____

To increase your sales and go toward your one- and three-year goals, what information do you absolutely need?
_____
_____
_____

What problem do you want the research to solve?
_____
_____
_____

Can you be more specific?
_____
_____
_____

What objectives do you wish to accomplish?
_____
_____
_____

For *strategic* information, collecting data involves reading and note taking at libraries, government agencies, and at the office or home. To get the data, you will telephone important resource people and have hard-to-get publications mailed to you.

To acquire *tactical* information about customers, your product or service, and pricing, you must design questionnaires. Then you either collect the information yourself or hire others. Customers, competitors, educators, suppliers, and the person on the street may be surveyed.

The ways of finding either tactical or strategic information will be discussed later within this chapter.

Analyze and Interpret the Data

Analyzing the data means simply outlining all the facts. Interpreting the findings involves determining what the results imply about the direction you should take. Interpretation is largely subjective, but an unbiased look at the facts will lead you to the best solution.

The purpose of analysis is the reduction of data to intelligible and interpretable form. Analysis is the categorizing, ordering, manipulating, and summarizing of the data. The interpretation takes the results of the analysis, makes inferences, and then draws conclusions. A meaningful analysis and interpretation will require the careful mixing of judgment, informed insight, statistical procedures, and a thorough knowledge of the decision alternatives under consideration.

Summarize Your Findings

The summary of research is a written report, whether it is a formal report covering several pages or an informally handwritten report on one sheet of paper. The basic purpose of the research report is to communicate the results, conclusions, and recommendations of the research project. If the findings have to be presented to management, the report should be more formal.

The *formal* report has the following format:

1. Title page.
2. Table of contents, charts, graphs, and illustrations.
3. Introduction.
4. Summary and highlights.
5. Conclusions and recommendations.
6. Complete findings of the study.
7. Supporting charts and tables.
8. Appendixes.

The *title page* includes the subject of the study, for whom it was prepared, by whom it was prepared, and the date. The *table of contents* is not required for reports of less than 10 pages. For longer reports, it aids the reader in locating key information. The *introduction* shows the basic purpose of the research and the specific objectives. It describes the methodology and the type of resources used. The *summary* presents the research highlights in a straightforward and precise manner. The *conclusions and recommendations* show what the research results imply. The *findings* show all the details of the study from which the recommendations are derived. The *supporting charts and tables* present the data in graphic form.

Finally, the *appendixes* are used to present copies of questionnaires, published information consulted, transcripts of conversations, or any other data that might be helpful to the report user.

PRIMARY OR SECONDARY INFORMATION

Research information falls into two broad categories: primary research and secondary research.

Primary research is research done directly with the customer or representatives of the customer. This type of research is usually for tactical, short-term information. Primary research usually takes the form of personal interviews, telephone interviews, or direct mail questionnaires. Usually it is conducted to determine: short-term forecasting of sales and inventory needs; motivational research; customer attitude; customer acceptance of product, packaging, and price; and strengths and weaknesses of competitors.

Strategic information may be gathered by primary research, too. Primary research may be used in such long-term strategic interests as determining and securing a new business location.

Secondary research is usually found in published public information, for example, looking at the U.S. Census is secondary research. Most strategic information is available from secondary, public sources. Information about long-term forecasting, acquisition, market potential, market share, customer characteristics, and analysis of channels of distribution can be found in secondary sources.

SECONDARY (STRATEGIC) RESEARCH

Secondary research is research carried out to solve a strategic, long-range problem. Secondary research helps you find the size of the market, the cost to enter or expand the market, and the best location for a business.

Secondary research is carried out in the following steps:

1. Determine published resources needed.
2. Research and document the resources.
3. Process and analyze the data.

Determine Published Resources Needed

Published information is information that is available to the public from private and governmental sources, including books and publications available at libraries or government buildings or through the mail. Published, public information may include information available on national computerized data bases such as Compuserve, Source, and *The New York Times*.

Published market information falls into three broad categories: industry, consumer, and competitor/industrial customer.

Some of the things you can discover from consulting general industry publications is your industry's growth rate and sales and expense figures. You can also discover new technological changes in your industry, general personnel salaries and policies, and the government controls and regulations that apply to you.

Consumer information publications divulge average consumer expenditures, number of consumers available to a company in your area, and the location of consumers. Published sources might be consulted to develop lists of consumers or to view their finances.

Competitor/industrial customer information can be found in public libraries, trade associations, and government libraries. Competitor or industrial customer information shows sales and operating figures, number of employees, and sales plans of specific companies.

Research and Document the Resources

Strategic (secondary) research usually starts in a library or at a government bookstore or by calling a trade association.

Most people know where a good local public library is. University libraries are also likely to have the published resources you need.

Publications are kept for reference and sale by the 43 U.S. Department of Commerce district offices and the 12 Bureau of Census regional offices. Government publications from all bureaus are sold by the U.S. Government Printing Office and its branch bookstores in 20 cities. These may be good sources of industry, customer, and competitor information. If there is no bookstore near you, you can call or write

SUPERINTENDENT OF DOCUMENTS
U.S. Government Printing Office
Washington, DC 20402

Trade Associations are organizations of businesses like yours whose purpose is to disseminate information about your industry. FTD (Florists' Transworld Delivery) is a trade association of retail florists. If you don't know the name of the trade association for your industry, you can look it up in *The Encyclopedia of Associations* from Gale Research Company, Detroit, which lists all major associations in the United States. Industry trade associations usually have the most complete information about your industry available, and they can be reached by a phone call.

A listing of the sources of consumer, industry, and competitor/industrial customer information you might consult follows this section.

Research Guide

When you go into the library or store or read industry information, it helps to have a written guide such as Form 3.2.

This form can be used to guide your research survey. In the first column write the general information category (industry information, consumer information, or competitor/industrial customer information). The second column is for a more specific area (industry sales, competitor operating figures, average customer expenditures, etc.). In the third column, write the title and source of the publication.

FORM 3.2   Research Guide

General Category	Specific Area	Resource

Process and Analyze the Data

Once you have done research and taken notes, outline the data on paper and then match your data to your outline. Make charts comparing contradictory results. Try to summarize your findings on one page.

Secondary information may be divided according to whether it applies to:

Industry research.
Consumer research.
Competitor/industrial research.

INDUSTRY SECONDARY (STRATEGIC) RESEARCH

Industry publications show your industry's growth rate and your industry's sales and expense figures. Industry information will give you general data about an industry, similar industries, population, and political realities.

Publications about industry conditions are available from the government, trade associations, and private sources.

Government Industry Information

The U.S. and state governments are good places to start industry research. They have hundreds of good publications, but here we will consider only a few of the best.

The best overview of an industry published by the government with historical growth trends, latest developments, government regulation, and pay scales is the *U.S. Industrial Outlook* for the latest year, available from Superintendent of Documents at the address given earlier. The book has data on over 200 industries. Any industry researcher will always start with the *Industrial Outlook*.

A handy resource if you want to be able to contact anyone at a government agency is the *Federal Statistical Directory*. It is a telephone directory, by agency, office, and individual of all information contacts in the federal government (available, also, from the Superintendent of Documents).

A much consulted government publication is the monthly *Survey of Current Business*. The *Survey* draws together the most important business statistics from the Department of Labor, the Federal Reserve Board, the Census Bureau, and other federal and private sources in a compendium of the latest measures of the U.S. business performance. This is an excellent source if you want to see sales performance in a given industry. It shows monthly sales for the last year with annual averages for the preceding two years. The *Survey* gives information on national personal consumption expenditures, private investment, new plant and equipment expenditures, and employment (with average hours and earnings per week). It's available from

U.S. DEPARTMENT OF COMMERCE
PUBLICATION SERVICES
Bureau of the Census
Room 1061
Building 4
Washington, DC 20233

Individual industries are surveyed by the Bureau of Census. Their surveys provide information on industrial production, productivity, and price levels. Business and industrial marketers use the data to make forecasts; to analyze sales performance; to lay out sales territories; to measure business competition; and to decide on the location of new plants, warehouses, and stores. These surveys also contain information on types of businesses, kinds of products, and competition in a given geographical area. Surveys are available for the following industrial groups:

Retail trade.
Wholesale trade.
Service industries.
Manufacturers.
Construction industries.
Mineral industries.
Transportation.

These publications are available from

DATA USER SERVICES DIVISION
Bureau of the Census
Washington, DC 20233

County Business Patterns is an annual publication useful in analyzing market potential, setting sales quotas and budgets, and making basic economic studies in small areas. It provides information on employment and payroll by county and industry. This employment information is assembled from the Internal Revenue Service and Social Security Administration records. Knowing the number of workers in an industry in your area, you can obtain an idea of what the market potential is by multiplying the average purchases per worker by the number of workers in that industry.

The federal government also has some special industry analysis services that can be reached by telephone. Two excellent reference guides to these offices, information available, as well as the names, addresses, and contact people of various governmental agencies are: The Washington Monitor's *Federal Yellow Book* or *Congressional Yellow Book* (a loose-leaf directory of federal departments and agencies). This can be obtained from

THE WASHINGTON MONITOR, INC.
1301 Pennsylvania Avenue, NW
Suite 1000
Washington, DC 20004
(202) 347-7757

Also the *Guide to Information from Government Sources* by Van Mayros and D. Michael Werner (Copyright © 1983) (listings for 77 departments and agencies, over 600 publications and data bases, thoroughly described and cross referenced to 113 functional specialties) can be obtained from

CHILTON BOOK COMPANY
Radnor, Pennsylvania 19089

The National Technical Information Service handles queries on more than one million government-sponsored technical reports of all kinds. For $100, they will do a search of your subject. If one has already been done, they will provide a copy for $25. The phone number for the order desk is (703) 557-4650. These and other federal telephone numbers are included in

A Researcher's Guide to Washington
Washington Researchers
910 17th Street, NW
Washington, DC 20005

Most states have agencies that collect state sales tax. In California, this agency is called the State Board of Equalization. These state agencies collect data on retail sales throughout the state. Their basis of information is every retail business in that state. In California, the State Board of Equalization publishes a report called *Taxable Sales in California*. These state sales tax agency publications break sales down to the city. The sales tax publication also tells you how many of a certain type of store (retail clothing, for instance) there are in a city. The publication shows the total sales of all (retail clothing) stores. Dividing total (retail clothing) sales in a city by the total number of (retail clothing) businesses in the area gives you the average dollar sales for each (retail clothing) store in that city.

Private Industry Information

To find out what has recently been published about the industry in the media, there is no better guide than the *Business Periodicals Index*. This source lists articles by subject heading from 150 or more business periodicals. If something has been published about your industry in the business press, it's listed here. This is available at almost all libraries or from

H. W. WILSON COMPANY
950 University Avenue
Bronx, NY 10452

Sources of State Information contains a list of public and private agencies that supply information about their states. *State Industrial Directories* includes a list of state directories of manufacturers' names, addresses, and other information. Both are available from

CHAMBER OF COMMERCE OF THE
UNITED STATES
1615 H Street, NW
Washington, DC 20006

If you are thinking of international markets, there's one that lists all kinds of business directories from all over the world. It also gives you the price, publisher, and a description of what each directory contains. It's called the *Bulletin of Public Affairs Information Service*, available from

PUBLIC AFFAIRS INFORMATION
SERVICE
11 West 40th Street
New York, NY 10018

INDUSTRY SECONDARY (STRATEGIC) RESEARCH

For information on manufacturers' agents and distributors, a good source is *Distribution Channels for Industrial Goods* by William M. Diamond, available from

BUREAU OF BUSINESS RESEARCH
Ohio State University
1659 North High
Columbus, OH 43210

For forecasting there are three excellent publications: *Robert Morris Annual Statement Studies*, *NCR Expenses in Retailing*, and the Accounting Corporation of America's *Barometer of Small Business*. These publications give you average expenses for several types of businesses. The RMA *Annual Statement Studies* lists the most industries of the three. *NCR Expenses in Retailing* has the most detail about the expenses of doing business in various retail businesses (drugstores, clothing stores, office supply, etc.). The *Barometer of Small Business* lists a variety of retail stores not included in the NCR book.

Another good book for forecasting is the *Almanac of Business and Industrial Financial Ratios*, published annually by Prentice-Hall. This source lists a number of business, sales, and operating ratios for many industries. The computations are from tax returns supplied by the IRS, and the data allow comparison of company's financial ratios with others in the industry. The Dun & Bradstreet *Cost of Doing Business* also has some costs as a percentage of sales for several types of businesses.

These books are available from:

Book	Address
RMA Annual Statement Studies	Robert Morris Associates P.O. Box 8500 S-1140 Philadelphia, PA 19178
NCR Expenses in Retailing	NCR Corporation Sales Promotion Manager Dayton, OH 45479
Small Business Barometer	Accounting Corporation of America 1929 First Avenue San Diego, CA 92101
Almanac of Business and Industrial Financial Ratios	Prentice-Hall, Inc. Englewood Cliffs, NJ 07631
Cost of Doing Business	Dun & Bradstreet, Inc. Business Economics Division 99 Church Street New York, NY 10007

Bacon's Publicity Checkers is probably the most complete source of print media available. Bacon's lists the names, addresses, and editors of all major magazines and newspapers in America. It is a two-volume directory published annually and revised three times a year. It tells not only the editor's name, but also the type of publicity releases used by each publication. Order from

BACON'S PUBLISHING COMPANY
14 East Jackson Boulevard
Chicago, IL 60604

Preparation for Finding Industrial Resources. Review the preceding list of resources and write down the name and publisher on Form 3.3.

CONSUMER SECONDARY RESEARCH

Consumer research sources show average consumer expenditures, number of consumers available to a company in your area, and the location of consumers. Published sources might be consulted to develop lists of consumers or to view their finances.

One of the best sources of information on who your consumers are and what they have to spend is the industry association of your particular industry. If you don't know what your industry association is called or where it is, consult *The Encyclopedia of Associations*, mentioned earlier.

Besides industry association material, other publications that will help you with your consumers are available from the government or private sources.

Government Sources of Consumer Information

The most well-known information about consumers is the general information about the whole population called the *Census of Population and Housing*, available from the U.S. Government Printing Office. The census provides information about the population characteristics of states, counties, cities, towns, and many neighborhoods. The 1980 census col-

FORM 3.3   Industry Research Guide

Publication	Publisher	Library

lected information on age, race, sex, education, income, occupation (including the industry to which that occupation belonged), and employment. It also covered housing characteristics, such as value of housing units, rent, kitchen and plumbing facilities, and household appliances.

One of the most important uses of the census is measuring market potentials (i.e., questions about age, income, ethnic balance, and so on) of a market. Population and housing data are useful in allocating advertising expenditures, delineating trade areas, and analyzing sales performance.

Marketing Information Guide, published monthly by the Department of Commerce, lists recently published studies and statistics that serve as useful sources of current information on markets.

County and City Data Book from the U.S. Government Printing Office gives statistics on population, income, education, employment, housing, and retail and wholesale prices for various cities and metropolitan areas.

Private Publications on Consumer Information

Guide to Consumer Markets is published by the Conference Board and provides data on the behavior of customers under the headings of population, employment, income, expenditures, production and distribution and prices.

Consumer Market and Magazine Report, by Daniel Starch, describes the household population of the United States with respect to a number of demographic variables and consumption statistics. The profiles are based on a large probability sample, and they give good consumer behavioral and socioeconomic characteristics.

Rand McNally Commercial Atlas and Marketing Guide contains marketing data and maps for some 100,000 cities and towns in the United States, including auto registrations, basic trading areas, manufacturing, transportation, population, and related data.

Market Guide, published by *Editor and Publisher* magazine presents data on the principal industries, transportation facilities, households, banks and retail outlets for some 1500 U.S. and Canadian newspaper markets.

Survey of Buying Power is published by *Sales and Marketing Management* magazine and gives information on population, income, retail sales, and buying power for all cities in the U.S. with populations over 10,000.

Mailing Lists. Once you have identified who and what your consumer is you can get mailing lists from trade publications, industry associations, and list brokers (listed in the telephone Yellow Pages).

Standard Rate & Data Service: Business Publication Rates and Data provides information about media publishers and local markets.

These books are available from:

Book	Address
Guide to Consumer Markets	The Conference Board 845 Third Avenue New York, NY 10022
Consumer Market and Magazine Report	Starch, Inra, Hooper, Inc. E. Boston Post Road Mamaroneck, NY 10544
Rand McNally Commercial Atlas and Marketing Guide	Rand McNally P.O. Box 7600 Chicago, IL 60680
Market Guide	Editor and Publisher magazine 575 Lexington Avenue New York, NY 10022
Survey of Buying Power	Sales and Marketing Management magazine 67 Atlantic Avenue Manasqua, NY 08736
Standard Rate & Data Service: Business Pub. Rates and Data	Standard Rate & Data Service 5201 Old Orchard Road Skokie, IL 60076

Preparation for Finding Consumer Information

Review the preceding list of resources and write down the name and publisher on Form 3.4.

COMPETITOR/INDUSTRIAL CUSTOMER SECONDARY INFORMATION RESEARCH

Competitor or industrial customer information is data about companies' sales and operating figures, their number of employees, their sales plans, and who their primary customers are.

Dun & Bradstreet Directories are lists of U.S. firms including information on products, annual sales, number of employees, names and

FORM 3.4 Consumer Research Guide

Publication	Publisher	Library
_____	_____	_____
_____	_____	_____
_____	_____	_____
_____	_____	_____
_____	_____	_____

titles of 75,000 key executives. Listings are cross-referenced by company name and product classification.

Also published by Dun & Bradstreet are the *Middle Market Directory* and the *Million Dollar Directory*. The first lists companies with assets in the range of $500,000 to $999,999. It offers information on 30,000 companies' officers, products, sales, and number of employees. The latter publication gives the same information for companies with assets over $1 million.

Fortune Plant and Product Directory of the 1,000 Largest U.S. Industrial Corporations is an annual list with addresses, sales, assets, profits, employment, and products.

Moody's Industrial Manual is an annual describing the operations, plants, subsidiaries, officers, directors, comparative income statements, long-term earnings record, and other financial and operating data on domestic and foreign industrial companies. Similar publications are also available on banking, utilities, government, and transportation.

Poor's Register of Corporations, Directors & Executives is a multi-volume service listing information on over 30,000 U.S. and Canadian corporations and key executives, with addresses, products, services, sales, number of employees, and standard industrial classifications. The *Register* lists over 260,000 prospects, including the job titles, business addresses, and telephone numbers of 70,000 top-level officers and directors.

Sweet's Catalog is an annual file of manufacturers' catalogs, including names, products, trade names, and market data for the following areas: architectural; light construction; industrial construction; plant engineering; metalworking equipment; and product design.

The *Yellow Pages* classified telephone directory, available from local telephone companies, lists local manufacturers and service firms.

Directory of Intercorporate Ownership by Simon and Schuster is in two volumes. Volume One contains parent companies, with divisions, subsidiaries, and American companies owned by foreign firms. Volume Two is an alphabetic listing of all the entries in Volume One.

Sheldon's Retail Directory of the United States and Canada published by Phelon, Sheldon, and Marsar supplies the largest chain, department, and specialty stores according to their state and city or their Canadian province and city. This source also includes merchandise managers and buyers.

The preceding books are available from:

Book	Address
Dun & Bradstreet Directories *Middle Market Directory* *Million Dollar Directory*	Dun & Bradstreet, Inc. 99 Church Street New York, NY 10007
Fortune Plant and Product Directory of the 1,000 Largest U.S. Industrial Corporations	Fortune, Time–Life Building New York, NY 10020

Book	Address
Moody's Industrial Manual	Moody's Investor Service 99 Church Street New York, NY 10007
Poor's Register of Corporations, Directors & Executives	Standard & Poor's Corporation 345 Hudson Street New York, NY 10014
Sweet's Catalog	Sweet's Catalog Service 330 West Forty-second Street New York, NY 10036
Yellow Pages classified telephone directory	Local telephone companies
Directory of Intercorporate Ownership	Simon and Schuster The Simon and Schuster Building 1230 Avenue of the Americas New York, NY 10020
Sheldon's Retail and Phelon's Resident Buyers Book	Phelon, Sheldon and Marsar Inc. 32 Union Square New York, NY 10003

Preparation for Finding Competitor/Industrial Customer Information

Review the preceding list of resources and write down the name and publisher on Form 3.5.

This completes the section on secondary (strategic) research. The publications listed are those that the authors have found to be valuable over the years. There are many more. The best research approach is to research these publications and keep your eyes open for anything else that will help your particular business. Often it is very helpful to talk about your project with a reference librarian. Finally, set aside at least 6 hours for this research. It can't be done in an hour during lunch.

FORM 3.5   Competitor/Industrial Customer Research Guide

Publication	Publisher	Library

TACTICAL (PRIMARY) RESEARCH

Primary research is research that is done one on one. It is not research that you may get from libraries, government, associations, or other repositories of publications. Primary research is *original* research done by you or an agency you have chosen.

Primary research is research done directly with the customer or representatives of the customer. This type of research is usually for tactical, short-term information. Primary research usually takes the form of personal interviews, telephone interviews, or direct mail questionnaires.

Usually primary research is conducted to determine short-term forecasting of sales and inventory needs; motivational research; customer attitude; customer acceptance of product, packaging, and price; and strengths and weaknesses of competitors.

Primary research is carried out by following these steps:

1. Determine sample size and makeup.
2. Determine sampling technique (telephone, person-to-person, mail).
3. Prepare questionnaire.
4. Conduct mailing or personal/telephone interviewing.
5. Process and analyze data.

Sample Size and Makeup

Sampling assumes that we can make a decision concerning the characteristics of a large number of items based on an analysis of a limited number of items from the larger group. The larger group of items is called the "population" and the limited number of items selected from the larger group is called the sample.

An example of sampling is to talk to 200 people to get an idea of how the population in general will accept your product. Another example is to ask certain of your customers questions to determine how your customers feel in general.

Whom and how many do I want to sample? is the first question you must ask yourself in primary research.

Sampling Techniques

There are three basic sampling techniques: personal interview, mail questionnaire, and telephone interview.

Personal interviews are well-suited to complex problems requiring extensive explanations and new products. The advantages of the personal interview are that it allows the interviewer to gain additional information from his or her own observations, there is better control, and the information gleaned is more detailed. Furthermore, you'll get a higher percentage of completed answers, you can use visual aids, it allows in-depth exploration, and questions may be adjusted to the respondent's general interest.

The disadvantages of the personal interview are its higher cost compared to the other methods, the direct influence of interviewer bias, and the detailed supervision of data collection required. Also it is time-consuming to find and train interviewers.

Telephone surveys are best when the information required is well-defined, nonconfidential in nature, and limited in amount. The advantages of the telephone survey are that it is fast, inexpensive, and has a wide geographical reach. The disadvantages are that it is limited to telephone subscriber locations, must require only a small amount of information, and is a difficult technique to use to obtain motivational and attitudinal information.

Mail surveys can be used to broaden the base of an investigation to supplement the firsthand knowledge gained by the other surveys. They are most effective when well-defined information is required and specific, limited answers are called for.

The advantages of mail surveys are that you can get wide distribution at a relatively low cost, they avoid interviewer bias, you can reach remote places, and the respondent remains anonymous.

The disadvantages of mail surveys are that up-to-date mailing lists are not always available, returns may not be representative of the entire group surveyed (only 5 to 20% are returned), questionnaire length is limited, and it is difficult to ensure that questions are fully understood.

PREPARING A QUESTIONNAIRE

To prepare a questionnaire you must (1) list the objectives, (2) determine the type of questionnaire and questions you will use, and (3) write the questions you want to ask.

Objectives are what you hope to accomplish with this questionnaire. For example, if you are a laser manufacturer who is concerned with the perceived superiority of your product technically, you might have as your objective to find out (1) if the subject thinks a better product exists, (2) what that product is, (3) how your product's technical superiority ranks with the competition, and (4) what technical improvement might increase your product's superiority.

It is a good idea to limit your objectives to no more than five. The smaller the number of objectives, the more effective the questionnaire can be.

What type of questionnaire means either: personal interview, telephone, or mail. Personal interviews may be either one on one or in a group.

Types of questions include yes–no or true–false, closed response, multiple choice, rating scales, and ranking types. Examples of each type follow:

Yes–No, True–False: "Are you responsible for laser purchases?" ( )Yes ( )No.

Closed Response: "List all brands of laser equipment with which you are familiar."

Multiple Choice: "If you were to buy laser equipment today, which of the following brands would you consider?" ( )Jax ( )Firebreather ( )Twentieth Century ( )Hayes ( )Elmore

Rating Scales: "How would you rate the quality of Hayes Lasers?" ( )Very good ( )Good ( )Average ( )Low ( )Very low ( )Don't know

Ranking: "How would you rank these lasers in regard to price (1 being least expensive, 2 second least expensive, etc.)?" ( )Jax ( )Firebreather ( )Twentieth Century ( )Hayes ( )Elmore

When writing the questions that you want asked, you should follow these simple rules:

No question should be over 20 words.

Ask no more than 15 questions, maximum.

Use simple, everyday words.

State questions in a specific, clear, direct manner.

Avoid ambiguous words and those that may be difficult to define or interpret (e.g., *quality, taste, service,* etc.) without first defining the terms yourself.

Avoid combining two questions into one.

Don't lead the respondent to a bias response.

Always start with a simple or general, yet interesting, question. End the questionnaire with more difficult and specific questions.

Encourage the respondents to give additional information that may enhance their individual reactions or qualify their remarks.

On Form 3.6, you may write your own questions.

HOW TO CONDUCT MAILINGS AND INTERVIEWS

Mailings

In mailings you should be concerned with (1) the appearance of the questionnaire, (2) ways to increase response, and (3) contents of the mailer.

The appearance of a mailer is enhanced when the questionnaire is attractive, looks easy, and is interesting. Use of white space gives the questionnaire an easy-to-complete look. Use of illustrations will help the looks, also.

FORM 3.6 Questionnaire Planning Form

Objectives

_____
_____
_____
_____
_____
_____
_____
_____

Type:__ Personal Interview __Telephone __Mail
       __One-on-One __Group

Questions

_____
_____
_____
_____
_____
_____
_____
_____
_____
_____
_____
_____
_____
_____
_____
_____
_____
_____

Response may be increased by asking questions of great interest to the respondent even when they are of no interest to the company sending the questionnaire. Premiums (gifts, money samples) often help increase response. The premium should be something the respondent will find desirable but that will not bias his answers.

The mailer should contain the questionnaire and a personal cover letter telling the importance of the respondent's answers and how he will benefit. Assure the respondent of confidentiality. The package should also contain a self-addressed, postage-paid envelope. A business reply mail permit, which allows your company to only pay for the letters that respond, is available at the local U.S. Postal Service office for about $50.

Conducting Telephone or Personal Interviews

With personal or telephone interviewing you can use in-house interviewers or hire a firm or individuals to conduct the survey. In any case you need to set ground rules and train and supervise the interviewers.

The list of ground rules each interviewer is given could include the following rules:

Read questions exactly as worded on the questionnaire and in the same order.

Always record an answer for every question. Note if the respondent refused to answer.

Always record answers in the proper space.

Don't explain or add questions.

Record answers exactly even if you must use abbreviations.

Always present a good appearance and pleasant manner.

Introduce yourself and the name of the organization, give the questionnaire objectives, and explain how answering the questionnaire will benefit the respondent.

In the training session give each interviewer complete written instructions on how to conduct the interview, how to classify respondents, the meaning of each question, how to record answers, and any other responsibilities. Also give the interviewers an adequate supply of questionnaires, directions to interviewing locations, identification cards, sheets on which to list interview data, time sheets, and an envelope in which to store all materials. Have interviewers read over the questionnaires until they are almost memorized. Have each interviewer give a test interview in your presence.

Ongoing and postinterview supervision are also important. Spot-check all fieldwork. Send a followup postcard to the respondent or telephone to ask if he was interviewed. Conduct some validating and editing of completed questionnaires early in the interviewing process to check for errors and misinterpretation. Supervisors need a copy of all materials given to the interviewers, the names and addresses of interviewers, a schedule of interview times and locations, and a file for keeping this material in order.

PROCESSING AND ANALYZING THE DATA

Processing and Tabulating Data

To process and tabulate the data the questionnaires must be edited, and the frequency response to each question must be tabulated.

ILLUSTRATION 3.1   Tabulation Form Example.

QUESTION: "If you were to buy laser equipment today, which of the following brands would you consider?"

SIZE OF COMPANY (gross sales)	JAX	FIREBREATHER	20th CENTURY	HAYES	BROOKS
10,000 - 50,000	////	///	////// //	//// /	///
50,000 -100,000	//// //	//// //// //	///	//// //// /	//// ///
100,000 -500,000	///	////	//// ////	//// //// ////	//// ////
500,000 and up	//	//// /	////	////	//// ////

Edit questionnaires to insure that entries are legible and answers completely consistent.

Tabulating the data means to state the question and count the responses in each category. Illustration 3.1 gives an example of the form used.

Form 3.7 is a blank form you can use for your tabulations.

Analyzing the Data

Data may be analyzed in many ways. Two of the simplest methods use mode distributions and the arithmetic mean.

Mode is simply that value which occurs most frequently (i.e., the most typical value). For example, to a particular question that rated a product from very good to very low, the respondents answer one choice more frequently. Say, to the question "How would you rate the quality of Hayes' Lazers?" the respondents answered the following:

Very good—5 Good—10 Average—7 Low—5 Very low—2

The mode is Good, which has 10, the greatest number of positive responses.

The *arithmetic mean* is the sum of the values for each answer divided

FORM 3.7   Tabulation Form

Question: "_____?"

by the number of people answering. For example, assume that there are five potential customers for your product, and they currently buy 500, 1000, 1000, 2000, and 2500 units, respectively. The average units purchased by these five companies would be:

$$\frac{500 + 1000 + 1000 + 2000 + 2500}{5} = 1400$$

There are many other methods for analyzing data including *scatter diagrams*, *percentage relative* methods, and *median* methods and several other statistical measurements. Given the scope of this chapter, we could not cover all of these. (For information on the statistical measurements, see *Statistic Methods* by Arkin and Colton, Volume 27 in the Barnes and Noble College Outline Series.)

SUMMARY

To do research, researchers should know the type of information they are looking for and the reasons (objectives) for the research. The research is normally secondary for strategic or long-range purposes. Usually information is available for strategic needs from secondary sources (published articles, books, pamphlets, etc.). If the needs are short-range or tactical, the research should be primary, that is, original research conducted one on one by means of questionnaires.

4

CUSTOMERS: YOUR BEST SOURCE OF MONEY

Yourcompany enjoyed a commanding share of the market for years, then noticed its share fast slipping away to lesser known competitors.

No one made a better product. No one offered a lower price. No one had a better reputation in the industry. John Your, owner of Yourcompany, decided to sample his customers informally and see why they were buying from the competition. He wrote down a series of questions to ask and phoned 10 customers whom he knew had switched.

The answer: Next-day delivery.

John Your quickly reorganized his shipping department to get the product out quicker with no increase in staff. He promoted a strong new relationship within the shipping department. He then advertised the new delivery to his customers by telephone and mail.

Sales increased to $6.3 million from $4 million in less than a year.

That a company can increase sales by paying closer attention to its customers is an important fact. Your customers are your best source of money. Not the bank, not the owners, but the customer. By locating your business in the right place in relation to your customers, by making continuous efforts to build your customer base, and by making an effort to communicate with your customers, you can develop a system for increasing sales.

YOUR CUSTOMER

Determining who your customers are may at first seem elementary. You may say to yourself, Since I know my product, I certainly know my customers. For example, someone in the jewelry business says, "My customers are, of course, women." Someone selling products to homes would say, "My customers are homeowners."

In a broad sense, each would be right. However, general categories are equivalent to "shot-gunning" rather than precision rifle shooting at specific targets. To small businesses, the difference between concentration and hit-or-miss can be the difference between success and failure. Concentrating your fire on one specific type of customer at a time can multiply your results many times.

You must ask yourself the following series of questions to get an accurate picture of what your customer base is or could be:

1. What is my product or service?
2. What groups of people could use my product or service? Consumer groups? Industrial groups?
3. Among these groups, where is the demand for my product or service highest?
4. Among these groups, who is serviced by the greatest number of competitors? The least?

When considering the groups of people who could use your product or service, try to think of as many as possible, even if it seems extreme at the time. If you are already in business, a good guide to these groups could be is your own record of customers. What groups do they fall into? What characteristics do they have in common? You can use the list of your customers and acquaintances to build an effective mailing list.

If you already have existing customers, which group seems to buy the most of your product or service? From secondary research (see Chapter 3) you can determine where the demand is strongest for your product. Probably you can make some good guesses as well.

Which of these groups are serviced by many other businesses like yours? Which group has the smallest number of firms serving their needs?

Form 4.1 is provided for your answers to these questions.

LOCATING YOUR BUSINESS

In retail and many service businesses, location is essential for sales. In manufacturing and businesses that distribute to a broad area, location is important in increasing efficiency of distribution.

In this section, we will discuss the factors important in locating your business, the advisability of leasing or buying, how to find your customers with strategic (secondary) research, and how to best choose your location on a tactical (primary) research basis.

One thing you must avoid in any case when finding a location is decisions based on personal, not business, reasons. Some businesses locate strictly on the basis of personal preference. Such preferences can mean anything from locating a business within walking distance of the owner's home to buying a building from a friend merely because that friend wants to sell.

FORM 4.1 Who Is My Customer?

1. What is my product or service?

_____
_____
_____
_____

2. What groups of people could use my product or service? Consumer groups?

_____
_____
_____
_____

   Industrial groups?

_____
_____
_____
_____

3. Among these groups, where is the demand for my product or service highest?

_____
_____
_____
_____

4. Among these groups, who is serviced by the greatest number of competitors?

_____
_____
_____

   The least number of competitors?

_____
_____
_____
_____

You should begin your location consideration by asking yourself: Do I need a specialized building or can I be satisfied with an available, existing facility? Would an existing building be just as profitable as constructing a new facility?

Important Factors in Determining Location

You should consider the following factors when you decide to locate or relocate your business:

1. *Your Market.* Perhaps the most important consideration in any location is *being able to satisfy your market* (customers). You must study your market to determine who is interested in buying your product. Your plant or store must be located so that you have convenient access to all your customers, present and potential, and the customers have

convenient access to you. A good method for evaluating this is to mark the location of your customers with pins on a large map. It might also be desirable to indicate the location of your major competitors. By examining the scatter of customers, you can usually determine the center of your market area and the location that will best serve your customers.

If you are going after a new market or you are just starting a business, where your customers are located can be found by secondary research, discussed later in this chapter.

2. *Your Labor Force.* Your next consideration is where your labor force will come from. Some areas do not have an adequate group of people to draw on. One rule of thumb is that the ideal site is in an area that can provide 10 persons for consideration for each position to be filled. Furthermore, prevailing wages in the area must be in line with what you can pay. In some types of businesses, the skill of the workers must also be considered. If you are locating a software company, you will want to locate in an area that will have a surplus of computer programmers.

3. *Transportation.* Another factor in relocating or locating your business is transportation. The growth of air shipping makes sites near airports attractive to companies that must ship outside their immediate area. Interstate highways have increased the popularity of trucks as a method of moving goods. Railroad access is indispensable in transporting some types of products.

In addition to determining what mode of transportation is important for your present needs, you should consider what will be vital in the next 10 years. Look at access to freeways, available rail service, barge or deep water transportation, and the possibilities of using or expanding air shipments.

Retailers and some service businesses should locate near major auto routes with adequate parking or within walking distance in areas with heavy pedestrian traffic.

4. *Raw Materials.* Mark the sources of your raw materials with pins on a large map. If they all come from one area, you should consider advantages a competitor located adjacent to your supply source has over a more remote facility. It may be more important to be closer to raw materials than to your customers. Are there facilities to bring the raw materials to you rapidly and economically? Can you always be assured of supply regardless of the season? Does the supply of raw materials from the area seem assured in the foreseeable future?

5. *Suitability of the Site.* Is there a site available in the general area in which you have decided to locate? Is the terrain suitable? Are utilities (water, gas, etc.) adequate? Is it properly zoned? How is the location taxed?

Form 4.2 is a rating sheet for possible sites. Grade your chosen locations on each of the 15 factors. Grade an A for excellent, B for good, C for fair, and D for poor.

FORM 4.2 Rating Sheet on Sites

Factor	Grade
Centrally located to reach market	_____
Raw materials readily available	_____
Quantity of available labor	_____
Transportation availability and rates	_____
Labor rates of pay/estimated productivity	_____
Adequacy of utilities (sewer, water, power, gas)	_____
Local business climate	_____
Provision for future expansion	_____
Taxation burden	_____
Topography of the site	_____
Quality of police and fire protection	_____
Housing availability for workers and management	_____
Estimate of quality of this site in 10 years	_____
Located to take advantage of customer transportation needs	_____
Estimate of site in relation to my major competitor	_____

Buy or Lease?

An important consideration in locating or relocating a business facility is whether you should lease or buy the facility. Your decision should be based on these factors:

1. Are your requirements going to change rapidly over the next few years? If they are, probably you should consider leasing.

2. Do you often find yourself short of working capital? Can you use your available money better if it is not tied up in a building? What return can you expect from your funds if they are invested elsewhere? If your capital is tight, leasing may be preferable.

3. Can you secure a favorable lease with an option to purchase from the owner of the building? Because of tax considerations, a property owner may prefer to lease his property rather than sell it. In such a case, he is apt to make the lease price more attractive than the selling price.

4. Your accountant can advise you on the financial aspects of how leasing or purchasing might affect your financial picture. If you can buy property at a favorable price and the purchase does not cause a shortage in your working capital, then purchasing may be indicated.

5. Consider resale. Is the building one that can be readily resold? If so, to purchase it may be wise. On the other hand, leasing may be better if there is something about the building (e.g., little or no adjacent land for parking and plant addition) that could impede the resale of the property.

Retail Location by Types of Goods and Services

Another factor that affects site selection is the customers' view of the goods sold by a store. Customers tend to group products into three major categories: convenience, shopping, and specialty.

Convenience means low unit price, purchased frequently, little selling effort, bought by habit, and sold in numerous outlets, for example, candy bars, cigarettes, and milk. Convenience stores depend heavily on foot and auto traffic, they draw from the immediate area, and visibility of the store from the street is very important. Convenience stores are usually freestanding or in neighborhood shopping centers.

Shopping means high unit price, purchased infrequently, more intensive selling effort usually required, price and features are compared, and sold in selectively franchised outlets, for example, men's suits, automobiles, and furniture. Shopping goods draw on the immediate neighborhood as well as people outside the neighborhood. They should be near other stores and be convenient for people to get to and park. They require more advertising than convenience stores.

Specialty usually means high unit price (although price is not a purchase consideration), bought infrequently, requires a special effort on the part of the customer to make the purchase, and no substitutes are considered, for example, jewelry, perfume, cameras (specific brands), antiques, unusual items. Specialty stores don't rely as heavily on traffic and may be in isolated locations because they generate their own consumer traffic.

SECONDARY AND PRIMARY RESEARCH IN LOCATION ANALYSIS

If your customer is the ultimate consumer, that is, if you are a retailer or offer a service to the general public, location research is very important. It can make the difference between success and failure.

The retailer or service must consider two things in locating: (1) Where is the best customer base geographically? (2) What is the best location in that geographic area? The first consideration involves secondary (strategic) research, the other consideration requires mostly primary (tactical) research.

Secondary research in the census tracts will tell where your customers are located. Secondary research will also tell what the auto traffic count is at the location you are choosing. Primary research will show what the pedestrian traffic count is and whether the location is properly situated in terms of visibility and customer draw.

Secondary Research—People and Traffic

Every retail or service store has a *trading area*—the geographic region from which it draws its potential customers. Generally, data for trading areas, regardless of their size, can be assembled by combining a number of census tract areas. These may be the best single source of information.

Answers to questions like the following can be found in the census reports:

How many persons or families are there in the trading area and how has this changed over time?

Where do they work?

How many young or old persons are there; how many children or teenagers?

How many one-person households; how many small or large families?

What is the income of the families or individuals?

What do they do for a living?

Is the area an older established one or one where most residents are newcomers?

How many families own their homes? How many rent?

What is the value of the homes? What is the monthly rent?

What is the age and quality of the homes?

Do the homes have air conditioning; other appliances?

How many of the families own an automobile? How many own two or more?

We will consider five characteristics here—the general, social, labor force, income, and housing characteristics of the marketing area.

The first step in doing a population study in the census tracts is to get a map of the area in which you wish to locate. With a protractor draw a line that extends from your location at the center. Extend it 1 mile for convenience stores (grocery, dry cleaner, hairdresser, shoe repair, restaurant, liquor, etc.). Extend it 1½ to 2 miles for shopping stores (flower shop, clothing store, appliances, records, etc.). Extend it up to 4 miles for specialty goods stores (antiques, doll clothes, miniatures, art galleries, etc.).

Compare your map with the Census Tract map to see what census tracts apply and then look up information for those tracts.

General characteristics of the population describe the population in terms of race, sex, and age. See Illustration 4.1. If you are a children's clothing retailer, you will be particularly interested in the number of children as a percentage of the population. A store that sells ethnic groceries will be interested in the ethnic mix (race). A lady's hairdresser will be interested in the number of women within a certain age group who are in the population.

Social characteristics of the population show nativity (country of birth), parentage (i.e., the country where parents were born), and years of school completed. See Chart 4.2. If your customer is someone with

ILLUSTRATION 4.1 General Characteristics of the Population. (Source. Louis H. Vorzimer, *Small Business Administration*, Small Marketers Aid No. 154, Using Census Data to Select a Store Site.)

	Tract A	Tract B
RACE		
All persons	5 649	5 636
White	4 684	5 468
Negro	448	58
Percent Negro	7.9	1.0
AGE BY SEX		
Male, all ages	2 795	2 754
Under 5 years	353	168
3 and 4 years	102	72
5 to 9 years	237	211
5 years	47	33
6 years	47	42
10 to 14 years	207	327
14 years	30	82
15 to 19 years	186	315
15 years	31	70
16 years	35	82
17 years	35	75
18 years	33	64
19 years	52	24
20 to 24 years	751	222
20 years	126	38
21 years	179	34
25 to 34 years	445	280
35 to 44 years	241	341
45 to 54 years	201	445
55 to 59 years	61	154
60 to 64 years	48	108
65 to 74 years	40	128
75 years and over	25	55

a college education, or someone who comes from Switzerland, this information will be helpful to you.

Labor force characteristics of the population reveal the total number of individuals employed who are 16 years old and over and their profession, including professional, health worker, teacher, manager or administrator, salesworker, clerical, craftsman, construction worker, mechanic, transport worker, laborer, service worker, and farm worker. If you are marketing your product to teachers, obviously you want to choose census tract areas that have a high population of teachers. Also, the more people in the tract over 16 years of age that work, the better your overall sales will be. See Illustration 4.3.

Income characteristics of the population show income broken down in groups (e.g., less than $1,000, between $10,000 and $11,999, $50,000 or more). It also shows the median income of the total population and by family, nonfamily. Income statistics are important to *all* businesses, regardless of the industry. See Illustration 4.4.

The three characteristics of *education, occupation,* and *income* have a strong interrelationship. Occupation is closely aligned with education, and generally higher income is associated with college graduates. Therefore, you would expect a tract with a high percentage of college graduates to have a population with higher-level jobs and higher income.

Low income is a limiting factor for the purchase of products beyond the necessities. Upper-income households account for disproportion-

ILLUSTRATION 4.2 Social Characteristics of the Population. (Source. Louis H. Vorzimer, *Small Business Administration*, Small Marketers Aid No. 154, Using Census Data to Select a Store Site.)

NATIVITY, PARENTAGE, & COUNTRY OF ORIGIN	Tract A	Tract B
All persons	5 649	5 636
Native of native parentage	4 393	4 465
Native of foreign or mixed parentage	809	884
Foreign born	447	287
Foreign stock	1 256	1 171
United Kingdom	103	95
Ireland (Eire)	—	16
Sweden	—	91
Germany	218	124
Poland	29	22
Czechoslovakia	7	6
Austria	18	9
Hungary	—	14
U.S.S.R.	13	23
Italy	7	22
Canada	121	209
Mexico	37	21
Cuba	—	—
Other America	17	—
All other and not reported	686	519
Persons of Spanish language	210	112
Other persons of Spanish surname	—	—
Persons of Spanish mother tongue	141	38
Persons of Puerto Rican birth or parentage	14	—
YEARS OF SCHOOL COMPLETED		
Persons, 25 years old and over	2 120	3 201
No school years completed	13	4
Elementary: 1 to 4 years	21	5
5 to 7 years	89	61
8 years	250	146
High School: 1 to 3 years	412	357
4 years	983	1 086
College: 1 to 3 years	210	729
4 years or more	142	813
Median school years completed	12.3	12.9
Percent high school graduates	63.0	82.1

ILLUSTRATION 4.3 Labor Force Characteristics of the Population. (Source. Louis H. Vorzimer, *Small Business Administration*, Small Marketers Aid No, 154, Using Census Data to Select a Store Site.)

OCCUPATON	Tract A	Tract B
Total employed, 16 years old and over	1 479	2 234
Professional, technical, and kindred workers	152	505
Health workers	71	91
Teachers, elementary and secondary schools	26	116
Managers and administrators, except farm	67	427
Salaried	61	367
Self-employed in retail trade	6	28
Sales workers	80	247
Retail trade	69	109
Clerical and kindred workers	365	340
Craftsmen, foremen, and kindred workers	135	179
Construction craftsmen	45	58
Mechanics and repairmen	34	47
Operatives, except transport	146	122
Transport equipment operatives	22	73
Laborers, except farm	134	95
Farm workers	5	—
Service workers	347	211
Cleaning and food service workers	203	110
Protective service workers	16	10
Personal and health service workers	119	88
Private household workers	26	35

ILLUSTRATION 4.4 Income Characteristics of the Population (Source. Louis H. Vorzimer, *Small Business Administration,* Small Marketers Aid No. 154, Using Census Data to Select a Store Site.)

INCOME IN 1969 OF FAMILIES AND UNRELATED INDIVIDUALS	Tract A	Tract B
All families	1 718	1 582
Less than $1,000	88	25
$1,000 to $1,999	59	20
$2,000 to $2,999	119	30
$3,000 to $3,999	199	20
$4,000 to $4,999	174	32
$5,000 to $5,999	143	36
$6,000 to $6,999	182	49
$7,000 to $7,999	170	30
$8,000 to $8,999	119	125
$9,000 to $9,999	96	92
$10,000 to $11,999	131	168
$12,000 to $14,999	119	235
$15,000 to $24,999	109	381
$25,000 to $49,999	—	239
$50,000 or more	10	100
Median income	$6 423	$14 094
Mean income	$7 640	$18 568
Families and unrelated individuals	2 215	1 948
Median income	$6 077	$12 508
Mean income	$6 981	$16 420
Unrelated individuals	497	366
Median income	$5 056	$5 394
Mean income	$4 703	$7 135

ately large shares of total spending for such product categories as home furnishings, equipment, and appliances. This also applies to alcoholic beverages, automobile products, recreation, and clothing.

The highest income market is made up of college graduates from the occupational groups of "professional, technical, and kindred workers" and "managers and administrators" who are in the 35- to 54-years-old age group.

Occupancy, utilization and financial characteristics of housing units include information about the value of the property (homes) owners occupy and the value of rents for rental units broken down by dollar amount. Homeowners create a market for lawn mowers, hardware, outdoor furniture, and many home maintenance products. The number of renters suggests a different market. Renters generally live in multiple dwellings where, usually, space is more limited. This creates a market for retailers of portable household appliances and other items necessitated by less space. See Illustration 4.5.

Primary Research—Site Evaluation

Primary research is research that is done directly one on one by questionnaire, in person, by mail, or by telephone. Once you pick the site, primary research will show you the true value of your location.

Before you go to the site and do an evaluation, there are still a few sources of secondary (published) information that you need to check. They are:

ILLUSTRATION 4.5 Occupancy, Utilization, and Financial Characteristics of Housing Units. (Source. Louis H. Vorzimer, *Small Business Administration*, Small Marketers Aid No. 154, Using Census Data to Select a Store Site.)

	Tract A	Tract B
All housing units	2 263	1 929
VALUE		
Specified owner occupied units[1]	429	1 341
Less than $5,000	5	—
$5,000 to $7,499	15	7
$7,500 to $9,999	44	15
$10,000 to $14,999	207	89
$15,000 to $19,999	103	275
$20,000 to $24,999	29	237
$25,000 to $34,999	13	223
$35,000 to $49,999	4	192
$50,000 or more	9	303
Median	$13 800	$27 100
CONTRACT RENT		
Specified renter occupied units[2]	1 442	486
Less than $30	6	5
$30 to $39	6	1
$40 to $59	24	11
$60 to $79	80	17
$80 to $99	244	65
$100 to $149	884	230
$150 to $199	164	80
$200 to $249	3	28
$250 or more	1	29
No cash rent	30	20
Median	$121	$131

[1] Limited to one-family homes on less than 10 acres and no business on property.
[2] Excludes one-family homes on 10 acres or more.

Maps. Street maps of the community and Chamber of Commerce or Planning Commission maps that show crime rate, income, age, family status, and planned development and zoning are available at your local City Hall. (See Illustrations 4.6 to 4.8.)

Auto Traffic Statistics. What is the density of traffic on the streets near your location? The traffic department of the city should be able to give you this information. The statistics show how many cars drove on a particular street in a 24-hour period.

The Yellow Pages. The name and locations of your competitors in a given area can be found in the Yellow Pages. Competitors include anyone who is selling similar goods (e.g., candy is sold at liquor stores, grocery stores, drugstores, and candy stores). Locate these competitors on the map and note the auto traffic they have on their street.

After studying the preceding resources, the next step is an in-person inspection. This inspection will give you a good idea of the immediate market area. The steps involved are:

1. Personally inspecting the building.
2. Walking around the neighborhood.
3. Visiting with the neighbors.

ILLUSTRATION 4.6 Street Map of Brentwood.

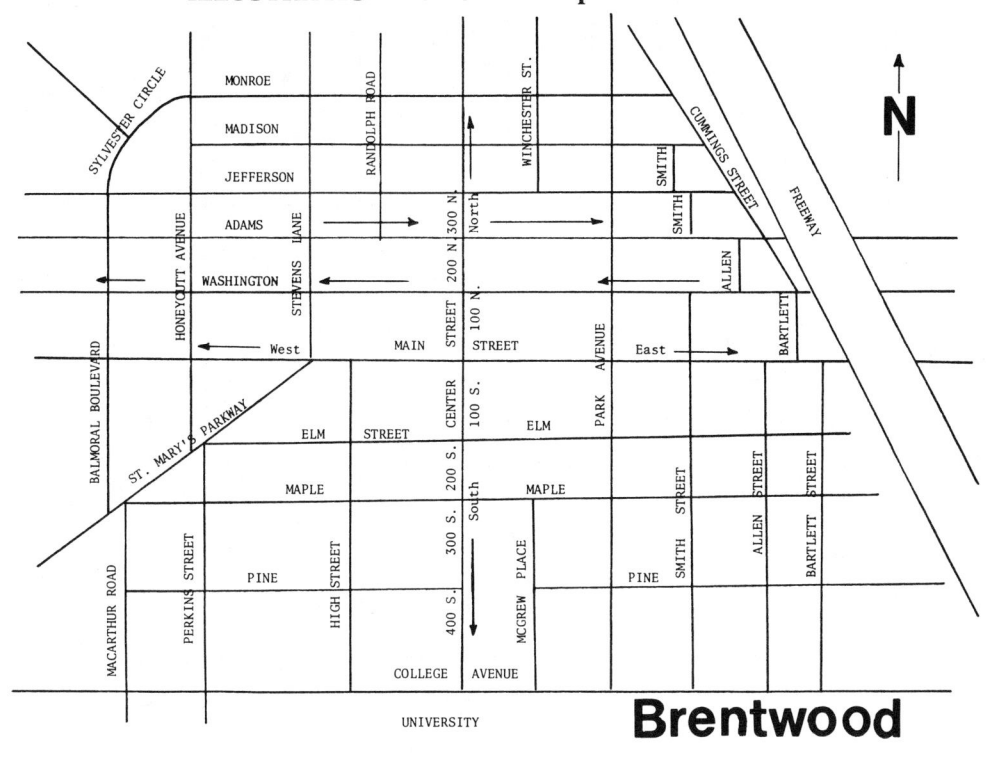

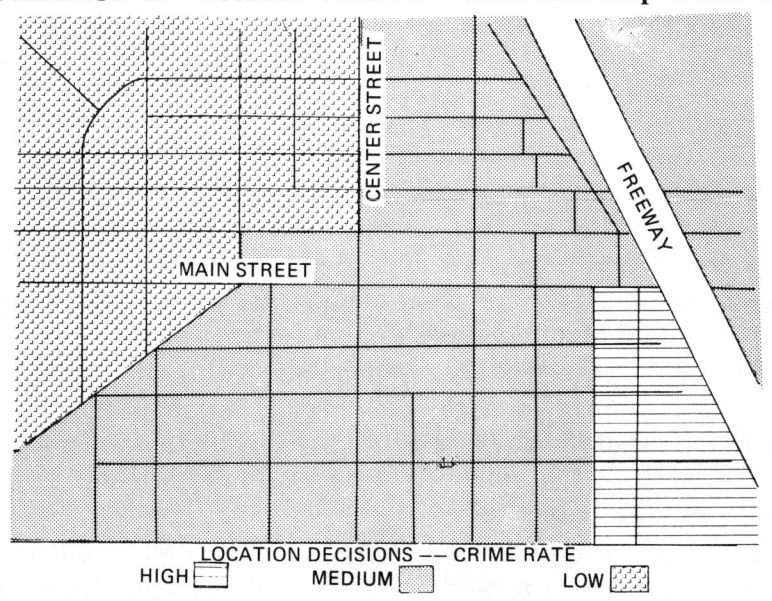

ILLUSTRATION 4.7 Location Decisions—Crime Rate Map of Brentwood.

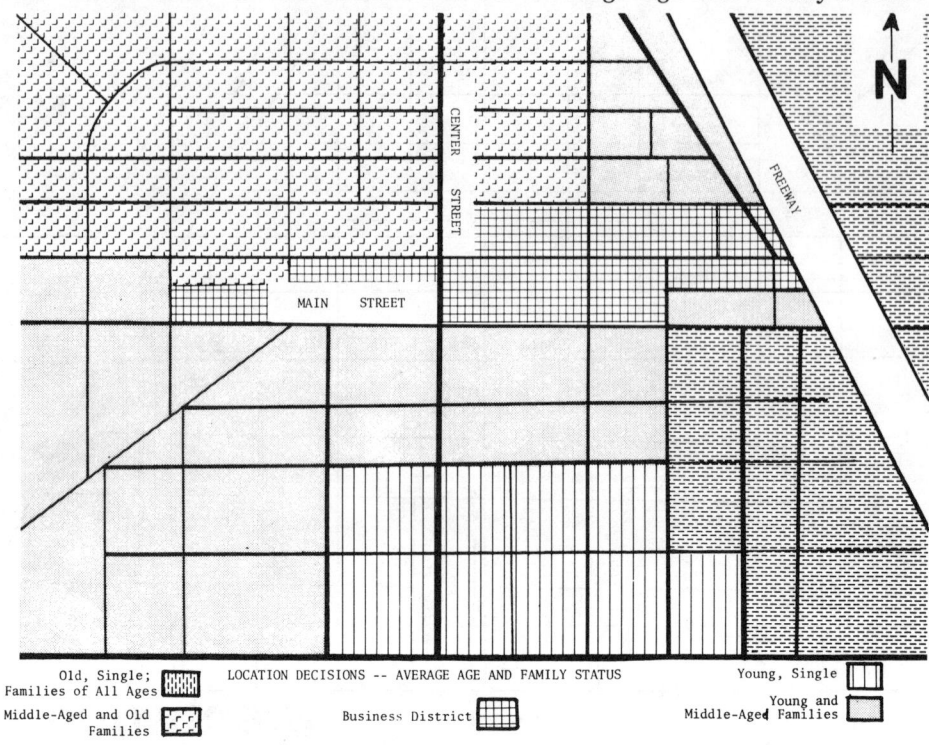

ILLUSTRATION 4.8 Location Decisions—Average Age and Family Status.

4. Visiting former tenants.
5. Visiting the neighborhood at least twice more at different times of day.

1. *Personal Inspection.* This means looking at the physical features of the building, checking its exterior, interior space, plumbing, electrical, and other existing fixtures, and parking space. If you think you will have to modify the interior, you should consider the costs. The more money you can keep in your business, the better. Even though modifications may improve the store image and storage, improvements are expensive and don't contribute directly to sales. Finally, when you are in your building, try to imagine yourself as a customer.

2. *Walk Around the Neighborhood.* Are all the shops open? How do they look on the outside and the inside? What kind of goods or services do the stores offer? What type of people shop there? How old are the employees? What are their skill levels? Is there plenty of parking space? What kind of automobiles do you see?

3. *Visit with the Neighbors.* When you go into stores in the neighborhood, talk with the manager. Ask him or her about the customers; the busiest times of the day and of the week; who the former tenants of your location were; the reliability of local employees; and, if you can get it, the average daily sales.

4. *Visit with Former Tenants.* You should get a list of former tenants from the landlord (or neighbors) and contact them. These could be

phone queries. You want to know about the landlord and customers. About the landlord, ask: How quickly are repairs made? What was the biggest problem(s) with the landlord? How can the premises be improved? About customers, ask: What seemed to sell the best? What was the best method for reaching new customers? Finally, ask for a detailed description of the typical customer.

5. *Followup Visits.* Visiting your new neighborhood at different days of the week and different times of day will give you a more complete picture of the location. A successful businessman swore that one of the most important things to do when deciding on a location was to take a walk through the neighborhood at midnight to see the quality of the neighborhood most clearly. You should also visit the neighborhood on a weekday and a weekend.

To assist you in your on-site inspection, take Form 4.3 with you and fill it out.

Pedestrian Traffic Count

If you own a convenience or shopping goods store, pedestrian traffic is important to you. No one keeps records of pedestrian traffic, so you will have to do the research yourself.

First, you must decide what types of people should be included in the count. It is frequently desirable to divide the pedestrian traffic into classes (men aged 20 to 30, women aged 40 to 50, etc.). To better determine what portion of the passing traffic represents your potential shoppers, some of the pedestrians should be interviewed about where they are coming from, their destination, and the stores in which they plan to shop.

The day of the week and the time of day should represent a period of normal traffic flow. Pedestrian flow accelerates around noon.

Data from the pedestrian traffic survey can give you information on whether the site would generate a profitable volume for your store. The steps are easy:

1. Calculate the number of individuals who would stop in the store as a percentage of the total who walk by.
2. Determine what the average expenditure of a daily customer would be. (Industry association material will tell you that.)
3. Multiply the total pedestrians counted per hour times the percentage that will come in the store times the number of hours in a work week times the average expenditure per person.

For example, if, out of 100 passers-by each hour, 5% will enter and each customer spends an average of $8.00. The total hours you are open per week is 60. Therefore, 100 × 0.05 × 60 × $8.00 = $2400. Sales should be $2400 per week.

FORM 4.3   On-Site Inspection Checklist and Questions

1. Personal Inspection of the Building (A—excellent; B—good; C—fair; D—poor; F—Forget it.)

Physical Features
Exterior looks _____   Interior space _____   Plumbing _____
Electrical _____   Existing fixtures _____ Parking _____

2. Walk Around the Neighborhood (Comments)

Are all the shops open?
_____
_____

How do the shops look on the outside and the inside?
Outside _____
_____

Inside _____
_____

What kind of goods or services do the stores offer?
_____
_____
_____

What type of people shop there?
_____
_____

What age are the employees? What are their skill levels?
_____
_____

Is there plenty of parking space for these stores?
_____
_____

What kind of automobiles do you see parked in the neighborhood?
_____
_____

3. Visit with the Neighbors (Ask them the following questions.)

Could you describe your customers?
_____
_____
_____

What are the busiest times of day?
_____
_____

What are the busiest days of the week?
_____
_____

Who are the former tenants of the location I'm investigating?
_____
_____

FORM 4.3 Continued

How reliable are the local employees?

What do you estimate is your average daily sales?

4. Visit with Former Tenants (Get a list of former tenants, contact them, and ask the following questions.)

About the landlord, ask:

How quick are repairs made?

What was the biggest problem(s) with the landlord?

How can the premise be improved?

About customers, ask:

Of the items you sold, which sold the best?

What did you find was the best method for reaching new customers?

Please describe, in detail, your typical customer.

5. Followup Visits (Findings)

Visit at midnight

Visit on weekend

Visit on weekday

FORM 4.4   Pedestrian Traffic Count

Type of Passersby:

Men _____   Women _____   Children _____

Age Group (Adults):   20s _____   30s _____   40s _____   50s _____

Sample Questions to Passersby:

What is the origin of your trip?
_____
_____
_____
_____

What is your destination?
_____
_____
_____
_____

What shops do you plan to visit?
_____
_____
_____
_____

Count

Time Period	Numbers
_____	_____
_____	_____
_____	_____
_____	_____

Calculations

Number pedestrians per hour	×	Percentage pedestrians coming in	×	Working hours per week	×	Dollars spent/ person	=	Average weekly income
_____		_____		_____		_____		_____

Once you have decided who and when, you must count the passersby and do the calculations. You can record your answers on Form 4.4.

METHODS FOR BUILDING A CUSTOMER BASE

Building a customer base is the process of developing new customers and larger orders from existing customers. You build your customer base six ways:

Word of mouth.
Trade-show attendance.

Mail.
Telephone.
Personal meetings.
Media.

Word of Mouth

New customers come to you on the advice of people they know. Regular customers come from this type of recommendation. Recommendations don't just happen; you must earn them. You must let customers know that you appreciate referral business. It also doesn't hurt to ask for referrals.

Earning word of mouth recommendations means having the right price, terms, delivery and service. To increase word-of-mouth recommendations you must also make your company known in the industry.

You should set your *price* very carefully so that it allows you sufficient profit, but is low enough to be competitive. Generally speaking, the lower the price, the higher the volume, and the higher the price, the lower the volume. Many industries have standard pricing for items. A search of the market will let you know the average price.

Terms of payment are usually set by the industry. Some require cash up front and some allow as short as 10 days or as long as 90 days for the customer to pay. If you allow your terms to be longer than the industry (45 days instead of the industry average 30 days), you will get more customers, but you also will have more of a cash squeeze. If your terms are lower than the industry average (cash up front vs. 30 days), you must either have a better price or faster delivery and service.

Delivery was the problem Yourcompany had at the beginning of this chapter. By speeding up delivery, Yourcompany increased sales significantly. After a certain point, the faster the delivery, the more the cost. Therefore, you should find out the delivery speed of the competitors so that you know what you are shooting for. In some businesses, fast delivery will justify a higher product price. If you can deliver a product in one week when the competition is backlogged two months with a similar product, you will expand your sales.

In the long run, *service* is the factor that will generate the most word-of-mouth referrals. Do your customers get immediate attention on their problems after the sale is made? Are they satisfied with your product or service months after they paid you? Are their problems taken care of quickly? Do you have sufficient service staff?

Making your company known throughout the industry requires:

The presence of your company in the industry for many years.

Active participation in industry activities (membership in trade associations and local clubs).

Advertising in trade publications.

Attendance at trade shows.

Publication of articles in trade magazines, newsletters, journals, and books.

To keep your name in front of your customers, you should communicate with them often. Communicate with old as well as new customers. Customers like to think that you remember them and appreciate information about your company. Every time there is a new model or a new development in your service, all your old customers should be notified. A rule of thumb is to communicate with them often enough so that they never move or change course without you knowing about it.

Telephoning old customers occasionally is a good method to keep in touch. Another easier method is to send literature out every month, whether it is a letter, a birthday card, a calendar, a newsletter, a company brochure, or a copy of an article about you or your product/service.

Trade Show

For most businesses not selling retail convenience goods, trade shows are a great source of sales leads. People who come to trade shows for a particular product (outdoor furniture, architecture, electronics, plants, etc.) are already qualified customers. They came to the show because they are interested in your type of product.

Just being in the show will get your name around in the industry. The trade show offers a great opportunity to sharpen your image and introduce new products.

At trade shows you get to see the competition firsthand, talk to the customer, evaluate what the customer is looking for, and develop a list of prospective customers. (For more detailed information about trade shows, see Chapter 7.)

Mail

Mail is a powerful tool for communicating with your customer and getting new customers. With automated techniques for mailing, you can reach a great number of selected individuals (from mailing lists) economically.

Using the names and addresses of customers, vendors, associates, acquaintances, friends, and family is a good starting place for a mailing list. You should mail material to every person you ever received a business card from. One small insulation contractor told me, "When I made my first mailing list, I had my secretary go through every file I had to get names and addresses. I mailed business cards to people I couldn't remember at all. Everyone, but everyone, found out about my service."

Mail may be used in the following ways to build customer goodwill:

1. Logos and letterhead should present a good image of your company.
2. All correspondence should be polite and businesslike.
3. All customer billing should be prompt and courteous.

4. All *current customers* should:
   (a) Be notified of all new company developments.
   (b) Get thank-you letters when they buy or even when they have been casually contacted.
   (c) Be sent gifts such as calendars and birthday cards.
   (d) Be notified of all sales and public relations events.
5. Build sales to *prospective customers* by mailing to selected mailing lists:
   (a) Brochures or catalog.
   (b) Promotional material.
   (c) Newsletters and copies of trade articles with a cover letter.

(For a more thorough discussion of mailing, see Chapter 7.)

Telephone

No sales effort gets serious until a phone call is made to the customer or prospective customer.

Regular customers should be telephoned to keep you in touch with their feelings about your company, to take new orders, and to keep communication going between them and you.

Prospective customers (prospects) should be telephoned to make an appointment leading to a sale, to keep communications going, and to apprise them of special company offers.

When using the telephone, (1) be courteous and polite, (2) create a warm image with your voice, and (3) stay in control of the conversation.

Here are a few ideas on how to increase sales with relatively little cost by using telephone marketing efforts:

1. *Up-Sell.* When a customer calls or orders, or asks for information, always make another offer or *up-sell*. If someone calls in about buying ornamental trees, mention fertilizing products that will help the tree grow. Selling more to your present customers is a top priority. It can build sales volume as much as 25% without extra cost.
2. *Consider an 800 Number.* An 800 (toll-free) number is good public relations and effective in space advertising. These numbers are relatively inexpensive and offer an ease to the prospective customer.
3. *Offer to Mail Gifts.* Suggest that your customers phone you with gift orders for holidays and special occasions.
4. *Survey the Market.* Use the phone to find who your customers are, where they live, and whether they are interested in your product or service. Call people similar to your customer and see if you can sell them. One hundred calls can give you a good consensus.

5. *Make Effective Use of the Yellow Pages.* You might want more than one listing. Use display ads in the Yellow Pages, or even dollars-off coupons in phone books. Give prospects a reason to call—to get a free estimate, to compare prices, or to get a brochure or catalog.
6. *Offer to Give Useful Information.* For instance, you may offer people who respond to your media advertisements an evaluation of several types of spread-sheet software for small computers.
7. *Solve Customer Service Problems Quickly.* Encourage people to call with any type of complaint so that it may be solved quickly by telephone.
8. *Qualify Prospects Before Seeing Them.* This will help you avoid a common problem of salespeople—seeing people who cannot buy.
9. *Systematize Your Phone Effort.* Many persons use a form to record all outgoing sales calls including the results of past efforts and reminders for follow up.

Personal Meetings

To sell most services or products, a personal one-on-one meeting is required. Your customers like to see the people they are dealing with (you).

The most frequent meetings with the customer are those involving sales. Other meetings can be on a more social level (a tennis game, a skiing trip, an outing to the theater). Some chief executives use the social meeting with their big customers as their most important sales strategy.

The important things to remember when you meet a customer face to face are:

Project a strong personality with your appearance (clothing and grooming).

Project pride in your product or service.

Radiate confidence.

Show genuine concern and warmth for the customer.

Believe in yourself and act with assurance.

Don't quit no matter how much pain or problems you encounter. Keep your desire high.

Overcome your fears.

Be enthusiastic.

Don't take rejection personally.

Always show your customer you care.

Remember when you go out to talk to customers, you are interested in what *they* have to say not in hearing yourself ramble on. If you can get them to talk about what benefits they want, then you can use these benefits to sell them on your product. When you *tell* customers something, they don't believe it, but when *they say it*, it is true.

Media

Using the media properly is a good way not only to attract new customers, but to give old customers more confidence in you and your product/service. *Media* include all third-party methods for getting your message to the people, such as magazines, newspapers, television, radio, and billboards.

All these methods will be covered in greater detail in Chapter 7. The best way to use the media is to get free exposure. Free exposure is usually created by a public relations program and press releases (discussed in Chapter 5). Every small business owner or manager should know how to write a press release and how to use the press to the company's benefit.

Media advertising can raise immediate sales by:

Announcing special promotions, such as sales.
Dispensing coupons that may be redeemed with purchases.
Urging people to come into your store.
Alerting people who might be interested in distributing your product.

Media advertising can increase customer awareness of your company through:

Telling people where you are located.
Extolling special product features.
Listing new products.
Publicizing special changes in price or packaging.
Emphasizing the company's service record.
Demonstrating the proper use of the product.
Drawing favorable comparisons between your product and competing products.

Characteristics of Different Media Types.

1. *Newspapers*
   (a) Eight out of ten Americans read them.
   (b) They lend a factual air to your advertising due to their overall news content.
   (c) They are local and allow you to reach specific geographic markets.
   (d) You can change your ads easily or submit them on relatively short notice.
   (e) They are good for dispensing discount coupons.

2. *Magazines*
    (a) They allow you to reach select audiences because they are often specialty magazines.
    (b) They can be even more select with special geographic or demographic editions.
    (c) The high quality of printing shows your ads well.
    (d) They are read more carefully and are kept around the house or business longer than most newspapers.
3. *Television*
    (a) Has enormous mass coverage. Over 95% of Americans own a television.
    (b) Filmed ads may have greater impact and are good for demonstrating the operation of your product.
    (c) Production and air time costs may be high.
    (d) It is not easy to change ads and only rarely can ads be done on short notice.
4. *Radio*
    (a) Since most stations have special listeners, you can reach specialty groups.
    (b) Messages can be changed on short notice.
    (c) It is relatively low-cost advertising.
5. *Trade Publications*
    (a) The main advantage of trade publications is that you can reach a very special market (e.g., machine-shop owners, chemical engineers, golfers, and woodcarvers).
    (b) It is especially good for industrial advertising.
6. *Outdoor Advertising*
    (a) It is best used as a supplement to advertising in other media.
    (b) It's a good technique for reminding customers of your product, but is not good for explanations.
    (c) It is especially good for a ground transportation user customer.

CUSTOMER REFERRALS

Customers who are referred to your company often become your best customers. Companies should always encourage referrals. You can usually close a sale twice as fast with a referred prospect than with a non-referred contact. Forty to sixty percent of the people who are referred to you will buy eventually.

Referrals are created two ways: (1) *networking* with known customers, suppliers, and associates, (2) collecting referrals at every sales call.

Networking

Networking is a word, a technique, that has gained a lot of currency of late. Networking is creating an interconnecting pathway among several elements and thereby collecting those elements together. The *Oxford English Dictionary* gives this definition of a network: "A piece of work having the form or construction of a net; a collection or arrangement resembling a net."

Networking is casual prospecting.

Andrew Smith from San Francisco works for a small investment banking company. The small company is just struggling to survive and must lay Smith off.

Smith spends 2 months calling everyone he knows in the industry and all his friends to tell them he needs work and is looking for a job. By the end of the second month Smith had received referrals to over 10 job interviews at some of the biggest companies in California. By the end of the third month, he landed a job that paid 20% more than he was making before. The job is with one of the largest commercial banks in the state, located only a block from where he used to work. He was referred to the job by a friend of a friend of his cousin Joe.

Mr. Smith demonstrates how networking is used in getting a job. It can also be used in getting customers for your own company.

Networking to get referrals is communicating with everyone you come in contact with and telling them what your company does. Tell them about your company and request that they call you if there is anyone they come across who might need your product or service.

When people call you or you call them, take time to talk about your company and what it does. Ask the following people to send you any person who might benefit from your product or service:

1. *Suppliers* when you order goods from them.
2. *Salespersons* who call on you to sell you something.
3. *Friends* and social acquaintances.
4. *Business associates* you run into in your industry.
5. *Salespersons* who work for the competition whom you might meet at a trade show or some industry function.
6. *Professional advisers* such as your attorney, CPA, banker, or consultant.

Referrals from Sales Calls

Once you contact that prospect who was referred to you or a "cold call" prospect or someone who just called in, then you should also get referrals from them.

Asking a prospect, "Do you know anyone else I can show my product to?" usually gets a no answer. When asking a prospect for a referral try a more subtle technique:

1. Isolate groups of people he or she knows.
2. Write the referral's name on a card.
3. Qualify the referral.
4. Ask for the address.
5. Ask the prospect to call and set the appointment. If the prospect shows nervousness, ask if you can use his or her name when you call the referral.

To isolate groups of people in the mind of the prospect, you might ask, "Do you attend any trade meetings?" or "Do you know the owners of the companies you buy from?" Either question will isolate groups of people in the prospect's mind. The next question is, "Is there someone (group) who has indicated to you that they might need a service (product) like mine?"

Writing the referral name and address on a card helps you get organized. Try to get as much information on the card as you can. This will help you when you talk to the referral.

It is of no use to have the name and address of someone who cannot buy your product or service. You must qualify the referral to see if he or she is capable of using and paying for your service or product.

Asking for the prospect to call the referral is a good strategy because, if the prospect is willing, this will give you a strong lead. You must at least be allowed to use the prospect's name, or the referral is useless.

SUMMARY

Customers are your best source of money. Not banks, not investors, *customers*. Relations with your customers have a direct effect on where you locate your business, how you build your customer base, and how you communicate with your customers.

If you are in a retail or ultimate consumer business, your business should be located close to your customer. If you know who your customers are you can locate them with the census tracts or community resources (Chamber of Commerce information). Once you find where they are, the next step is finding a location that will suit their needs.

The best methods for building a customer base are: by word of mouth; attendance at trade shows; mailing; telephone calls; personal meetings; and using the media.

Customer referrals are built through networking with your associates and making a referral request at every sales call.

5

IT'S ALL IN THE IMAGE—WELL, MOST OF IT, ANYWAY!

At the pinnacle of the marketing triangle introduced earlier is the *image*. Image in marketing is the long-term element, the one aspect that will be a guide to many of the decisions to be made. Image is not just important. To most customers, your image is *everything*. Image is the company's major asset; it is the economic power that does not show on your balance sheet.

The image of your company to the customer may not be a true image. What customers think of your company (their image of it) may be better or worse than the truth. But so can your own image of the company. Many business owners have never taken a hard look at their business's image. They don't even think of an image in its complete sense. They may respond when asked about their image, "... well, I think my logo is pretty good lookin'...." They may tell themselves that their image is all right because the company is making money.

Image is a more deep-seated concept than just the superficial, the visual or the bottom line. The image deals with product, place, price, people, and promotion. The composite of these five must be consistent with the overall image of the business based on the target market that you feel is where your sales are going to come from. It must reflect the same objectives as the strategies you have developed in your marketing plan.

You don't have to be in business long to have seen at least one example of a company that has been hurt by their bad or incomplete image to the customer. You may have seen a company that has an excellent product, but their delivery or service is too slow to build a base of satisfied customers. Perhaps you have been lured to a company with an attractive price only to find the product quality unacceptable. How do your customers see your company?

Image is not something that has to be haphazard. Image is something that can be engineered carefully by means of a three-step process:

1. Determine the image you wish to have and can maintain.
2. Determine what your market image presently is.
3. Develop a program whereby you build company credentials through some planned image-building activities.

CHOOSING AN IMAGE

What are the areas that someone considers important when buying a product or service? If you think about it, these are the same areas around which you should build your image. Five of the most important areas of concern to anyone making such a purchase are: price, quality, availability of service, terms of payment, and delivery. You might like to have your company known for low price; high-price, high-quality; fast service; a durable product; friendly service; convenient service; an easy-to-use product; fast delivery; or favorable credit terms. All these ideals are variations on the theme of price, place, product, promotion, and people.

To begin to formulate your company's image, the following list of image-related questions was compiled by William H. Brannen, author of *Practical Marketing for Your Small Retail Business*. The beauty of this exercise is the complete range of elements that the business owner can consider to choose his or her company's image.

1. Target market elements of image.
    (a) Type of clientele served.
    (b) How customers dress.
    (c) What customers say in the store.
    (d) How customers act in the store.
    (e) Whether or not customers smoke.
    (f) How much time customers spend in the store.
    (g) Whether different types of customers visit the store at different times of the day.
    (h) How many (or how few) customers are in the store at different times of day.
    (i) With whom the customer shops (e.g., with family or alone).
    (j) How much do customers handle products, and interact with employees and other customers.
2. Product elements of image.
    (a) Quality of merchandise or service.
    (b) Merchandise or service assortment.
    (c) Availability.
    (d) Fashionability of service or product.

    (e) The number and level of customer services offered and who pays for them.
    (f) Packaging.
    (g) Brands carried.
3. Place elements of image.
    (a) Business location.
    (b) How long business has been at that location.
    (c) Neighboring businesses.
    (d) Parking facilities, cost, and availability.
    (e) On-premise signs.
    (f) Business front appearance.
    (g) Physical appearance of building.
    (h) Fixtures.
    (i) Width of aisles.
    (j) Location and appearance of product displays.
    (k) General cleanliness.
    (l) Atmospherics, such as color and lighting.
4. Price elements of image.
    (a) Price levels.
    (b) Range of prices.
    (c) How prices are marked physically.
    (d) How price is featured in advertising.
    (e) Price/quality relationship.
    (f) Discounts.
    (g) Credit terms available.
5. Promotion elements of image.
    (a) Advertising media used.
    (b) Amount of promotion.
    (c) Institutional versus item price promotions.
    (d) Size and layout of advertisements.
    (e) The advertising message communicated.
    (f) Believability of advertisements.
    (g) Types of sale promotion used.
    (h) Frequency of sales promotion events.
    (i) Characteristics of sales or marketing personnel.
    (j) Extent of involvement in community activities.
    (k) Membership in trade associations.
6. Human elements of image.
    (a) Personality of owner/manager.
    (b) Personality of other employees.
    (c) How employees get along together.
    (d) Physical appearance of personnel.

(e) How your employees relate to customers.
(f) How well your employees get to know customers.
(g) How your employees treat customers.

Use the preceding outline to help you determine your business's image. Professor Brannen's list of image-related topics was designed for a retail-oriented business, but there is little difference in the impact of these items for either a manufacturing or service type of business.

Use Forms 5.1 to 5.6 to help you consider the various elements of image as they relate to your target markets, product, place, price, promotion, and people.

Images may be created. They need not necessarily be real. If you wish to create an image of your company as an established firm, an office filled with antiques might help. Or you may desire to specify a modern appearance. This might involve linoleum floors and shiny chrome furniture.

FORM 5.1 Target Market Elements of Image

(a) Who are your clientele?

(b) How do your customers dress?

(c) What do customers say in the store?

(d) How do customers act in the store?

(e) Do your customers smoke?

(f) How much time do customers spend in the store?

FORM 5.1 Continued

(g) What types of customers visit the store at different times of day?

(h) How many (or how few) customers are in the store at different times of day?

(i) With whom do the customers shop?

(j) Do customers handle the product(s)?

(k) Do customers talk to the other customers?

(l) Do customers talk to the salespeople?

FORM 5.2 Product Elements of Image

(a) What is the quality of the service or merchandise?

(b) Is there an assortment of merchandise or services?

(c) What is the availability of the product or service?

FORM 5.2 Continued

(d) How fashionable is the product or service?
___

(e) Is customer service available?
___

Who pays for it?
___

(f) What is the packaging like?
___

(g) What other brands are carried?
___

FORM 5.3 Place Elements of Image

(a) What is your current business location?
___

(b) How long has your business been at that location?
___

(c) What are the neighboring businesses?
___

(d) Is there enough parking space for customers?
___

FORM 5.3 Continued

Do you validate if there is a charge for parking?

(e) Is there a visible sign with your company name on it?

(g) Is the physical appearance of the facility neat and clean?

(h) Are furniture and fixtures attractive?

(i) Is there adequate space between the aisles?

(j) Are there product displays?

(k) Are the displays clean and attractive?

(l) Is there adequate lighting?

(m) What is the color scheme? Is it appealing?

FORM 5.4 Price Elements of Image

(a) What are the price levels?

(b) What is the range of prices?

(c) Are prices clearly marked?

(d) Do you feature price in your advertising?

(e) What is the relationship between price and quality?

(f) Do you offer discounts other than advertised specials?

(g) What are your credit terms?

FORM 5.5 Promotion Elements of Image

(a) What advertising media do you use?

(b) What special promotions do you use?

(c) Do you offer institutional price promotions?

(d) What are the sizes of your advertisements?

(e) What is your advertising message?

(f) Are your advertisements believable?

(g) What types of sales promotions do you use?

(h) How often do you have a promotional event?

(i) What are the characteristics of your salespeople?

(j) What community activities do you participate in?

(k) What trade associations do you belong to?

FORM 5.6　Human Elements of Image

(a) What are the personality characteristics of the owner/manager?

(b) What are the personality characteristics of the other employees?

(c) Do the employees get along with each other?

(d) Are your employees neat and attractive?

(e) Do your employees relate well to your customers?

(f) How well do your employees get to know your customers?

(g) Do your employees treat your customers courteously?

YOUR COMPANY'S PRESENT IMAGE

If you ask the average small businessperson what his or her company's image is, you may be met by a blank stare. Another person might answer the same question by going on and on about what that image is when in fact every sentence uttered *is* believed by the marketplace.

Your economic power derives from the marketplace. This marketplace has a certain view (image) of your company; therefore, your economic power resides in your image. Your company is known for certain things. The smart entrepreneur finds out what these things are and promotes them. On finding negatives, he or she will do what can be done to turn them into positives and then promote them.

The best way to find out the market's view is to sample it. One of the authors discovered that fact one summer when he was too busy to develop a new product brochure. So he had a newly hired field service representative and an assistant, a college student home for summer vacation, conduct a telephone survey of a sample of product users. The object of the survey was to find out why the users had made their initial purchase.

In this case the findings were somewhat of a surprise—the product advantages that the company had not been promoting, especially service availability, turned out to be the very ones that the customers liked. After the findings of the survey were in, it was easy to design the brochure around them. In a sense, the company's customers wrote the new brochure.

Finding out what your customers and vendors think of when they think of your company can be accomplished very simply. Just follow these steps:

1. Determine what questions you want to ask.
2. Design a simple questionnaire for mailing or a telephone survey.
3. Gather, compile, and evaluate the data.

Questions should center around the various elements of product, place, price, promotion, people, and target market outlined previously. Don't clutter the questionnaire with too many questions—stick to a few key ones. Make sure some of the questions are open-ended such as, What do you think are your company's strongest points? Weakest points? Also ask how the company could improve.

The two sample questionnaires (Forms 5.7 and 5.8) may help you. They can be adapted to most businesses. There is one for use with your customers and a second for vendors and subcontractors.

Improving Company Credentials

To build your reputation in the industry, here are some rules to follow:

1. Stay in contact with allied competitors.
2. Don't knock the competitors; it will come back to you.

FORM 5.7 Sample Customer Questionnaire

How do you rate Yourcompany, Inc.?

```
                        Key:
         don't know 0    1    2    3    4    5
                        poor ─────────── excellent
```

Accuracy in estimating job	0 1 2 3 4 5
Organization of company	0 1 2 3 4 5
Financial strength of company	0 1 2 3 4 5
Communication between you and Yourcompany	0 1 2 3 4 5
Reliability (i.e., finishing the job on time)	0 1 2 3 4 5
Invoices and billing formats	0 1 2 3 4 5
Quality of work	0 1 2 3 4 5
Quickness of solutions to problems	0 1 2 3 4 5
Quality of advertising material	0 1 2 3 4 5
Quality of sales program	0 1 2 3 4 5
Overall rating	0 1 2 3 4 5
Overall rating compared to other vendors	0 1 2 3 4 5

What do you think is Yourcompany's biggest problem? _____
_____

What do you think is Yourcompany's best characteristic? _____
_____

If you were the management of Yourcompany, what suggestions would you have to improve customer relationships? _____
_____
_____

3. Be active in trade associations. Go to their meetings, seminars, and so forth. The dues that you pay will be returned many times over in the good advice, referrals, and contacts you can glean.

4. Join the Chamber of Commerce. This can give you the clout with City Hall and banks (since their personnel are usually members). It is also a source of good marketing information that may be helpful in doing other marketing research described in this book.

5. Be friendly with bankers, suppliers, unions, and all of your customers.

FORM 5.8 Sample Vendor and Subcontractor Questionnaire

How do you rate Yourcompany, Inc.?

```
                        Key:
        don't know 0    1    2    3    4    5
                        poor _____ excellent
```

Quality of communication between Yourcompany and you	0	1	2	3	4	5
Promptness of payment from Yourcompany	0	1	2	3	4	5
Accuracy of delivery date	0	1	2	3	4	5
Financial condition of Yourcompany	0	1	2	3	4	5
Quickness of solutions to on the job problems	0	1	2	3	4	5
Overall rating of Yourcompany	0	1	2	3	4	5
Overall rating of Yourcompany compared to other customers	0	1	2	3	4	5

What do you think is Yourcompany's biggest problem? _____
_____
_____

What do you think is Yourcompany's best characteristic? _____
_____
_____

If you were the management of Yourcompany, what suggestions would you have to improve vendor relationships? _____
_____
_____

CREATING AN IMAGE OF YOUR COMPANY

The image that you are going to create for your company will make the difference between the successful and the unsuccessful business. The word and concept may sound simple, but its meaning is not. It is both tangible and intangible; it is everywhere! *Image is essentially the collective impression created in the mind of the viewer.* The successful image is for the most part the successful business enterprise. The business that is not doing well has a ho-hum image and lack of appeal.

This may seem to be a simplistic generalization, but as you explore your own company's operation, you will see the power of this thing called image. Your image is made up of the people you employ, the building you occupy, the business card you hand out, the letter you send, and the way the phone is answered. We could go on infinitely with examples of image, but you should get the idea without it.

Image affects the decision-making process of the customer from the point of making the initial decision to buy or not to buy from you until the next time the customer makes the decision that your product or service is needed again. Image makes the difference between constant repeat business and the one-time or casual sales pattern.

So, you ask, how do I get an image? Part of the process begins with a feeling of goodwill that comes from a positive attitude about every aspect of your business. Every business has its faults and weak spots. The successful ones have a proactive attitude about making these weaknesses better. The power of a positive attitude from the top down will create the basis of the most favorable image you can find. Create in your mind's eye the image that you wish to attain. The power of that alone will project itself to others. This doesn't happen overnight, but the sooner you begin, the sooner the results can be seen, felt, heard, and appreciated. There is no better atmosphere than one you have worked at—the rewards are worth every ounce of effort put into it.

To begin the process of building the positive and professional image you need, use the following list of ideas to help your awareness of the simple things that can make people choose to do business with you rather than someone else. Take the time to read over these image-building components. How many of them are you aware of? How many of them can you honestly say you practice?

ILLUSTRATION 5.1   Image Reinforcers.

Remember names and places.
Be a joiner.
Be a good listener.
Play up the "you" appeal.
Be helpful.
Always demonstrate your integrity.
Be consistent.
Give specialized attention and personalized service.
Think about your customer creatively.
Be systematic, neat, and organized.
Be self-motivating and keep a positive attitude.
Be affirmative, not negative.
Be thoughtful and considerate.
Be alert.
Be neat.
Be patient.
Be logical.
Be specific.
Be authoritative.
Show humility.
Be generous.
Be punctual.
Display good manners.
Be original.
Be cheerful.
Be a graceful loser.
Be brief.
Don't be a lecturer.
Anticipate.
Take notes.
Be friendly, but not overfamiliar.
Derive fun from your work.
Display self-respect.
Be forthright.
Exercise polite persistence.
Don't misuse the hard sell.

Illustration 5.1 is by no means the complete list of image reinforcers, but it can begin to make you think about the many simple yet diverse activities that play a part of the image-building process. Probably you have been doing a lot of these things for a long time. A little concentration will give you the edge by allowing you to utilize even more of these handy image-building blocks. Each reader should be able to add to the list or expand on the depth of the ones given.

PUBLIC RELATIONS

Now that the ideas of an image are fresh in your mind, it's time to look at the use of public relations as a means to enhance the image or promote the goodwill of the company. Public relations usually includes any effort that promotes goodwill and enhances the company image. It is often confused with advertising. Many times when a business owner says, "... my advertising isn't working," it is more than likely that public relations is not working. One problem with public relations is that it is very hard to measure its results.

Public relations means many things to many people. Fundamentally, it involves communication: establishing communication, improving communication, and solving communication problems. It can be thought of as the eyes, ears, and mouth of an organization, communicating inward in a consulting capacity to management and communicating outward as a spokesman for management. Public relations is just about as broad as that, using many means of communication to transmit an infinite variety of messages to widely diverse groups, usually in an attempt to build an impression of the sender and/or to motivate the receiver into some kind of action. Public relations operates on many levels—governmental, political, community, personnel, sales, and just plain business relations.

Every business has public relations; the PR may be good, bad or in-between. A good PR program starts with the owners of the business and permeates the organization in good employee relations as well as good company relations with the outside world.

Use the following simple rules as a guide to good PR:

1. Work actively at getting as much PR as you can.
2. Submit all newsworthy events about your business.
3. Make sure someone knows how to write a news release and does it well.
4. Try not to con the press or media too often.
5. Always issue counter-statements to negative press.
6. Don't forget the trade and industry publications.
7. Don't forget to build a rapport and relationship with your politicos.
8. An upset customer is bad PR.
9. Good service is good PR.
10. Successful PR is greatly dependent on whom you know.

Perhaps the most effective and definitely the most reasonably priced PR activity is publicity. The advantage of publicity is that it is free and positive exposure for your business. It is one of the most effective promotional techniques you can use, and it's easy to do yourself. Press and other media coverage about your firm is advertising that can't be bought and it's read with interest by both customers and prospective customers alike. The PR material for your company must be in line with the image you wish your company to possess. Think of the impression you take with you to the polls on voting day. It's the image created by the candidate's PR staff.

For publicity to be effective, the person in charge must perform some basic functions. These include, but are not limited to:

Establishing relations with key media personnel

Developing mailing lists of trade publications, general community publications, community officials and leaders, competitors, customers, and sources of mailing lists

Keeping a file of releases and articles

Keeping a file for press release information

Recording publicity of effectiveness

Keeping a file of your competitors' releases and articles

Use Form 5.9 to help you begin to formulate a PR program for your company.

FORM 5.9 PR Program Work Sheet

1. Is good community relations a matter of concern to the management of the firm?

2. How do you guard against your business activities conflicting with public policy?

3. What are the groups that make up your firm's public?

4. What is special about these groups?

5. What steps do you take to see that each of these groups receives the attention and appreciation it needs?

6. Do you maintain an employee relations program? Does it include the temporary or subcontract help?

7. What is your system or policy for informing employees and others of what your company stands for and how it functions?

8. What do you do to remain in touch with what the public thinks of your firm?

9. Do you try to check what you hear? How do you do this?

10. How do you make needed improvements?

11. What community relations activities are you involved in?

12. What is done on an ongoing basis to maintain and improve community relations?

FORM 5.9 Continued

13. How does the government affect your business?
_____
_____
_____

14. What do you do for the improvement and maintenance of government relations?
_____
_____
_____

15. Do you insist that all your company's actions be completely honest and sincere?
_____
_____
_____

16. What community activities do your employees participate in?
_____
_____
_____

17. Do you encourage both employee and company involvement in community organizations of their choosing?
_____
_____
_____

18. Do you make it a point to consider what is best for the public at large as well as for your own private interest when major business decisions are being made?
_____
_____
_____

19. Do you feel that selling, serving, and good community relations are inseparable?
_____
_____
_____

20. Do you make the above-mentioned decisions yourself? If not, who else is involved?
_____
_____
_____

THE PRESS RELEASE

The press release is a short account of an activity or event that your company wants to publicize. It's about your new firm, a new partner, your new capabilities, an award, a new contract, a new line of products, promotions, an open house, financial news, or even the death of an important person. Anything that you can convince the media is newsworthy may be material for a press release.

Writing a press release is easy, economical, and not to be feared by anyone. In a lot of cases, the material you submit in the press release is at the mercy of the media editor, who elects whether to use the information or not. Sometimes the result will surprise you due to its newfound texture or spirit, but the key is to make it into printed form.

THE PRESS RELEASE

Before you actually start to write a press release, it is a good idea to use a fact sheet to compile the background information. Forms 5.10 and 5.11 can be used for this information. We will refer to these as press information questionnaires (PIQ). Usually these forms will be in a question-and-answer format, so leave plenty of room for notes you may want to take in addition to the information requested. Such notes can be particularly helpful if you are responsible to do an interview of a person to gather information before you write the release.

FORM 5.10 Biographical Data Sheet

Information from this form helps us prepare accurate news releases for media use. When you've filled out the form, please return it to the above address.

Company: _____
Division or branch office: _____
Main product or service: _____
Name: _____ Age: _____
Title: _____
Responsibilities: _____
_____

Date assumed new position: _____
Previous positions, titles, dates with current employer: _____
Previous two employers, titles, and dates (For all employers, briefly describe their business, e.g., major appliance manufacturer): _____
_____

Other employment history, include firms, titles, responsibilities, and dates: _____
_____
_____
_____

Education. Include dates, degrees, school names: _____
_____

Military experience, rank: _____

Home address, phone and city: _____

Spouse's name: _____
Additional Information. Social, civic, fraternal, professional participation, awards that might be of interest to readers: _____
_____
_____
_____
_____
_____

Adapted from *Marketing Problem Solver* by Cochrane Chase and Kenneth L. Barasch. Copyright © 1977 by the authors. Reprinted with permission of the publisher, Chilton Book Co., Radnor, PA.

FORM 5.11   New Product Information Sheet

Your firm:
Proprietary name of new product:
Generic name:
It uses: 1. Primary:
          2. Secondary:
          3. Other:
Who would use it?

Industries   Applications

_____   _____
_____   _____
_____   _____

List job title(s) held by persons we want to influence (e.g., design engineer, lab technician, housewife):
_____
_____

What need does the product fill?
_____
_____

Give a narrative description of all its key features *in order of priority*:
_____
_____

List those features that are unique when compared with conventional products:
_____
_____

How does each of these features help a customer do a job faster, at less cost, more accurately, or efficiently, etc.?
_____
_____

List specifications that you feel would interest buyers:
_____
_____

What is the price?
_____

What is delivery time in days?
_____

Add any other details you feel are important?
_____
_____

Give name of person to contact for more information:
_____
_____

Adapted from *Marketing Problem Solver* by Cochrane Chase and Kenneth L. Barasch. Copyright © 1977 by the authors. Reprinted with permission of the publisher, Chilton Book Co., Radnor, PA.

How to Write Your Press Release

Your company has a noteworthy event that is going to take place, so you need to produce a press release. To write a press release yourself is not hard and should not seem a mystical happening. There are distinct advantages to writing them yourself. First, a well-written press release will be published a lot sooner than if you have to wait for a reporter to appear, or get the initial release past the editor, who may tell you it needs to be rewritten. Second, you the writer can control the tone or image that you desire to project to the readers.

Before actually beginning to write the release, remember these basic guidelines:

1. State the facts. Don't make claims or pitches or present promotional ideas.
2. Only put into your release what you want to appear in print.
3. Use as few adjectives as possible, but use action verbs.
4. Give as much interesting factual information as necessary. Too much is better than a lack of information. The press can always edit your release, and they will!
5. Be straightforward, but don't overkill. Editors receive lots of releases. Most of them do not make it into print, so keep it interesting.
6. Enclose clear black-and-white photographs whenever possible.
7. Don't be afraid to use a quote.... often they liven up a news release.

With the use of a completed PIQ (Form 5.10 or 5.11), you are ready to write. The information you will include should answer the following questions:

Who?
What?
Where?
When?
Why?
How?

All this information can be gleaned from the completed PIQ.

Organize your release with the most important information at the beginning. Then work down to the less important facts. Some people prefer to end the release with something catchy to keep the interest of the reader. Generally, the concluding paragraph should give general information about the firm. This informational paragraph can remain the same for all of your releases.

Write in simple, fairly short sentences and try to avoid the use of technical language. Certain buzzwords are appropriate when you need to keep the attention of a more technical audience. The reader of the release will determine the level of sophistication of the language used. Generally speaking, try to keep it nontechnical and easy to read.

The paragraphs you use after the headline and opening will vary depending on the event or activity being reported. If you are telling about more than one central figure, be sure to give pertinent information

ILLUSTRATION 5.2 Sample News Release Format.

```
                    BROOKS ASSOCIATES
                    3525 CAZADOR STREET
                  LOS ANGELES, CALIFORNIA 90065

                                        NEWS RELEASE OR
                                        PRESS RELEASE HERE

   FOR FURTHER INFORMATION:             FOR IMMEDIATE RELEASE
   CONTACT PERSON
   TITLE AND ORGANIZATION
   TELEPHONE NUMBER
                                              ↑
                                           10 lines
                                              ↓

                      HEADLINE HERE; ONE OR TWO LINES

   BEGIN COPY HERE...
   (DATELINE OPTIONAL)




        AT BOTTOM OF PAGE TYPE "MORE" OR "-30-" AS APPROPRIATE...CENTERED.
```

on each person. The same format can be used for a simple or a more involved release. Remember to be concise, but also try to provide more information than the news media will probably use rather than too little. Illustration 5.2 is a sample news release format; Illustration 5.3 is a sample press release.

Rules for Writing Your Own Copy

Writing your own copy is quite simple. However, the editor of the publication might rewrite it—even if you write it well! If you write the copy poorly, the editor will trash your release and you'll never know what happened to it. Here are some simple rules for writing good copy:

1. Superlatives (words ending in "er" or "est") are forbidden unless demonstrably true.

ILLUSTRATION 5.3 Sample Completed Press Release.

BROOKS ASSOCIATES
3525 CAZADOR STREET
LOS ANGELES, CALIFORNIA 90065

NEWS RELEASE

FOR FURTHER INFORMATION:

CONTACT GREG ELMORE   FOR IMMEDIATE RELEASE
PROGRAM COORDINATOR
(213) 222-7222

SOUTH AMERICAN MUSIC ENSEMBLE TO PERFORM AT LOYOLA MARYMOUNT

Sukay, a four member musical ensemble that performs the traditional ethnic music of Peru, Bolivia, Ecuador, Chile and Argentina, will perform in Loyola Marymount University's Gersten Pavilion on Friday, May 20, at 8:30 p.m. Tickets are $6 for general admission and $4.50 for seniors, students and children under 18 years.

"Sukay" is the Quechua word meaning "to open up the earth and prepare it for planting." Through its presentations, the group Sukay seeks to foster a growing awareness of the Inca empire cultures and share the mysteries of the ancient Quechua and Aymara civilizations.

The group consists of folk musicians Quentin Badoux and her husband Edmond, who have traveled together for 15 months in South America researching the music of the highlands, and two native Bolivians, Javier Canelas and Gonzalo Vargas.

In concert, the members of Sukay present more than 25 instruments, many of them ancient, such as the antara, sicus, rondador, and other pan-pipes; notched flutes such as the choquellas and the lechewuayos, and a selection of drums and rattles such as the tinya and ch'ullus. The Spanish influence is seen in the fabrication of native stringed instruments, including the charango, which is fashioned from the shell of an armadillo.

Further information on the Sukay performance is available by contacting the Loyola Marymount University Central Box Office at (213) 555-5555.

2. Vague statements are bad also. Quantify as much as possible. Back your statements with numbers and statistics.
3. Avoid long sentences. Keep sentences short and factual. A good rule is to write no sentence over 17 words long.
4. Begin with the most important information and end with the least important.
5. Answer the journalist's six questions: who, what, where, when, why, and how.
6. Use photos of new products, new personnel, or a new building. Even if you have to wait for the photos, it's worth it. A picture *is* worth a thousand words, especially in the printed media.
7. Avoid unproven claims. Stick to what you know from field-

tested experience. Unproven claims will come back to haunt you.
8. Write about something new. You can say it with flowers, but avoid superlatives.
9. Keep the writing as simple as humanly possible. Aim for an eighth-grade reading level.
10. Study similar published news items for ideas, style, and format.

Sending the Release

All releases should be typed, double-spaced, and, if necessary, photocopied on a plain white bond paper. Leave margins on all sides so that an editor can make modifications or write printing instructions. If the press release is more than one page long, print each page on a separate sheet. Staple both pages together.

If you have a photograph to accompany the release, you should remember:

1. The prints should be sharp black-and-white glossies.
2. They should be 5 in. × 7 in. or larger.
3. If the release includes a photo of an individual, put the person's name, correctly spelled, on the reverse side of the photograph.
4. If the subject of the photo is action, a scene, a building, or even an artist's rendering, make sure a descriptive caption is placed on the back that clearly describes:
   (a) The project name.
   (b) What is going on.
   (c) Names of all individuals (in the order shown).
   (d) Any photo credit to be given.

The cover letter sent with the release can be used to give additional information that may be important. This is especially useful when the information is sent to a person or organization that knows you (e.g., an alumni association).

Direct your press release and cover letter to the editor unless you have the name of a specific person who should receive the release. If the publication is large, use your best judgment as to which department editor would be the most appropriate. *Do not* ask for your release to be returned or for a copy of the issue when a story appears.

If you haven't already compiled a list of places to send the release, you should take the time to do this. It will be used every time you decide to send out information in the form of an article or press release. Your list should include:

Trade associations (both local and national).
General business community organizations.

TV stations.
Radio stations.
Newspapers (both major metro area and neighborhood).
Financial and business periodicals (local and national).
Public interest groups (including community leaders and local government officials).
Personal membership and interest groups.

Sources for these can be found in the Yellow Pages and also in the directories listed in Appendix 2. *The Encyclopedia of Associations*, mentioned elsewhere, is also an invaluable source.

Allow enough lead time when submitting a dated release. This means at least 7 days for a newspaper or as much as 90 days for a periodical. Check with each source on your list to determine the necessary press dates for publication. Note these lead times as well as valuable contact people or special requirements for the list that you will maintain.

ARTICLES FOR TRADE PUBLICATIONS

Most types of small businesses can be grouped into an industry. Most of the industry groups have myriad trade associations or interest groups that can be joined. These organizations vary in size and also offer many different services to their members. However, despite the differences, what these trade associations have in common is that they are reliable sources of information relative to the particulars of their respective industries.

Some of these organizations publish newsletters, magazines, and brochures; they maintain valuable marketing statistics; provide special discounts on travel and group insurance; hold seminars and training sessions; and have referral services. The benefits will be different for each organization. If you are interested in an organization, they will provide you all the information you need to evaluate their benefits.

Because trade and business associations are hungry for information about their members, the releases that you prepare have a good chance of inclusion in their publications.

THE PRESS KIT

As you begin to develop the PR program for your company, preparation of a press kit becomes an important step in the process. This packet of information can be used for press conferences, seminars, or trade shows. It can even be mailed directly to prospective customers. Once produced, this packet can be sent to trade magazines, local newspapers, or specialty publications that the company decides are an important way to reach a target market.

The press kit serves several purposes: It is an excellent introduction to the local media. It provides background on your company, its products, capabilities, and personnel. A press kit is helpful when it accompanies a news release. It can always be left behind after making a marketing visit, much like the brochure and business card. Remember that the press kit must maintain the same image as any other piece of printed company material.

The kit usually contains a data sheet describing the complete company history, a list of the products or services, copies of articles published about your product or firm; biographies of the principal officers and key employees, any good photographs that are representative of company activities, and, of course, news releases pertinent to the happenings of your firm.

All of this information should be compiled, edited for content, and then neatly typed. Be sure to indicate the name and telephone number of a contact who can supply additional information. The press kit is a growing, changing marketing tool. Every major change at a company should be reflected in the press kit. Keep updating the materials, so that you can alter the kit to suit the reader. For example, the local newspaper will not need distributor information, but it will require more information than other recipients about local projects and so forth. Prepare a press list of where publicity information can be sent. You can make note of the information most appropriate for each.

6

DESIGN ADVERTISING: BROCHURES AND PRINTED MATERIAL

People will buy your product or service if you give them good reasons to do so. Consequently, the advertising you develop should attempt to give consumers these reasons. Since the customer usually wants to buy the things he sees that he likes, advertising bears the responsibility of presenting the message and the image of your company to the marketplace in an attractive light.

Advertising is paid-for communication to the public(s) designed to develop favorable attitudes and reactions from the consumer. This favorable reaction may not necessarily mean a sale. It is a bringing together of the advertiser and the reader or listener. Besides the expectation of closing the sale, the advertising process also includes personal contact, realization of benefits the product or service will provide, a comparison of value, promotional ideas, and intelligent salesmanship.

This chapter will help to make you aware of the process that printed advertising material must go through in its development. The brochure will be the main focus. We will try to use its development as a guide for all printed materials that might be used as marketing tools.

At the heart of all printed material is a look or an image that's worth a thousand words. If it successfully conveys to customers that your product or service is what they are looking for, no words are necessary. Your image is constantly being strengthened or weakened by the company material that your customer sees. This includes your logo, business cards, letterhead, and brochures. For a small business wishing to grow, the proper choice of image may be crucial to survival. We place a lot of emphasis on the image since it plays a part in so much of the business. But keep in mind, you must have a product or service that generally lives up to its reputation. A product that fails to do so will create its own, more persistent image—that of a bad product.

LOGO, LETTERHEAD, AND BUSINESS FORMS

Your logo and letterhead design are nonverbal communications—a crucial part of your image. Even so, logos are more important to those who live with them than to the customer. It is easy to get into an ego trip when deciding on a logo. Two things must be kept in mind: stay cheap when you have it created and be prepared to spend money to present it in the proper manner.

Logos are extremely important to a company because they are used everywhere a customer is exposed to your company. So take great care in choosing the design and typeface because you'll have to live with them for a long time. If you have a logo now and want to change it and your look/image, pick one and stick with it. Experimenting with different logos/images will confuse your customer.

Logos are not only used for business cards, letterheads, envelopes, memos and ads in the media, but also on your building sign, signs on your vehicles, give-aways (e.g., calendars), flyers, and on notebook binders. If your company's product is a report or some other paper presentation, it is especially important to use a presentation that reflects the company's logo.

Logo Design

When you design a logo, keep it simple. The effective presentation of letters or a shape can be most appealing. A fancy design may confuse your customer. Think in terms of the minimum information required to have the customer remember your company. Illustration 6.1 shows some sample logos (printed by permission).

The idea of a logo is to have a picture, a symbolic image that will be remembered by the customer. Simpler images are usually easier to retain than complex ones.

If you pay for a logo design it might be cheap or very expensive. In the late 1970s NBC paid several million dollars for a triangular red and blue N. On unveiling the new logo after ditching their peacock, NBC discovered a radio station in Chicago had the exact same logo. The radio station had paid a lot less for their logo, but had been using it longer. The radio station sued and got an out-of-court settlement of over $4 million. In 1980 NBC went back to the peacock.

Finding someone to design your logo at a reasonable price is not that hard to do. You can ask local printers for their recommendations. You can approach local universities with art departments. You can go to the Yellow Pages. From the names you choose, talk to more than one of them, look at their portfolios and look especially at the previous designs they have done. The choice of a designer is yours. You must feel comfortable with his or her artistic ability foremost, but the designer should also have a sense of the kind of image you want to portray.

ILLUSTRATION 6.1 Business Cards (Logo Samples).

115

ILLUSTRATION 6.1 Continued

Edward Scott
President

Sun Metalsource Corporation
P.O. Box 3757
Santa Monica, CA 90403
(213) 395-4985

Betty Lee
Photographer

THE PERFECT IMAGE
Post Office Box 641 · San Francisco CA 94101 · 415 885-6160

(213) 658-8770

Theodore Front Musical Literature

155 N. San Vicente Blvd.
Beverly Hills, CA 90211

PUBLIC RELATIONS FOR ARCHITECTS/DESIGNERS/ENGINEERS

PR ADE

F. WESTON STARRATT, P.E.

ONE SUTTER ST., SUITE 505 SAN FRANCISCO CA 94104 (415) 982 5448

DELOS RECORDS INC.
855 VIA DE LA PAZ
PACIFIC PALISADES, CA 90272

(213) 454-0524

DELOS

AMELIA HAYGOOD *DIRECTOR*

MONTEZ
Landscape Contracting, Inc.

John Montez

2120 Oswald Road
Yuba City, CA 95991
916-674-5297

Vera Robles De Witt
Vice President

POSSE

POSSE POLICE PRODUCTS, INC.
1700 DAISY AVENUE, LONG BEACH, CA 90813 • (213) 437-016

(213) 764-8334
(213) 764-3015

THE
CATAMARAN
STORE

DICK SIMS

11629 VANOWEN
N. HOLLYWOOD, CA. 91605

ILLUSTRATION 6.1 Continued

PATRICK ASSOCIATES
SALES CORPORATION

372 Brannan Street
San Francisco CA 94107

(415) 543-6556

Stephen Crivello

JON MESSER
Illustration · Design
11138 Aqua Vista #C10
N. Hollywood, Cal. 91604
760-0932

Research for Children

Unique Sewing
1867 Mission Street
San Francisco, CA 94103
415 861-4771

500 E Street, Southwest
Washington, D.C. 20024

RAVEN

Business Cards

One of the first uses of the logo is on the company's business card. A business card must look important. If a customer is likely to keep *any* of your company's materials, it is the business card. Many people glue your business card directly to a Rolodex card that will be used every time they call.

Most people understand the importance of the way a business card looks, but unfortunately very few of them pay any attention to the way the card is handled. Some people throw their card out as if pitching a piece of trash. You've seen the type. They stand in front of your desk and are ready to fling it even before you've been introduced. How much better it is if the card is presented as if it *means* something. Handle your business card with dignity.

The Japanese present their card with a ritual. The card is handed to you, not thrown down. The Japanese company's card is held in the upper left corner either between thumb and index finger or with index and middle fingers. These motions are only a portion of the Japanese business card ritual. This is not to advocate that Westerners adopt the whole ritual—with bow. The point is that handling your card with a sense of pride and presenting it face up may be as important a component of the company image as the card itself.

BROCHURES

The brochure is probably the most important marketing tool the businessperson has besides his or her business card. It not only presents the introductory picture of your company's capabilities, but it is the "leave-behind" item that must paint the picture of your firm in your absence. It must also be able to sell without you! Brochures take on many different forms, shapes, sizes, and artistic temperaments.

The two most common types of brochures are the company brochure and a less comprehensive product brochure. We will describe the two types and then explain the developmental processes for both.

The Company Brochure

When most people think of a brochure, they picture the company brochure. It is a fairly comprehensive view of the company in which you are trying to promote the company through a look at just what makes it tick, including:

- The company's history.
- Its purpose and philosophy.
- The motivations of the company (growth plans).
- Staff skills and education.
- Corporate skills.

Special capabilities.
Facilities and equipment.
Successful contracts fulfilled.
Client list.
Pictures, drawings, or meaningful graphics.

Paramount in the decision process to develop the company brochure is looking at the brochures of your competitors and also the industry as a whole. Do they use full color? How many pages? Try to collect samples of them. Make note of ones you like or particular aspects that are appealing. If you determine the need for visuals, these should be done by the best professional that you can afford. Often pictures can be substituted for written explanations. After all, your customers are busy people!

Color is another aspect that can aid in the potential substitution mentioned above. It is a tremendous cost consideration. Have a graphic designer or a printer give you an idea of the differences in price between two color and full color. The need for full color is debatable. If cost is a consideration, make the layout carry the necessary impact.

The Product Brochure

If you are in the business of manufacturing, selling, and/or distributing products, then a product brochure will be more useful to you. The overall thrust shifts from the company to its products and their specifics. That is, tell all the customer will need to know about the product. This means that the company is made to sound credible, but not at the expense of valuable product information. This can include:

Performance information.
Specifications.
Drawings/details.
Design information.
Construction information.
Endorsements.
Photographs (especially in use).

These brochures are not as elaborate as a company brochure. They can be smaller in size. Photographs are of utmost importance. It is the pretty pictures that sell the product here. Falling in love with a picture is the battle won! Going along hand in hand with good visuals is the necessity for color. It is expensive, but it must be shown as lifelike as possible. The product brochure is important to the customer who buys on impulse.

Since the product brochure is smaller in size and number of pages, the layout becomes even more important. Because there is less space, you have to be more resourceful. Using a central theme is helpful. It has to be sexy, not cluttered and intimidating.

STEPS TO PREPARING A BROCHURE

Before you make a final decision on which format to use and what the brochure will contain, take time to ask yourself some questions and write down your responses. This will aid in the planning you will want to do. Questions you should ask yourself are shown in Form 6.1.

FORM 6.1 Brochure and Printed Media Questionnaire

1. Who is going to receive and/or read my brochure?

2. What do the potential readers already know about my company?

3. What do the potential readers already know about my industry?

4. What are these readers/customers interested in knowing about my company or capabilities?

5. If I were going to buy the services or products that my company sells, what would I want to know?

6. What do I need to tell the potential customers to make them interested in my firm?

7. Are my experience and credentials important? Yes No Why?

8. How much can the company afford to pay for brochure development? (This should include the cost of printing, too.)

Use the following basic steps in preparing a brochure or printed media piece:

1. Planning.
2. Creating a rough of the brochure.
3. Designing the brochure.

4. Copywriting.
5. Layout and typesetting.
6. Printing.

Time needed to complete these steps will vary. Much will depend on the amount of work to be done by you. If you choose a graphic designer to do the work, your approvals will also affect the time needed to complete the job. In addition, any work that must be contracted out (e.g., typesetting and printing) will have a separate time schedule based on the contractor. Allow yourself enough lead time so you can avoid panicking over deadlines.

Planning

In concert with completing the brochure questionnaire (Form 6.1), you should examine the brochures of your competitors to see what is already out there. Go to a trade show and get every brochure you can find. Order brochures from all of your competitors. If your business is in a market that makes it hard to identify the competition, take a look at whatever you can get. Analyze the material you gather. You will begin to find common traits, things you like and things you don't like. Make notes of these things. They will be very helpful to a graphic designer if you choose to use one.

An earnest study will show you that the best impressions are made by a slick quality brochure, with simple copy, and strong illustrations or photos, done in more than one color (perhaps using halftones).

The planning process will involve two other decisions besides how many colors to use. First, you need to decide if you will use an outside consultant or graphic designer to assist you. If you are experienced with brochure design and production, you may want to handle the project yourself. If you have no experience it is best to find and retain a designer. To find a graphic designer, the best sources are referrals from printers or other small business people. Call several designers, meet with them, look at their portfolios, speak to their previous clients and get quotes from them. Graphic designers can help you avoid costly mistakes. The brochure they design will also have professional supervision throughout its development. These graphic design pros will be invaluable in the numerous decisions that must be made. Besides, they will also have the contacts to get any of the outside work completed.

Second, you need to establish a budget. If you choose to work with a designer, his or her company will be helpful in outlining the costs that will be involved. Use Form 6.2 as a work sheet on which to record estimated and actual costs for the project.

Creating a Rough of the Brochure

You've seen the competition. You've chosen a designer. You can't put off the brochure any longer. Start to put your thoughts on paper. This is sometimes the hardest thing to do, just like writing! If it is difficult,

FORM 6.2 Printed Material Budget Form

Brief description of item: _____

Date of estimate: _____
Budget prepared by: _____
Budget approved by: _____

Cost Item	Budgeted	Actual
Planning and administration	_____	_____
Data gathering	_____	_____
Creative artwork		
Artwork	_____	_____
Layouts	_____	_____
Photography	_____	_____
Copy	_____	_____
Illustrations	_____	_____
Paste-up	_____	_____
Legal fees	_____	_____
Miscellaneous	_____	_____
subtotal	_____	_____
Printing		
Typesetting	_____	_____
Engraving	_____	_____
Press charges	_____	_____
subtotal	_____	_____
Production:		
Paper	_____	_____
Printing	_____	_____
Binding	_____	_____
Collating	_____	_____
Special features	_____	_____
subtotal	_____	_____
Total	$_____	$_____

block out the words and picture spaces. This exercise is to help the graphic designer have your ideas to work with, too. After all, it's your company, and you have to use this marketing tool.

With this draft in hand, start to get some ideas and comments from as many other people as you can. This is an exercise in initial reaction, questioning, constructive criticism and a check for omissions. Take note of these impressions. They should be shared with the graphic designer. Also ask yourself:

Have I left out anything that would motivate my customer?
Have I identified my product or service completely?

Now is a good time to consider the format for your brochure. What impact do you want the brochure to have? What size should it be? These questions should be discussed with the designer. Some of these imply additional costs, some will give better use of the brochure for mailings and so forth. Take the time to discuss these and get any cost estimates that you can to compare prices.

Designing the Brochure

If you have retained a designer, work closely with him or her. Don't be afraid to make your comments or ask them to redo an idea or approach if you don't like the one they suggest. At your first meeting, you will discuss your rough draft, the image, color, pages, and approach. Subsequent meetings and conversations will move toward an agreed-on design, production, and completion date.

Copywriting

Whether you are writing your own copy or not, refer to the questions that you answered on the brochure questionnaire (Form 6.1) before you begin the project. Decide what information about your company, projects, personnel, and so on is important to the potential readers/customers. Write down these facts.

The text for your brochure should be well organized, client-oriented, and easy to read. The use of bulleted words and phrases makes for quick scanning of the main points. You should have others read over the draft of the text. Several rewrites may be necessary to assure a smooth flow of words.

Illustration 6.2 provides a list of 39 tips for do-it-yourself copywriting as compiled by William H. Peeler, marketing consultant and author of *Mail Order, Direct Mail Advertising Manual*.

After your brochure copy has been written, it may be well to use the following as a checklist:

Is it arresting?

Is it clear?

Is it simple?

Does it give the information that the reader would expect at this point in the decision making?

Is it believable?

Does it deliver the message about the product or service it was meant to deliver?

If a piece of copy can pass this test, it should do even better with the visuals.

ILLUSTRATION 6.2   Tips for Do-It-Yourself Copywriting.

1. Short sentences pack more punch, jump out at the reader, and grab his attention.
2. Short paragraphs enable the reader to understand and more readily absorb your selling message. When you use a paragraph with more than six lines (when printed), reader comprehension suffers at that point, and comprehension after that point (in a sales letter) is usually lower. It's OK to use as many as nine lines in column format on a brochure, because the lines are usually shorter.
3. Use simple sentences, without a lot of commas and other punctuation, to make the reader's job easier.
4. Vary sentence length to prevent boredom.
5. Prefer nouns and verbs to adjectives and adverbs. The former two sell the reader more.
6. For maximum impact, place the emphasis or strong point at the beginning or end of sentence, not the middle.
7. Use the active voice rather than the passive voice.
8. Don't tell a lot about yourself or your company. Use no more than two to three sentences about you. Talk much more about the reader. He is first and foremost interested in himself.
9. Don't address copy to groups of people (e.g., to all our customers). Rather, address an individual. The reader wants to feel like he's not just another number.
10. Get a "you slant" into your copy. Most of your copy should be addressed to the reader, covering what your products(s) or service(s) is (are) going to do for him.
11. Speak the language of the typical prospect you are writing to. English teachers expect a certain style; coal miners expect another.
12. Write conversationally. Your writing must sound as if you were sitting comfortably across from an individual prospect, talking casually with him. Avoid trying to sound more intellectual in your writing. It turns off most people.
13. Make your writing sound warm and friendly. This gives your reader the idea he is dealing with a human being.
14. Appeal to readers' senses.
    Wrong: "Pick strawberries in your own garden."
    Right: "Pick juicy, red strawberries in your own garden."
15. The most effective copy is logico-emotional. Most readers will maintain they purchase most things for a given reason. Usually an emotional appeal is what really made them buy.
16. Readers respond better to sincere rather than sophisticated copy.
17. Don't talk down to your readers. They may be impressed. But they also will feel alienated from you.
18. Don't be a slave to grammar. Feel free to end sentences with prepositions. Use contractions. Begin paragraphs with conjunctions. Use sentence fragments. The purpose of copy is to sell, not to please your English teacher.
19. Don't just cite facts about your product or service. Use examples. Examples reinforce the claims you make.
20. Avoid superlatives. People don't trust that something is really the best—especially when the seller makes that claim. To use superlatives is to shift reader focus away from benefits to him and on to thinking about you as someone trying to proposition him.
21. Be specific. Reader wants to know exactly what your offer is. You waste a lot of money on printing when, for example, you aren't specific in a lead getting ad.
    Wrong: "Earn $500 per month."
    Right: "Earn $500 per month selling tires."

ILLUSTRATION 6.2 Continued

22. Get to the point right away. Don't build up to the offer. Say what it is right away and begin building benefits immediately.
23. Use subheadings. They act as an outline for skim readers and enable you to present information twice in one piece: once in a body copy, once in the subheadline.
24. Use many of the 10 magic words of copywriting. These extra powerful words pull better than other words. The magic 10 are: (1) *new*, (2) *free*, (3) *now*, (4) *win*, (5) *easy*, (6) *introducing*, (7) *today*, (8) *save*, (9) *guarantee*, and (the biggest of all) (10) *you* [italics added].
25. Repeat primary and secondary benefits as much as possible. The repetition acts hypnotically on reader and makes your sales message sink in emotionally.
26. The fear of loss is just as powerful (if not more so) as the desire for gain. Push both these themes in your copy.
27. In the first paragraph, make reader want to read more. Accomplish that by offering him a major benefit right away.
28. Ask for the order. Readers respond to directions. Tell reader to read your copy and send for the product.
29. Don't be hesitant about using long captions under your illustrations. Don't just identify your product; use a motivating caption. This is important, because captions receive a great deal of attention. Also, readers believe captions more than regular body copy.
30. When using a lead ad to generate inquiries, don't give reader too much information about your product or service. He must know what your offer is. But too much information often spoils his sending for more details in followup package.
31. When you offer inquirers free booklets, information, etc., stress there is no obligation and more inquirers will respond.
32. Use of three dots can create suspense and enhance the drama of your offer. For example, the teaser copy on an outside envelope might read "You can save $20 on your next trip to the supermarket if you . . ." This practically forces reader to open your mailing, where you end the sentence possibly as the main headline in a letter: "Bring the copy of this letter to your nearest dealer for 20% off on any food purchase."
33. Use a startling statement or an exclamation to get reader's attention.
34. Point out the inflation-fighting aspect of your product or service.
35. Tie the copy about your product or service in with a major event, holiday, something current in the news, etc.
36. Describe your product or service as a problem solver.
37. Identify reader as a member of a select group, thus appealing to his desire to be snobbish.
38. The words "Not Sold in Stores" enhance the desirability of your product.
39. Make an appeal to nostalgia in your copy.

Adapted from "Direct Marketing Expert Lists—Tips to Polish Copy Writing Technique" (September 1, 1980) with permission of *Los Angeles Business Journal*. Copyright © 1983.

Layout and Typesetting

The layout stage of brochure development is putting the copy together with the visuals. The manipulation of the elements to tell the story with the desired effect is the goal. A graphic designer must take the parts and assemble them into a pleasing, meaningful arrangement. Unity is achieved with all of the parts working to maintain one central image. A balance of these elements must be made. This could be left/right or up/down, for example. Perhaps the most important layout characteristic is the flow. The reader's eyes move through the brochure, drawn to a particular spot by the arrangement of pictures, words, lines, and so forth.

Color plays an important part in the layout. Certain colors have their own psychological language.

Here is an example of some basic colors and the responses they elicit:

Red	Activity, warmth
Blue	Serenity, coolness
Purple	Richness, dignity
Green	Nature, harmony
Yellow	Sunshine, cheerfulness
Pink	Good health

Although color plays a significant part in the impact of advertising, most small businesses have to give the added printing costs for color separations and stripping a second look.

Another costly part of the brochure development process is the typesetting or typography. This step in the process is taking the copy and translating it into type. Most designers and printers do not do their own typesetting. Usually this process is contracted to the typographer. The designer will have a book that shows all of the different typefaces available.

Choosing the typeface is fairly simple. It is important to find a style that is easy to read. The typographer or the designer will be able to determine the size (pitch) to fit the spaces available. Also, it is a good idea not to mix too many styles of type together. The type style you use for your logo and business card should remain the same for all printed material that displays the name and address of your company.

One other area that you may consider in the development of the brochure is border space. A cluttered brochure or flyer may never be read. Use of borders and blank space can be very soothing to the reader. It may help soften the impact of the printed word.

Printing

Printing costs have soared in the last few years. So an underlying objective of this survey of printing is to save some money. A large portion of the production costs for a brochure can be saved if you handle the entire project as if you were sort of a "general contractor" subcontracting most of the work to other specialists.

If you have elected to use the services of a graphic designer, you must still maintain control and awareness of what is going on. Each step of the process should have a "sign-off" or approval for that particular portion of the work.

When you do get the paste-up of your brochure, check it thoroughly ... and then check it again. Mistakes that are corrected after the printer receives the camera-ready artwork will cost you.

When you are faced with finding a printer to do work for you, shop around. Not only for price, but also for quality. Printers span the gamut of excellent to poor. Get competitive quotes and look at samples of each printer's work. Also, ask for an estimated completion date.

Allow plenty of time for the printer to complete the job, especially if you are having color printing done. A printing shop has to schedule its presses around similar work. If your printer can notify you in advance of the scheduled printing date, you or your designer should be present to see the test run. This allows some control over the quality, particularly the colors. Printers have to mix the ink colors just as a paint store mixes paint, so the color is rarely exactly the same twice in a row.

Another price consideration is the paper stock that will be used. There are three main categories of paper: writing paper, book paper, and cover stock. These come in different weights and sizes. The printer or designer will be able to assist you with these decisions.

One other consideration is the cost per thousand or the "quantity breaks." Quantity breaks are the increments that show a substantial per unit cost decrease based on an increased number of units printed. For example, the cost per thousand of a brochure for the first thousand might be $100. If you order two thousand units, the cost per thousand may drop to $75. This point indicates a "cost break." Regardless of the quantity, you have paid the same development costs. Look at and compare these prices.

PACKAGE DESIGN

The packaging of a product is a physical experience that, hopefully, encourages consumer contact. A product's package has shape, color, and recognition value. You see it on billboards, in magazines, on television, or in store displays. The package conveys the most immediate impression on the consumer's mind. Moreover, the package is a medium that can carry the message to a consumer even after other exposures have failed.

Package design is in a state of change. Due to the litter concern, recyclability, and so forth, packaging has taken a direction that makes disposal of some containers increasingly difficult. Despite these limitations, changes in color, shape, and material are introduced into a product's packaging every time a new idea comes to mind.

A package must attract attention and look special or, as it has been dubbed, have a "buy-me" look!

Here are some trends that will affect packaging in the 1980s:

1. The single-person household or smaller family unit—especially in food packaging.
2. The concern for energy efficiency due to higher costs of energy.
3. The concern for rising costs of all consumer and industrial products.
4. The increase in eating away from home as more consumers lack food preparation time.
5. Trends toward natural foods and health because of growing health or weight consciousness.
6. Trends toward increased leisure and the expanded variety of leisure activities.

These trends are forcing dramatic innovations in packaging that should be well planned, questioned, and tested. Consumer research can assist in the development of product name, color, package shape, package verbiage, size, and so forth. These results coupled with a close review and monitoring of production costs are vital.

Package design should:

Communicate honestly (e.g., use representative photographs or drawings).
Communicate naturally (e.g., use a natural setting).
Communicate quickly (i.e., organize material in a simple way).
Communicate readably (e.g., use color contrasts that enhance legibility).

A package design that lives up to these goals will be repurchased as long as the product lives up to the expectations suggested by the package.

Packaging has one distinct advantage over the other media. It is very effective when used in a multiple unit display. Use this technique to the fullest. A display of this type will enhance brand identification. Package shape and the accompanying logo or identity will also aid in the identification (e.g., the Coca-Cola bottle shape).

Just as with other printed material, color is important, since it can arouse instant response. Color can convey emotion, action, style, comfort, as well as draw attention.

It is evident that the package is much more than a container. It must protect, identify, and dispense the product, attract the consumer, and comply with any federal regulations.

SUMMARY

Do not rush the process of brochure and printed material development. Plan the process and its related costs. Take the time to make the copy speak to the reader. This means numerous rewrites or fine-tuning adjustments.

Learn as much as you can from the development process. As you can see, there is money to be saved at various stages. Try to keep a time schedule for the activities. This can be compared with the budget form. This is an artistic activity, so learn to be particular.

A sampling of brochure styles and formats is shown throughout Illustration 6.3 (see individual pieces for descriptions).

ILLUSTRATION 6.3 SAMPLE BROCHURE FORMATS
(See pages 130–164. Descriptions accompany each sample.)

$8\frac{1}{2} \times 14$ inch. Three-fold mail-out style brochure. Effective use of both photography and halftones. Note U.S. Postal Service Bulk Mail Permit, as well as detachable information request card.

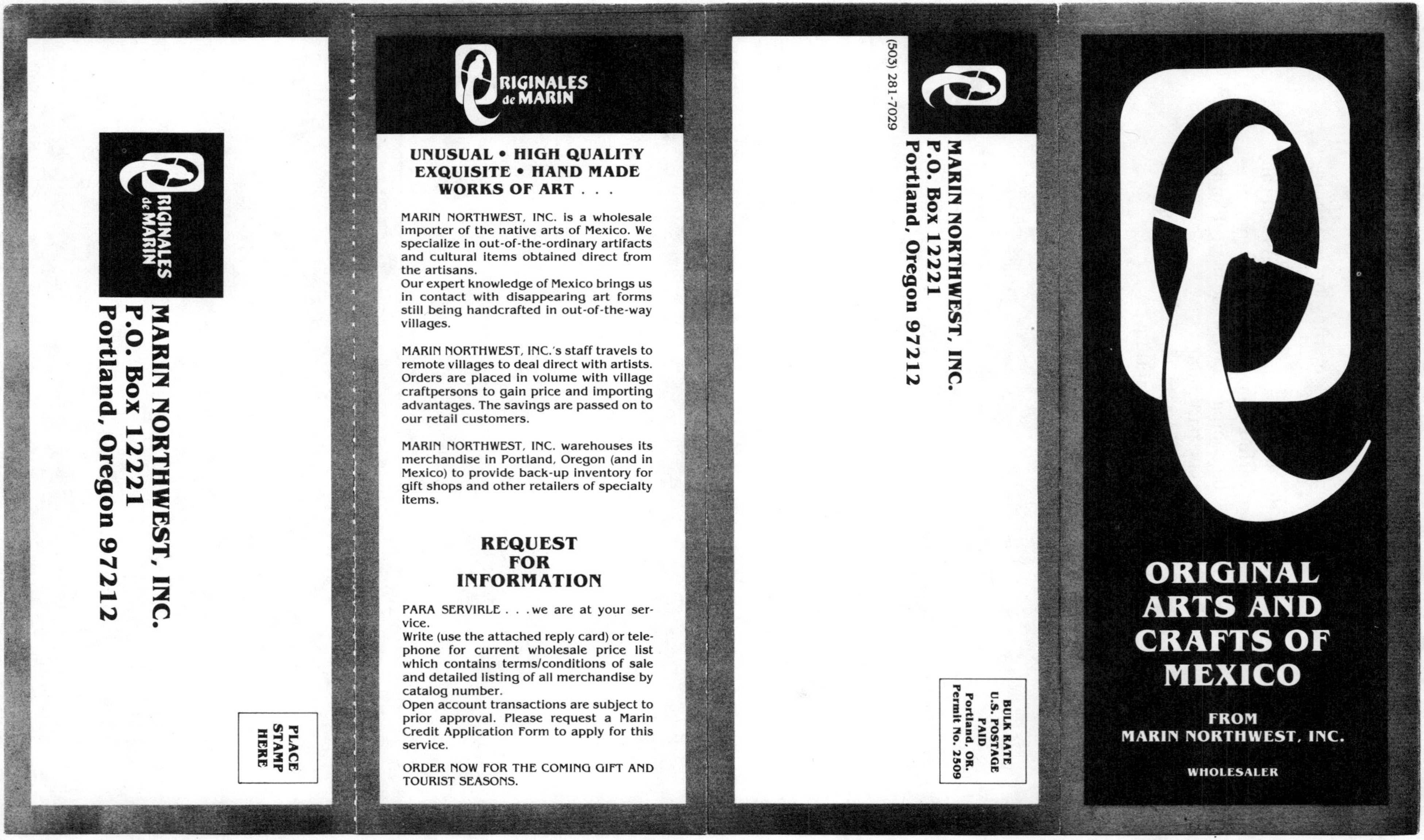

ORIGINAL ARTS AND CRAFTS OF MEXICO

FROM
MARIN NORTHWEST, INC.

WHOLESALER

MARIN NORTHWEST, INC.
P.O. Box 12221
Portland, Oregon 97212

(503) 281-7029

BULK RATE
U.S. POSTAGE
PAID
Portland, OR.
Permit No. 2509

RIGINALES de MARIN

UNUSUAL • HIGH QUALITY
EXQUISITE • HAND MADE
WORKS OF ART . . .

MARIN NORTHWEST, INC. is a wholesale importer of the native arts of Mexico. We specialize in out-of-the-ordinary artifacts and cultural items obtained direct from the artisans.

Our expert knowledge of Mexico brings us in contact with disappearing art forms still being handcrafted in out-of-the-way villages.

MARIN NORTHWEST, INC.'s staff travels to remote villages to deal direct with artists. Orders are placed in volume with village craftpersons to gain price and importing advantages. The savings are passed on to our retail customers.

MARIN NORTHWEST, INC. warehouses its merchandise in Portland, Oregon (and in Mexico) to provide back-up inventory for gift shops and other retailers of specialty items.

REQUEST
FOR
INFORMATION

PARA SERVIRLE . . . we are at your service.

Write (use the attached reply card) or telephone for current wholesale price list which contains terms/conditions of sale and detailed listing of all merchandise by catalog number.

Open account transactions are subject to prior approval. Please request a Marin Credit Application Form to apply for this service.

ORDER NOW FOR THE COMING GIFT AND TOURIST SEASONS.

PLACE
STAMP
HERE

RIGINALES de MARIN

MARIN NORTHWEST, INC.
P.O. Box 12221
Portland, Oregon 97212

8½ × 14 inch Three-fold mail-out style brochure (continued).

REQUEST FOR INFORMATION

I am interested in receiving information about the following Mexican Imports.

(PLEASE CHECK ITEMS OF INTEREST)

- ☐ Credit Application
- ☐ Ceramics/Dinnerware
- ☐ Lacquer Work
- ☐ Featherwork
- ☐ Textile Items
- ☐ Traditional Clothes
- ☐ Plaques
- ☐ Arbol de la Vida
- ☐ Price List
- ☐ Paper Mache
- ☐ Straw Weaving
- ☐ Bark Paintings
- ☐ Copper/Bronze/Tincrafts
- ☐ Oil Paintings
- ☐ Wall Hangings
- ☐ Greeting Cards

COMPANY _____

ADDRESS _____

CITY _____ STATE _____ ZIP CODE _____

PHONE (AREA CODE) _____

YOUR NAME _____

FEATHER WORK

Works of art created by small groups of Mexican artists to keep this disappearing art form alive. Natural feathers are colored and arranged in exquisite manners to depict exotic birds. Size is approximately 16 x 8 inches for display on wall, mantle or shelf. No feathers used are from endangered species.

LACQUER WORK

Artifacts in plate, box and other forms, each handcrafted from Tzirimo wood. In creating these items, the artisans adhere to the original process handed down by the Tarascan Indians. The lengthy process (some items take months) involves hand carving, oil rubbing using natural color pastes and finally manually burnishing to a bright luster finish.

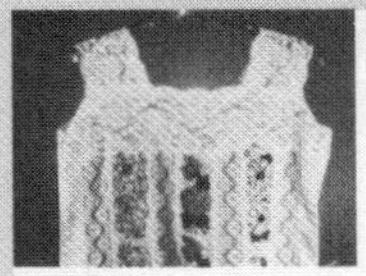

TRADITIONAL CLOTHING

Stylized native clothing that incorporates handcrafted designs and colorful ornamentations. These items are worn in Mexican society today, as well as by sophisticates around the world.
Blouses
Dresses
Sarapes (shawls)
Guayaveras (men's shirts)

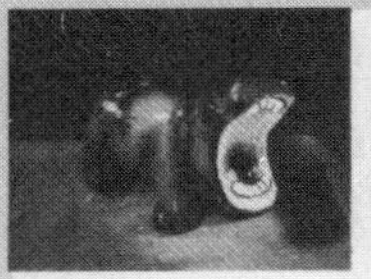

PAPER MACHE

Artistic figurines of animals, birds and other objects. Crafted by Mexican artisans in traditional designs and motifs to give a unique Mexican flavor. Over 24 different types, each available in several sizes, from small to life-size.

COPPER/BRONZE TIN CRAFTS

Copper artifacts are based on shapes of household articles. Each is hammered and shaped by hand. Artisans follow an age-old process to prepare each copper block for shaping. Over 10 types of copper items are available in traditional and contemporary designs.
Other metal objects include bronze works, tin crafts and metal jewelry.

STRAW WEAVING

A Mexican art form that has flourished for centuries. It is traditional in Michoacan villages for parents to pass straw weaving skills on to their offspring. Today's highly skilled straw weavers create intricate figures to form mobiles, Christmas ornaments and other artistic objects. Sizes vary from 3 inches to 5 feet.

CERAMICS AND DINNERWARE

Ceramic items and dinnerware sets are produced utilizing century-old pottery techniques. Each piece is individually shaped, hand painted, glazed and fired in ancient-type kilns. Designs are traditional to the areas of Mexico where they are produced. Although designs are repeated, no two sets are identical.

VERACRUZ BIRD STATUETTES

The unique figurines are creations of 4 Veracruz Indians who search the jungle for mushroom-like growths on trees. These growths and attached bark are shaped to form different birds with legs and stand added to make them freestanding. A clear lacquer finish retains the original texture.
The time and effort of these workers create special gifts of limited number.

PAINTINGS HANGINGS

Original oil paintings by well known and yet-to-be-recognized artists of Mexico. Each painting is an exquisite rendition of Mexican life style. Mexican artists excell in portraying their country's culture utilizing traditional and modern art forms.

8½ × 11 inch Single-sheet flyer or information mail-out brochure. Full color graphics and black and white typeset information on reverse side. Note use of both logos of the company and the particular show.

8½ × 11 inch Single-sheet flyer (continued).

The Music Of Black America

UNPRECEDENTED ADVERTISING OPPORTUNITY	**The Music of Black America** provides you with an unprecedented advertising opportunity to capture the lucrative Black consumer market. This 24-hour radio special will air on major Black radio stations nationwide during February, 1982 — **Black History Month.**
IN-DEPTH LOOK AT BLACK MUSIC	The program itself will, for the first time ever, give Black audiences an in-depth look at, and listen to, every aspect of Black music — from the unique stylings of **Billie Holiday** and **Scott Joplin,** to the melodic music of **Stevie Wonder** and the **Commodores.** Each hour will feature a mix of contemporary music and hits from the past, along with intriguing interviews with great artists of today and yesterday.
THOROUGHLY RESEARCHED BY WRITERS FROM NEW YORK TO LOS ANGELES	**The Music of Black America** is being thoroughly researched and written by writers from New York to Los Angeles, promising to make it a truly historical program.
120 MINUTES OF ADVERTISING	There are 120 minutes of advertising in the 24-hour program reserved for national advertisers. Exclusive sponsorship and billboards are available with minimum buys.
DESIGNED TO AIR ONE HOUR A DAY	**The Music of Black America** is designed to air one hour a day for 24 days during the Month of February. Some stations may elect to air more than one hour daily. Each advertiser will be provided with affidavits of performance.
NUMEROUS MERCHANDISING AND PROMOTIONAL POSSIBILITIES	There are numerous mechandising and promotional possibilities connected with the airing of **The Music of Black America,** including a poster and/or calendar giveaway using the beautiful illustration depicted on the front of this sheet.
RKO RADIO SALES — OFFICES	For information regarding advertising opportunities on the 24-hour Radio Special — **The Music of Black America,** contact **RKO RADIO SALES** at any of the offices listed below:

HEADQUARTERS:
NEW YORK
1440 Broadway, 15th floor
New York, NY 10018
212-764-6800
Attn: Jerry Kelly

REGIONAL OFFICES:

ATLANTA
1365 Peachtree St., N.E.
Suite 308
Atlanta, GA 30309
404-881-0095
Attn: LinaJean Trosper

DETROIT
3221 S. Big Beaver Rd.
Suite 207
Troy, Mich. 48084
313-643-7655
Attn: W.F. (Terry) Grimme

CHICAGO
401 N. Michigan Ave., Ste. 3200
Chicago, ILL 60611
312-836-8300
Attn: Linda Packer-Spitz

LOS ANGELES
5670 Wilshire Blvd., Suite 2140
Los Angeles, CA 90036
213-934-6531
Attn: Bob Bordonaro

DALLAS
3626 N. Hall St., Suite 711
Dallas, TX 75219
214-522-5650
Attn: James D. Allen

SAN FRANCISCO
1 Market Plaza, Suite 1504
San Francisco, CA 94105
415-777-5722
Attn: Sonny Mitchell

SYNDICATE IT, INC.

THE MUSIC OF BLACK AMERICA IS PRODUCED AND DISTRIBUTED BY SYNDICATE IT, INC.

Letter size file folder for company rates, corporate presentation or proposal. Full color cover. Inside map and service routes use entire inside of folder. Sample insert sheets can be changed and duplicated as needed with minimal expense.

P & H TRUCKING
5127 South Maywood Avenue
Maywood, California 90270
Phone (213) 583-4855   (800) 421-6409

134

8½ × 11 inch Rate sheet for insertion in file folder.

ICC PNHT 401	PASCUZZO & HONEYMAN TRUCKING, INC. 2ND REVISED PAGE 13 Cancels 1ST REVISED PAGE 13 LOCAL FREIGHT TARIFF NO. 2

Section 4	POINT-TO-POINT CLASS RATES RATES ARE STATED IN CENTS PER 100 POUNDS FOR APPLICATION OF SCALES, SEE TITLE PAGE TO THIS SECTION

Between
Los Angeles, CA, and its Commercial Group

And	Scale	Classes								
		100	92½	85	77½	70	65	60	55	50
Portland, OR Commercial Group	AQ	2114	1955	1796	1638	1480	1374	1268	1163	1057
	5C	1710	1582	1454	1325	1197	1112	1026	941	855
	1M	1351	1250	1148	1047	946	878	811	743	676
	2M	1162	1075	988	901	813	756	697	639	581
	5M	948	876	806	734	663	616	569	521	474
	10M	791	731	672	613	554	514	474	435	395
	20M	767	710	652	594	537	498	461	422	384
Seattle, WA Commercial Group	AQ	2250	2081	1913	1744	1575	1463	1350	1238	1125
	5C	1820	1683	1547	1410	1274	1183	1092	1001	910
	1M	1439	1331	1222	1115	1007	935	863	791	719
	2M	1237	1145	1052	959	867	804	742	680	619
	5M	1009	933	858	782	706	656	606	555	505
	10M	843	780	717	654	591	548	506	464	422
	20M	817	755	694	633	572	531	490	449	409
Spokane, WA Commercial Group	AQ	2464	2279	2094	1910	1725	1601	1478	1355	1232
	5C	1994	1844	1694	1545	1396	1296	1196	1097	997
	1M	1576	1458	1340	1222	1103	1025	946	867	788
	2M	1355	1253	1152	1050	948	880	813	745	677
	5M	1106	1023	940	857	774	719	664	608	553
	10M	924	855	786	716	647	601	555	508	462
	20M	894	827	760	693	626	581	536	491	447

For explanation of abbreviations and reference marks, see last page of tariff.

Issued: June 6, 1983   Effective: July 11, 1983

Issued by: Peter Sowa, President
            5127 Maywood Avenue
            Maywood, CA 90270

Correction No. 49

Inside of letter size file folder (continued).

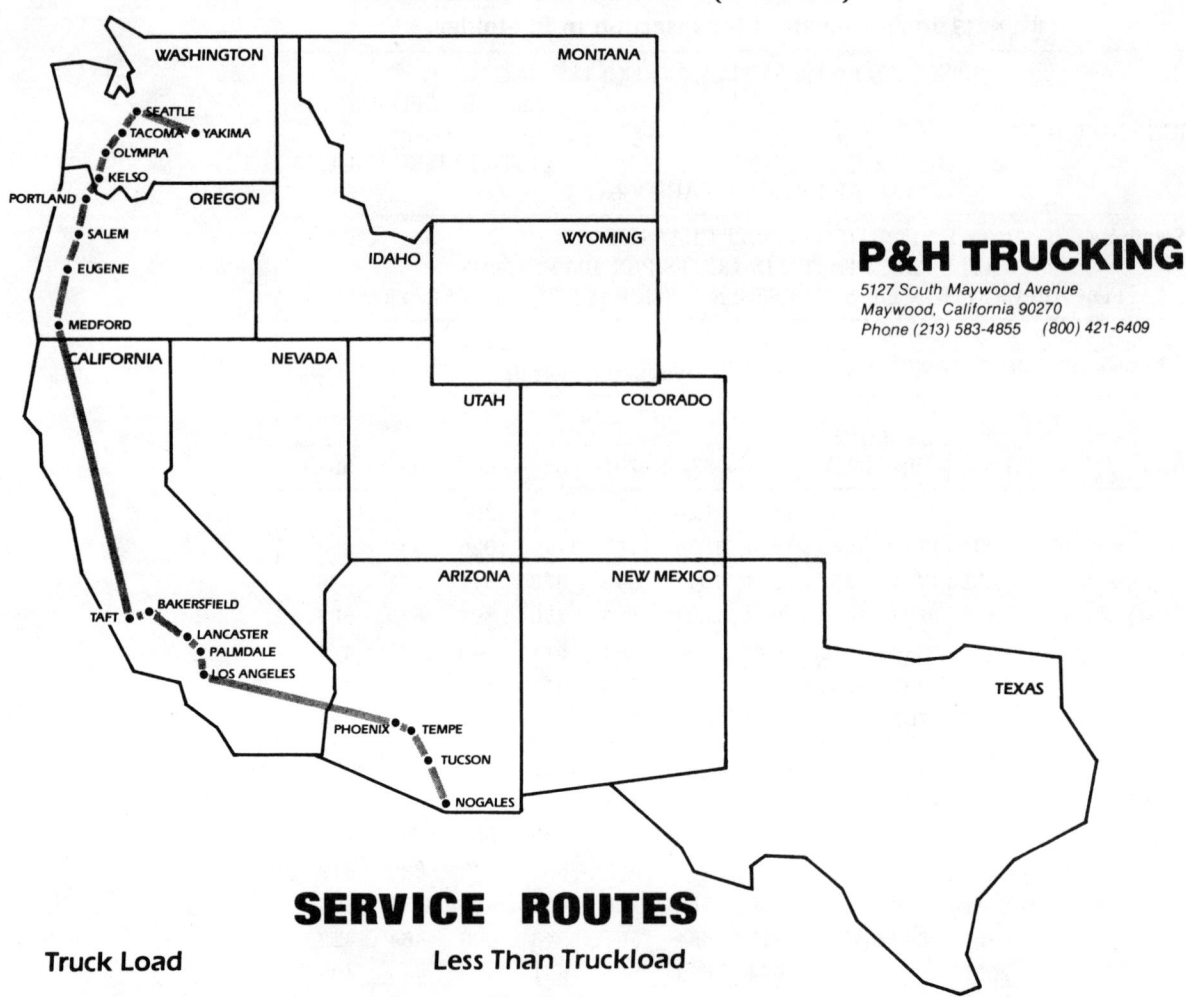

P&H TRUCKING
5127 South Maywood Avenue
Maywood, California 90270
Phone (213) 583-4855 (800) 421-6409

SERVICE ROUTES

Truck Load

Washington
Oregon
California
Idaho
Nevada
Arizona
Montana
Wyoming
Utah
Colorado
New Mexico
Texas

Less Than Truckload

WASHINGTON
Olympia
Auburn
Sumner
Puyallup
Parkland
Kent
Federal Way
Des Moines
Renton
Bellevue
Mercer Island
Riverton
Redland
Kirkland
Selah
Yakima
Union Gap
Seattle
Tacoma

OREGON
Portland
Beaverton
Salem
Corvallis
Eugene
Albany
Kelso

CALIFORNIA
Hanford
Visalia
Tulare
Earlimart
Delano
McFarland
Bakersfield
Lamont
Taft
Ford City
McKittrick
Buttonwillow
Di Giorgio
Arvin
Weed Patch
Pumpkin Center
Old River
Hillcrest Center
Wasco
Shafter
Palmdale
Lancaster
Lost Hills

ARIZONA
Phoenix
Glendale
Tempe
Scottsdale
Mesa
Peoria
Tucson
Nogales

$8\frac{1}{2} \times 11$ inch Corporate capabilities brochure. Excellent use of photography, graphics, and written copy. Technical information is presented in a well-planned and expensive brochure (sample pages shown through page 146).

≋GRC

Geo/Resource Consultants, Inc.

Principals of GRC in a strategy meeting. Left to right: Warren W. Wong, Vice-President and Chief Geotechnical Engineer, Alan D. Tryhorn, Vice-President and Chief Geologist, and Alvin K. Joe, Jr., President.

Left: The Port of San Francisco's Ferry Building — an historic landmark and site of GRC's geotechnical studies for its renovation. Architect: I. M. Pei, Developer: Continental Development Co.

Geo/Resource Consultants, Inc. (GRC) is a diversified earth sciences consulting corporation specializing in geotechnical engineering, engineering geology, geophysics, exploration geology, geohydrology, seismology, and the environmental sciences. The firm is certified 8a by the U.S. Small Business Administration, and is also certified as a Minority Business Enterprise (MBE) by the EPA, DOT, DOE and other agencies.

Founded in early 1977 by Alvin K. Joe, Jr., President, and Alan D. Tryhorn, Vice President, as engineering geology and environmental geology consultants, the company has since grown to add other principals and associates specializing in the fields of geotechnical engineering, seismology and geophysics, hydrogeology, and mining geology. Principals and associates are California licensed professionals in civil engineering, geology and engineering geology, and geophysics.

The firm's corporate headquarters is located in San Francisco near the northeast waterfront area, with branch offices in Redding, Oakland, and Los Angeles, California, Reno, Nevada, Tucson, Arizona, and Denver, Colorado. Since our professional staff have varying technical specialties, GRC can pool the technical resources from any office to provide the client with a full professional service organization.

GRC maintains its soils testing laboratory at its San Francisco office. The firm has its own geophysical equipment and downhole shear wave hammer, and maintains a pool of field equipped vehicles for exploration and field testing purposes. In addition, the firm is equipped with its own computer for word processing and slope design, and has recently developed its own Earthquake Data Bank. GRC also utilizes a portable video camera and video cassette recorder (VCR) for geologic/geotechnical field reconnaissance and documentation and for inhouse corporate training programs.

GRC is a member of the Consulting Engineers Association of California, Association of Soil and Foundation Engineers, Society of American Military Engineers, Soil and Foundation Engineers Association, Asian American Architects and Engineers, and the Association of Minority Consultants. Our professionals regularly publish and present technical papers and are actively involved in the ASCE, AEG, Society of Mining Engineers, Seismological Society of America, GSA, American Geophysical Union, Geothermal Resources Council and Earthquake Engineering Research Institute.

The firm's primary expertise lies in the diversified geologic and geotechnical engineering backgrounds of its key professionals. GRC's professional staff has been involved in many geotechnical studies concerning regional geologic and seismic hazards mapping, sedimentation and erosion studies in both inland and coastal areas, stream scour studies for pipeline and bridge crossings, siting studies for highrise, commercial and industrial buildings, landslide classification mapping, tunnelling for rapid transit and sewer transport, and historic rehabilitation studies of landmark structures. In addition, GRC's staff has been involved in numerous coastal EIRs, dam and reservoir engineering studies, and regional geoplanning studies for the purpose of analyzing mining impacts in forested areas, transmission line and pipeline right-of-way studies, acid mine drainage abatement studies, seismic safety elements, geothermal assessments, and economic geologic studies of rock and gravel quarries.

(GRC) Organization Chart

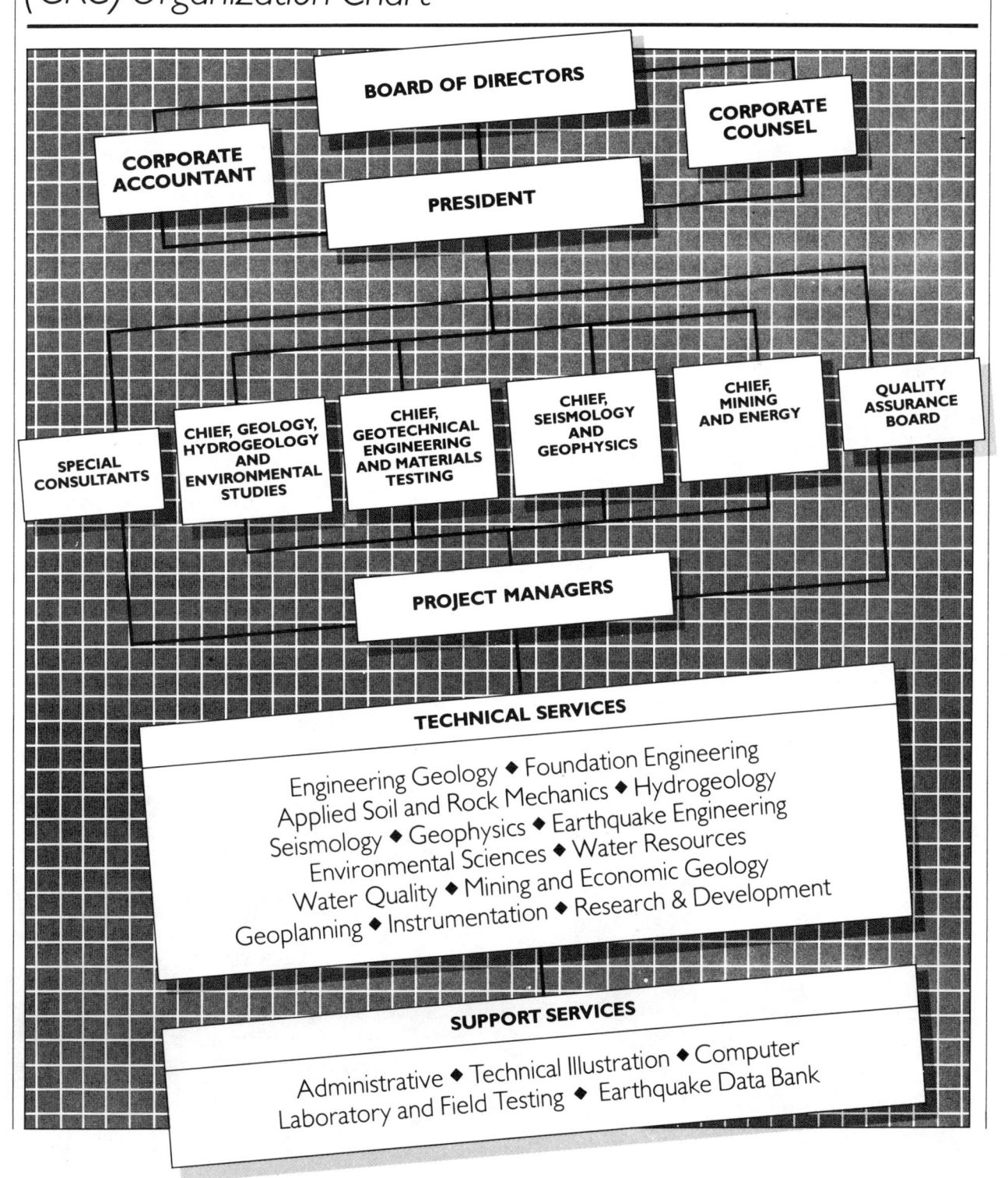

```
                    BOARD OF DIRECTORS
                              |
  CORPORATE  ─────────────────┼───────────────── CORPORATE
  ACCOUNTANT                  |                  COUNSEL
                         PRESIDENT
                              |
   ┌──────────┬───────────────┼───────────────┬──────────┐
SPECIAL    CHIEF,         CHIEF,           CHIEF,      CHIEF,        QUALITY
CONSULTANTS GEOLOGY,      GEOTECHNICAL     SEISMOLOGY  MINING        ASSURANCE
           HYDROGEOLOGY   ENGINEERING      AND         AND ENERGY    BOARD
           AND            AND MATERIALS    GEOPHYSICS
           ENVIRONMENTAL  TESTING
           STUDIES
                              |
                       PROJECT MANAGERS
```

TECHNICAL SERVICES

Engineering Geology ◆ Foundation Engineering
Applied Soil and Rock Mechanics ◆ Hydrogeology
Seismology ◆ Geophysics ◆ Earthquake Engineering
Environmental Sciences ◆ Water Resources
Water Quality ◆ Mining and Economic Geology
Geoplanning ◆ Instrumentation ◆ Research & Development

SUPPORT SERVICES

Administrative ◆ Technical Illustration ◆ Computer
Laboratory and Field Testing ◆ Earthquake Data Bank

GRC

Engineering Geology and Related Investigations

CAPABILITIES

- Geo-Planning
- Geologic hazards evaluation
- Seismic risk analyses
- Landslide and slope stability considerations for forested and mined lands, and urban areas
- Land planning and development studies
- Fault studies for critical facilities, i.e., dams, pipelines, power plants, hospitals and schools
- Transportation facilities (subways, sewer transport), structures, storage facilities, and water-related investigations
- Solid and hazardous waste and disposal site evaluations (toxic, nuclear, non-ferrous)
- Surface fault rupture studies
- Location and evaluation of borrow and rock quarry sites
- Surface mine reclamation studies (aggregate, massive sulfides, coal, etc.)
- Professional review services
- Geologic resource inventory studies
- Expert witness/litigation studies
- Hydroelectric facilities (pumped storage and small hydro)

TECHNICAL SERVICES

RESEARCH AND REVIEW
- Locate and interpret existing published and unpublished geologic data developed by federal, state, county and city agencies, universities and private firms.
- Retrieve available data in our files from previous investigations.

AERIAL PHOTOGRAPHIC INTERPRETATION
- Identify and delineate geologic features, such as faults, landslides and boundaries of bedrock formations and soil deposits, by analyzing stereopaired aerial photographs of various types, scales and flight dates.

FIELD GEOLOGY
- Detailed and reconnaissance geologic mapping to field check aerial photograph interpretations, to gather additional geologic data, and to evaluate the impact of geologic conditions on landuse planning
- Exploratory borings to evaluate subsurface conditions, including sampling and logging of rock cores and soils

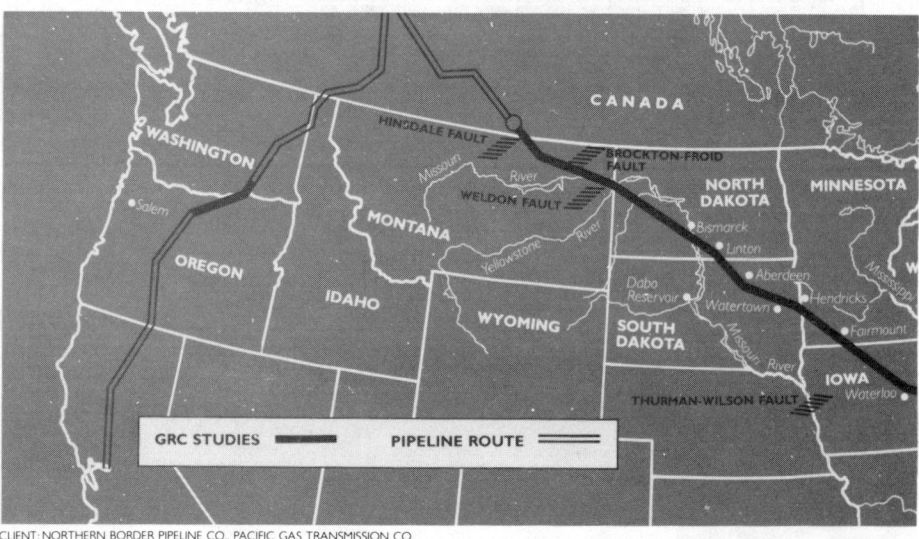

Top: Rock coring for seismic evaluation of existing dam and reservoir; bottom: Geologists examining core samples.

Map illustration of the Western and Eastern route of the Alaskan Natural Gas Transportation System. GRC studies involve: geologic, seismic, geotechnical, environmental and stream scour.

CLIENT: NORTHERN BORDER PIPELINE CO., PACIFIC GAS TRANSMISSION CO.

◇ Geophysical surveys and trenching to locate and delineate faults and other geologic features of engineering significance.

REPORT PREPARATION
◇ Analyze and synthesize geologic data gathered during research and field activities
◇ Prepare geologic maps, cross-sections and three-dimensional illustrations
◇ Prepare geologic hazard and seismic risk maps
◇ Present results, recommendations and conclusions in a final report
◇ Emphasis on clearly presenting geologic data to personnel not practicing in geoscience

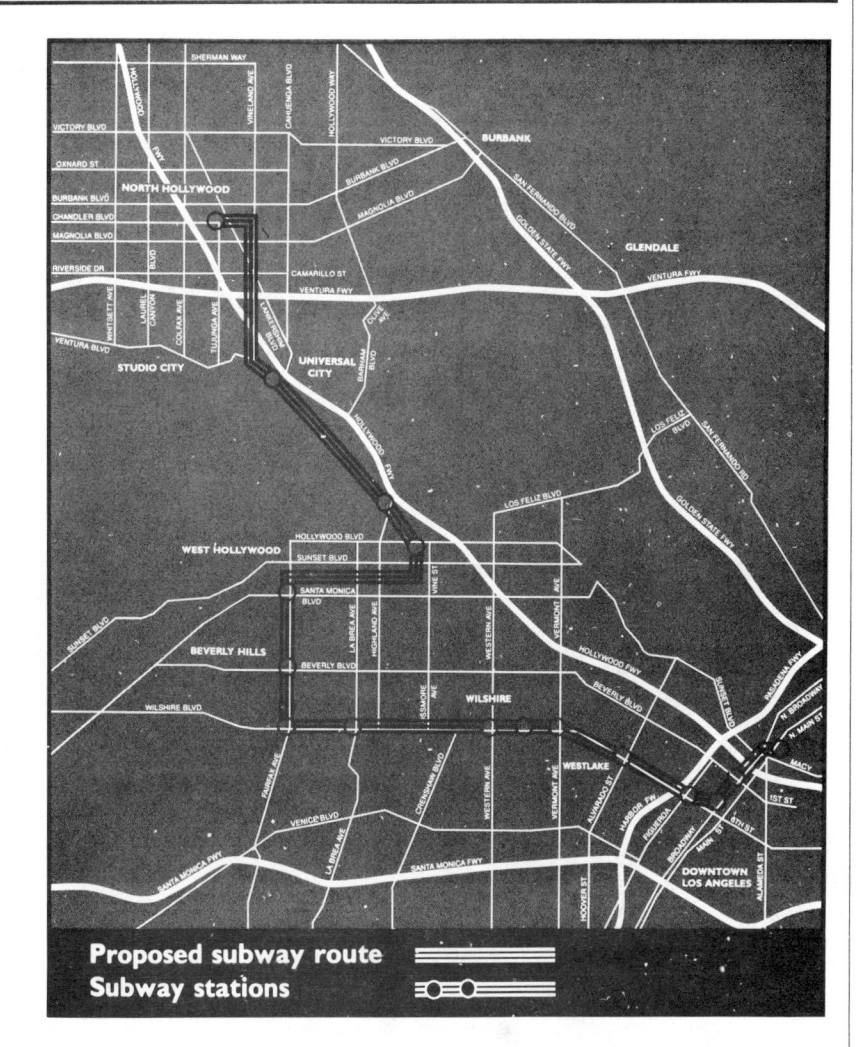

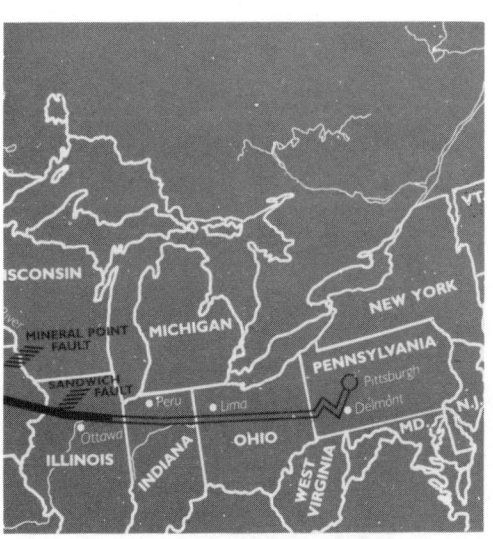

Proposed route of the Los Angeles Metro Rail Subway. GRC conducted geotechnical and engineering geologic studies, and geophysical surveys (downhole/crosshole seismic) for the entire subway route.

GRC

Geotechnical Engineering Investigations

CAPABILITIES

- Land planning and development for commercial, light and heavy industrial and residential subdivisions
- Transportation facilities including bridges, roadways, pavements, airports, mass transit facilities and pipelines (gas, oil, water and sewerage)
- Structures including highrise and midrise buildings, industrial plants, retaining structures, research centers, hospitals, small hydropower facilities
- Storage facilities including reservoirs, tanks and silos, dams (both earth and tailings)
- Water-related facilities including marinas, harbors, piers, wharves, tunnels, and offshore facilities
- Embankment and slopes for open pit quarries and special excavations

TECHNICAL SERVICES

FIELD
- Exploratory borings and seismic surveys to evaluate subsurface conditions
- Resistivity surveys to evaluate corrosion potential of soils
- Retrieval of both bulk and undisturbed samples of representative soils
- Slope indicator installation for measurement of ground movement
- Settlement marker installation to measure ground settlement
- Piezometer installation for measurement of soil pore-pressures

LABORATORY TESTING
- Soil Classification characteristics
- Physical strength properties under either static or dynamic loading conditions
- Suitability for anticipated usage
- Strength characteristics under pavements
- Water sensitivity and expansion characteristics
- Other engineering properties
- Water quality analyses

ANALYTICAL ENGINEERING
- Support characteristics, suitable foundation types, and necessary design data
- Seismic risk analysis
- Degree and rate of consolidation under loading
- Stability of cut and fill slopes
- Rock reinforcement systems
- Consultation and review services

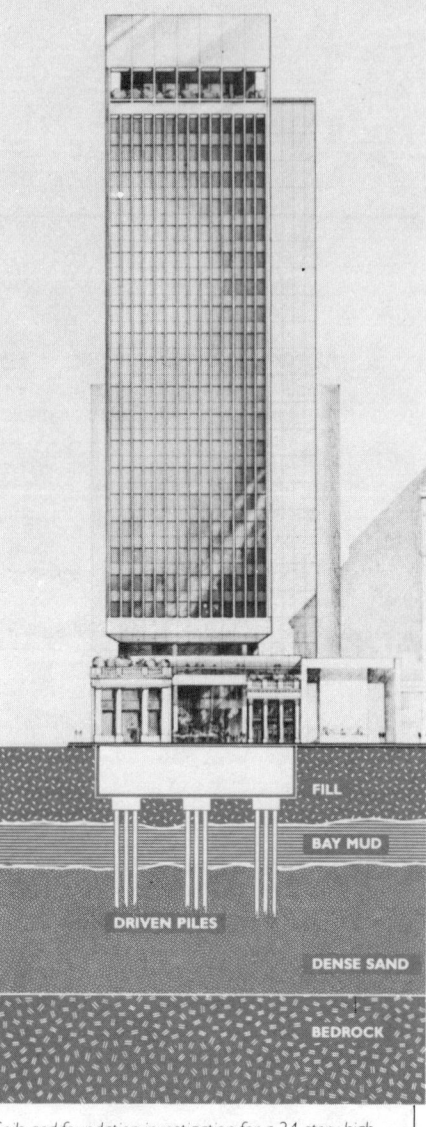

Soils and foundation investigation for a 24-story highrise in downtown San Francisco, including historic preservation of the Sutro Building Facade, was performed; followed by a geophysical downhole seismic survey and seismic response study.

Engineering Geology and Geotechnical Engineering investigation of a landslide in the Berkeley Hills for the city of Berkeley. GRC was involved in landslide repair and earthwork monitoring phases.

All terrain tract-mounted drill rig sampling on dam embankment. Project: Seismic reevaluation of East Bay M.U.D.'s Seneca Reservoir, Oakland, CA.

GRC

Seismic Studies

A stream offset by the San Andreas Fault in central California.

View of San Bernardino Mountains and city of Banning, looking north, where the San Andreas and Banning fault zones are exposed. Project: Geologic resource inventory of the San Bernardino National Forest for the U.S. Forest Service.

CAPABILITIES

- Seismic hazards evaluation
- Land planning and development
- Professional review services
- Analysis of historic and/or instrumental seismic data to be used to obtain engineering criteria for a design earthquake
- Seismic hazards evaluation, including fault rupture hazards, liquefaction, ground failure, ground shaking, and tsunamis
- Fault investigations (regional or site-specific) that will satisfy local and state requirements
- Seismic Safety Elements, preparation of city or county planning and technical documents and maps
- Siting of critical structures
- Risk analyses
- Evaluation of design earthquake; development of criteria for design earthquake
- Investigation of linear features to ascertain relationship, if any, to faulting
- Evaluation of maximum earthquake based upon geologic and seismic factors

TECHNICAL SERVICES

EVALUATION OF SURFACE FAULTING POTENTIAL
- Topographic and geomorphic geologic studies
- Aerial photography and imagery interpretations
- Lineation investigations
- Exploratory borings and piezometer installations
- Seismic surveys
- Magnetometer surveys
- Resistivity surveys
- Trenching and test pits

INVESTIGATION OF SEISMICITY
- Listing of worldwide earthquake epicentral data, with emphasis on U.S. earthquakes (GRC Earthquake Data Bank)
- Geographic search of earthquake epicenters
- Listing of major earthquakes in historic time
- Evaluation of historic intensity data
- Evaluation of fault activity or capability
- Monitor microseismic activity
- Determine frequency, magnitude, and probable displacement along a particular fault and suggest setbacks for structures
- Develop probable rock motions for the anticipated earthquake, including the maximum amplitude, the predominant period, and the duration

SAN ANDREAS FAULT

BANNING FAULT ZONE

EVALUATION OF GROUND FAILURE POTENTIAL
- Evaluate liquefaction potential and recommend engineering measures to reduce such potential
- Estimate differential settlements due to densification of granular soils caused by ground shaking, and recommend engineering measures to minimize such settlements
- Analyze the seismic safety of an open slope (i.e., slope failure, landslide, lateral spreading, etc.), and recommend engineering measures to increase the safety factor of the slope
- Evaluate the possibility of lurching and delineate susceptible areas

EVALUATION OF GROUND SHAKING POTENTIAL
- Evaluate subsurface conditions as required by either interpreting available data or performing field exploration and lab tests
- Based on the developed hypothetical rock motions and the local subsurface conditions, evaluate ground surface response and subsurface soil stress-strain conditions by computer analyses
- Based on the evaluated ground surface response, study the distribution of the maximum accelerations and the fundamental periods and develop recommended building distribution criteria
- Slope indicator installation for measurement of ground movement
- Settlement marker installation to measure ground settlement
- Piezometer installation for measurement of soil pore-pressures

ANALYSES OF SEISMICALLY INDUCED WAVES (TSUNAMIS)
- Discuss the possibility of seismically induced waves along a coastline
- Evaluate the extent of such waves and define probable affected areas

SEISMIC SAFETY ELEMENT FOR LAND PLANNING
- Discuss code requirements and other public regulations with regard to seismic safety elements, and evaluate seismic protection provided through the building codes, grading ordinances, general plans, and other regulations. Develop acceptable risk levels for land and building uses.
- Determine appropriate range of land uses in each risk zone, and prepare seismic risk maps and supportive text to satisfy seismic safety element requirements

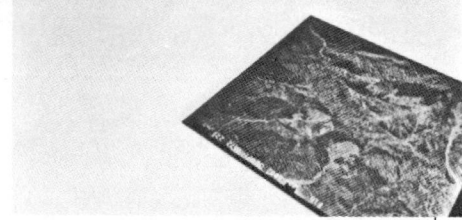

Geologist using stereo-paired photographs to interpret local and regional geology.

Hydrogeology

CAPABILITIES

ENVIRONMENTAL ENGINEERING
◇ Evaluation of ground water quantity, quality, flow directions and rates, geologic controls, recharge and discharge areas
◇ Evaluation of surface and ground water impacts on community leach field systems
◇ Site selection for dewatering cutoff trenches
◇ Assessments of septic, toxic, and radionuclide migration in ground water
◇ Acid mine drainage abatement programs

WATER RESOURCES ENGINEERING
◇ Development of industrial and municipal water supplies
◇ "Cut off" walls
◇ Basin management
◇ Siting and design criteria for artificial recharge
◇ Ground water system modeling

GEOLOGICAL AND GEOTECHNICAL ENGINEERING
◇ Dewatering Systems
◇ Seepage studies
◇ Fault location studies using ground water barriers
◇ Liquefaction and subsidence studies
◇ River scour analyses

TECHNICAL SERVICES

FIELD SERVICES
◇ Surface and ground water sampling
◇ Geological and geophysical surveys for ground water supply
◇ Test borings to determine aquifer properties
◇ Pump testing for aquifer analyses
◇ Observation and monitoring well networks
◇ Electrical resistivity logging
◇ Fluorometer testing of ground water for trace studies
◇ Direct ground water temperature readings
◇ Spinner tool testing for direct measurement of ground water flow directions and velocities
◇ Permeability Packer testing

LABORATORY SERVICES
◇ Coefficients of permeability
◇ Sieve and hydrometer analyses
◇ Water quality testing

ANALYTICAL SERVICES
◇ Trilinear plots of water quality to determine regional ground and surface quality trends
◇ Evaluations of aquifer properties
◇ Ground water simulation models
◇ Ground water recharge potential mapping
◇ Evaluation of ground water flow directions and velocities
◇ Ground water basin analyses
◇ Bedrock fracture system analyses
◇ Ground water flow and mass balance models
◇ HEC 1, 2 and 6 hydraulic engineering analyses for river scour

PLANNING AND DESIGN SERVICES
◇ Evaluation of safe yield
◇ Well and well field design
◇ Site selection assistance for waste disposal facilities
◇ Artificial recharge system feasibility and design
◇ Cutoff trenches and cutoff walls
◇ Horizontal well design for gravity flow water supply

ENVIRONMENTAL SERVICES
◇ Assessment of trends in ground water quality
◇ Flood control studies
◇ Acid mine waste abatement programs
◇ Ground water extraction related to subsidence
◇ Ground water monitoring
◇ Toxic and radioactive waste disposal

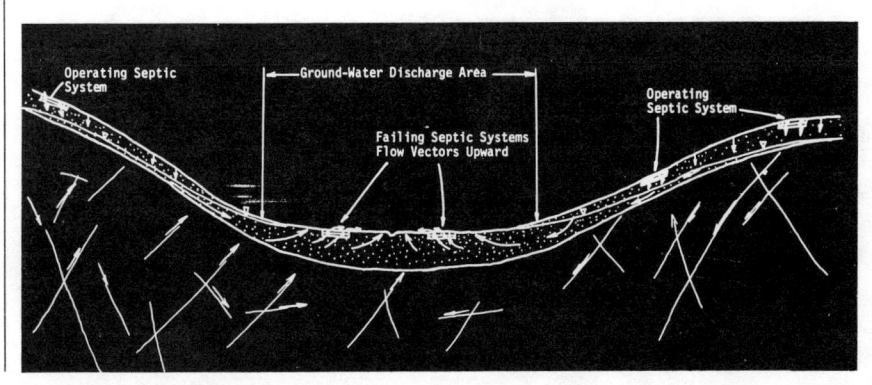

Schematic diagram for on-site waste disposal in Amador County, California.

Mining Geology

CAPABILITIES

- Provide assistance to Mine operators regarding environmental permitting and reclamation planning
- Interpret recent OSM and SMARA regulations from State and Federal Agencies regarding mine reclamation
- Evaluate economic value of mineral resources by exploratory methods, i.e., drilling, testing, geophysics
- Develop field mapping, sampling and exploration programs
- Provide remote sensing interpretation of targeted areas
- Provide consultation regarding techniques to control acid mine drainage
- Analyze rock stability within underground and surface mines, i.e., spiling effectiveness and functional classification of gouge materials
- Analyze geochemistry of mineral deposit
- Evaluation and effectiveness of tunneling methods and tunnel boring machines
- Investigate potential borrow sites for construction aggregates

TECHNICAL SERVICES

- Research and development projects
- Mine site selection, borrow pit suitability
- Feasibility studies for mining companies
- Underground shafts, tunnels, adits
- Mineral resource surveys

ASSOCIATED SERVICES

- Marine geologic studies
- Soil Surveys
- Hydraulic Engineering Studies
- Geothermal Resource Evaluation
- Underwater photography and construction monitoring surveys
- Marine and aquatic biology surveys
- Materials engineering and testing
- Instrumentation programs
- Revegetation plans
- Air/water quality studies
- Master planning and site selection analysis

Geophysics

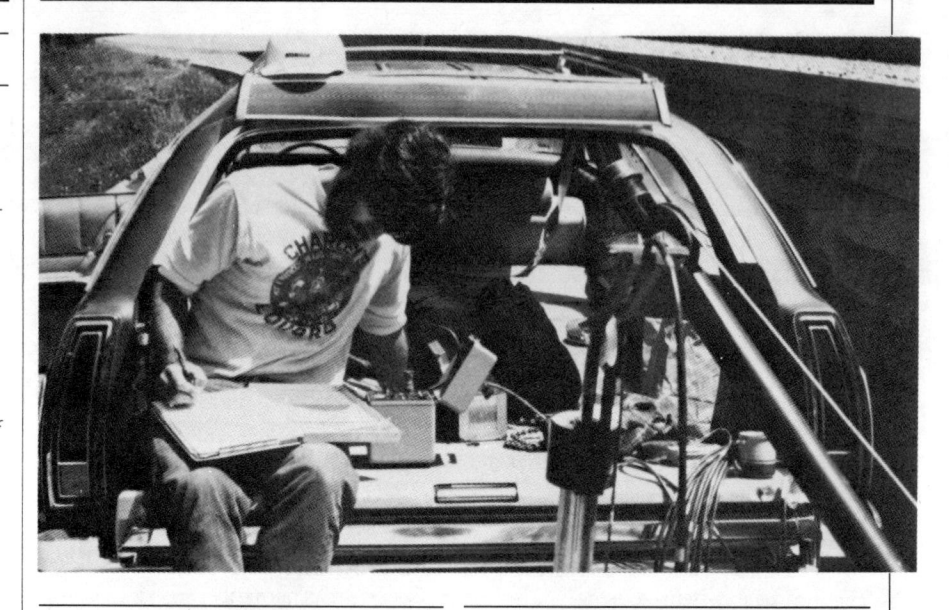

CAPABILITIES

- Highrise structures, foundation investigations
- Nuclear power plants, safety analysis report preparation
- Pipelines, seismotectonic hazards and corrosion protection
- Geothermal studies, subsurface exploration
- Dams, foundation design and geologic hazards determination
- Lifeline facilities, tectonic and geologic hazards
- Minerals exploration, resource evaluation and inventory

TECHNICAL SERVICES

GEOPHYSICAL FIELD SURVEYS AND INTERPRETATION

- Refraction and reflection, mechanical or explosive sources
- Crosshole and downhole shear wave surveys, mechanical or explosive sources
- Gravity surveys
- Magnetic surveys
- Resistivity and self-potential surveys
- Seismic instrumentation, earthquake monitoring networks/strong motion
- Earthquake Data Bank, catalogs and seismicity maps
- Seismic risk analysis, maximum earthquake estimates, time histories, response spectra, probabilities, and recurrence intervals

Above: Geophysicist recording data gathered in downhole seismic survey.

8½ × 11 inch Product catalogue. Original graphic concept that enhances the marketing of the complete line of products. Note simple graphic depiction of uses as it carries a theme of simplicity throughout the entire catalogue (cover below and sample pages shown through page 158).

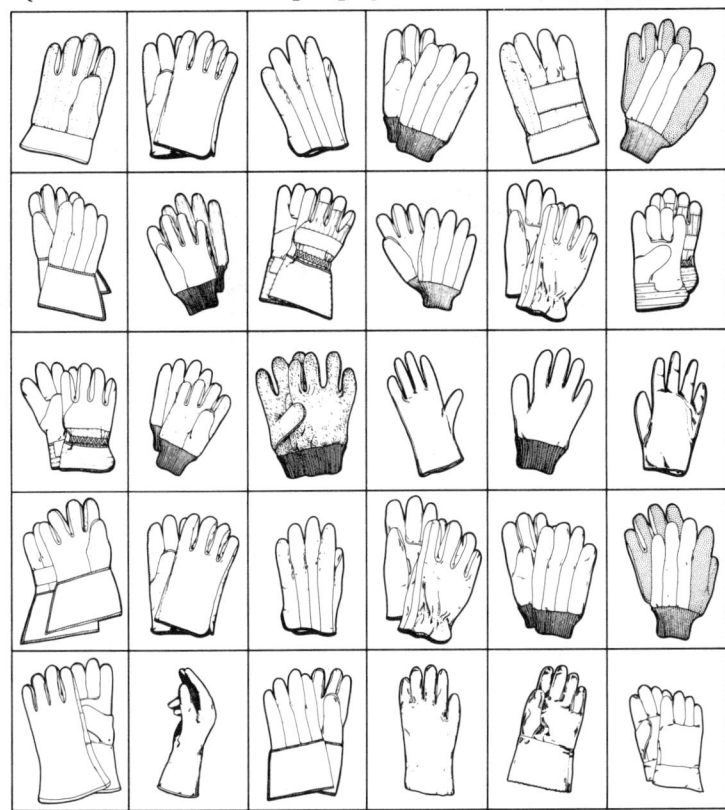

PANAMA ▲ GLOVES
Panama Glove Company, Inc., 1911 Fourth Avenue, Los Angeles, California 90018 (213) 737-8420

A GLOVE FOR EVERY INDUSTRY

Industrial Symbols

At Panama Glove Company, we specialize in the protection of your hands, no matter what your needs. We have a wide variety of gloves, suitable for use in a wide variety of industries.

The symbols below represent the various industries in which our gloves are used. These symbols appear throughout our catalog, to help you identify the glove that meets the job requirements of your industry.

Foundry
Welding
Metalworking
Glass
Electronics
Automobiles, etc.

Forestry
Lumber
Paper, etc.

Film Processing
Film Editing
Record Production
Tape Production, etc.

Food Processing
Poultry Handling
Fish Handling
Meat Handling, etc.

Glossary

The following abbreviations, which appear throughout the catalog, are used for ease in ordering, and represent the variety of styles, materials and sizes that are available. Where standard sizes are not indicated, or where special order sizes are required, please check with us.

Cuff Styles:	Materials:	Rubber Gloves:
KW – Knit Wrist	**J** – Jersey	**U** – Unsupported
BT – Band Top	**L** – Lisle	**S** – Supported
SC – Safety Cuff	**C** – Canvas	
G – Gauntlet	**T** – Terry Cloth	**Ln** – Lined
SO – Slip-On	**SN** – Stretch Nylon	**UnL** – Unlined

Cuff Styles

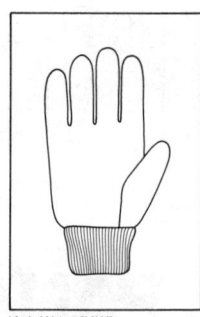

Knit Wrist (KW)

Agriculture
Fruit Picking
Food Packing
Canning, etc.

Manufacturing
Shipbuilding
Aircraft
Railroad
Machining and Tooling
Repairs and Parts, etc.

Construction
Painting
Repairing
Wood Handling
Glass Handling

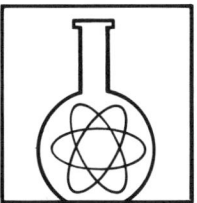

Chemical
Pharmaceutical
Medical/Hospital
Cosmetic
Nuclear
Dust-free, etc.

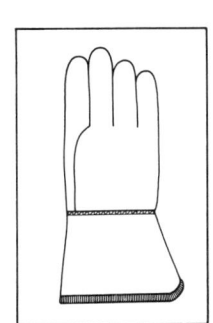

Gauntlet (G)

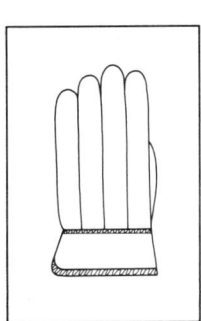

Safety Cuff (SC)

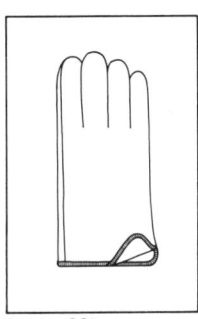

Slip-On (SO)

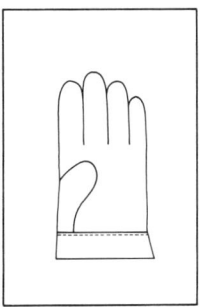

Band Top (BT)

BASIC GLOVES

How to select a Basic Glove

Among the basic gloves, you have a choice of cotton, nylon, jersey and terry. Each is available in a variety of weights to satisfy the degree of dexterity required. The basic gloves also have use as liners under heavier gloves.

Cotton Inspection Glove
100% cotton knit
Reversible
White
Sizes:
Men's M/L/XL/Jumbo
Ladies S/M/L
Style: **100** Lightweight
105 Interlock
150 Mediumweight
170 Heavyweight
(MIL-G-3866)

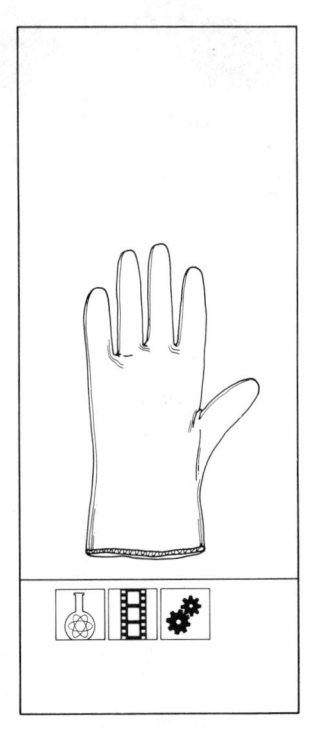

CANVAS GLOVES

White Canvas Glove
Clute pattern
Gauntlet style
Sizes:
Men's M/L/XL
Cadet
Style:
7610 G 10 oz.
7612 G 12 oz.

White Canvas Glove
Clute pattern
Knit Wrist
Sizes:
Men's XL and Jumbo
Style:
7608 KW 8 oz.
7610 KW 10 oz.
7612 KW 12 oz.
(MIL-G-1008G)

White Canvas Glove
Reversible
Knit Wrist
Sizes:
Men's
Cadet
Style:
7608R KW 8 oz.
7610R KW 10 oz.
7612R KW 12 oz.

FLANNEL GLOVES

White Flannel Glove
Double quilted palm
and thumb
Also available in
BT, SC, G
Style:
516 KW 16 oz.

Hot Mill Glove
White flannel
Quilted palm, thumb
and index finger
Gauntlet
Style:
524 G 24 oz.
530 G 30 oz.

Brown Flannel Glove
Double quilted palm
and thumb
Canvas back
Safety Cuff
Style:
618 SC 18 oz.

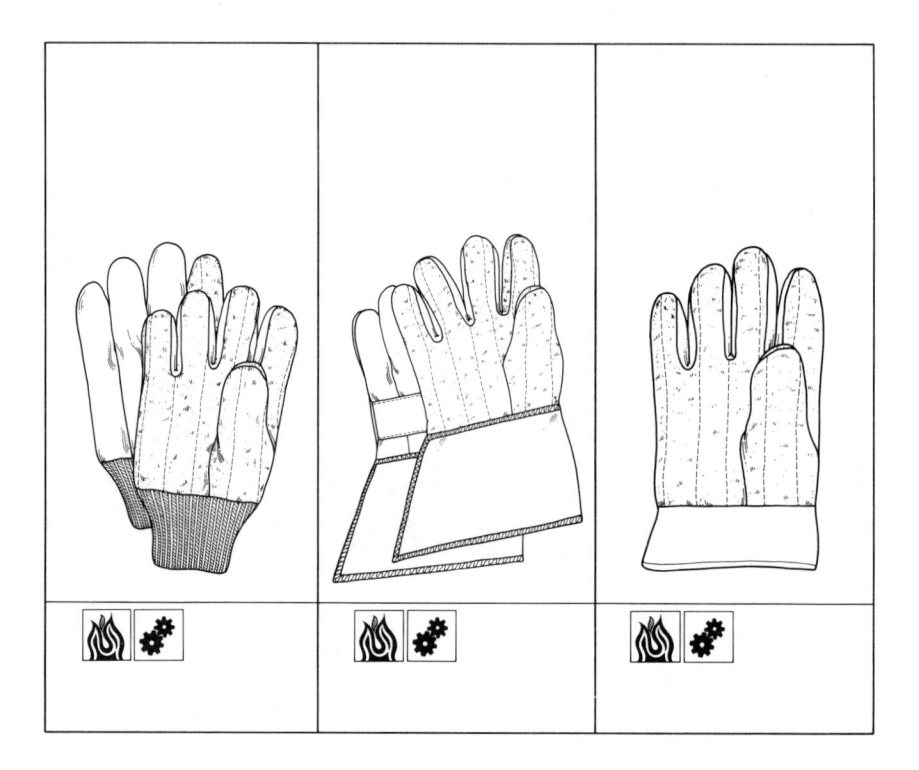

LEATHER GLOVES

Leather Palm Features

Wing thumb eliminates seam in palm area allowing longer, more comfortable and more flexible wear. Welt stitching provides additional reinforcement for longer wear.

How to Select a Leather Glove

Leather gloves perform best for general purpose and heavy materials use. They offer the highest degree of protection from heat and cold. Select a leather glove based on the degree of protection versus dexterity required.

For example, gloves with proportionately more leather area offer a greater degree of protection. For a greater degree of dexterity, choose a leather glove with canvas back or finger areas.

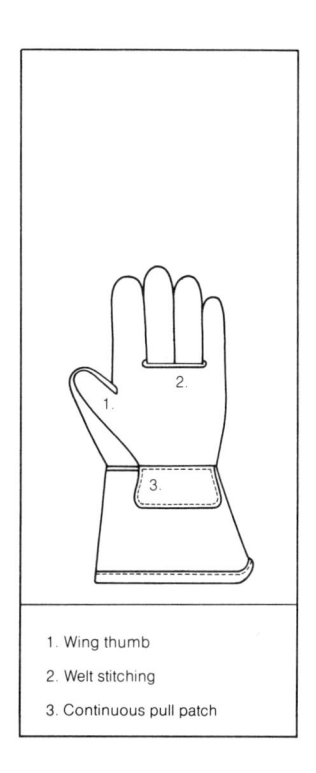

1. Wing thumb
2. Welt stitching
3. Continuous pull patch

LEATHER GLOVES

Leather Palm Glove
Pearl gray
Split leather palm
Clute cut pattern
Knit Wrist
Style: **800 KW**

Leather Palm Glove
Pearl gray
Split leather palm,
knuckle strap,
index finger and
fingertips
Continuous pull
Gauntlet
Style **800 G**

Leather Palm Glove
Pearl gray
Split leather palm,
knuckle strap,
index finger and
fingertips
Continuous pull
Safety Cuff
Style: **800 SC**

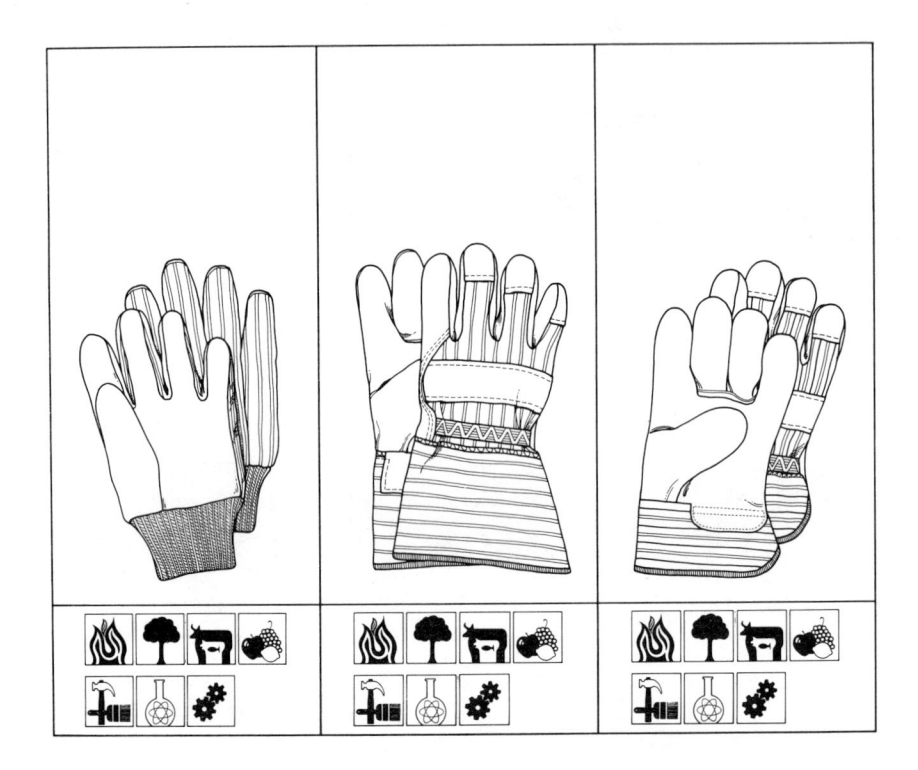

LEATHER GLOVES

Leather Driving Glove
Top grain leather
Driver style
Sizes: S/M/L
Style: **1700**

Leather Driving Gloves

These all-leather driving gloves are made from top grain leather. They are smooth, soft and pliable, for dexterity, yet durable and longwearing. This makes them suitable for other hand protection purposes in addition to driving, such as handling heavy equipment, dock and railroad work, loading and unloading. As you can see, they have applications in almost every industry.

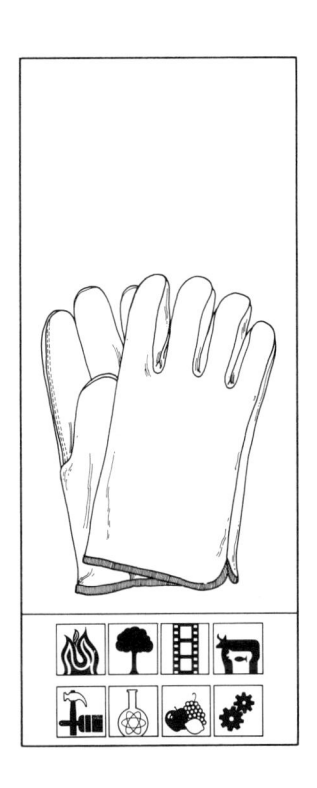

COATED GLOVES

Latex Surgical Glove
For inspection and
clean room use
Smooth finish
Form fit for
maximum dexterity
Style: **EE**

Neoprene Glove
Safeguards against
acids, oils and caustics
Positive grip
Flock-lined
Supported (S) or
Unsupported (U)
Style: **GG-S**
GG-U

**How to Select
a Coated Glove**

Determine the degree of protection and dexterity required for the job. The lighter, unsupported glove offers maximum dexterity while a heavier glove offers greater protection from extreme temperatures and caustic chemicals.

There are three main types of coating available: vinyl, natural rubber and neoprene. Your selection should be based on the material that performs best for the required job (see glove descriptions, right).

A variety of lengths and weights are available, in addition to those pictured. Please specify requirements when ordering.

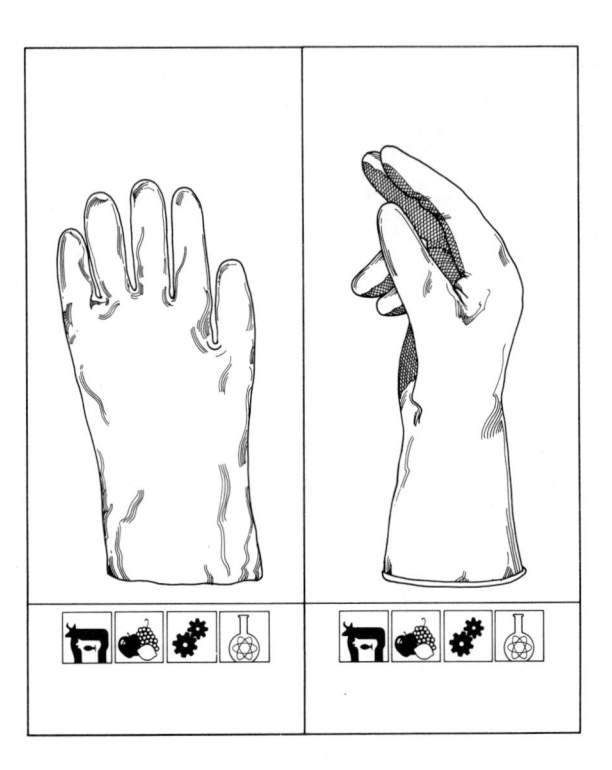

PROTECTIVE SLEEVING

Glove with Sleeving
Canvas glove with
clute pattern back
Protective canvas sleeving
With elastic forearm
Style: **1300**
(MIL-G-2874)

Protective Sleeving
Protective canvas sleeving
Elastic wrist and forearm
Style: **1310**

Glove with Sleeving
Leather palm glove
with canvas clute
cut back
Protective canvas
sleeving
Elastic forearm
Style: **1320**

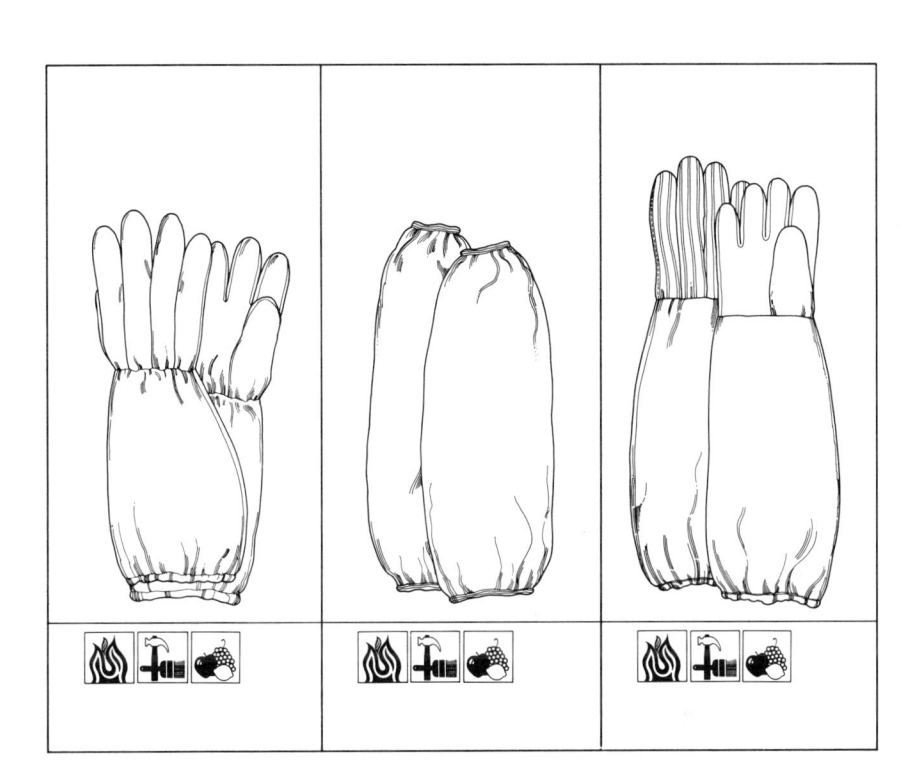

APRONS

Truckers Apron
4 pockets
Single leg strap
Olive drab or
Blue denim
Also available
flameproof,
waterproof,
weatherproof
Style:
PTR 36 (36" length)
PTR 42 (42" length)

Carpenters Waist Nail Apron
5 pockets
1 hammer loop
Duck, natural
Also available
with riveted
pockets (PC 12R)
Style: **PC 12**

Shop Apron
3 pockets
36" length
Blue denim, or
Duck, natural
Style: **PBS 40**

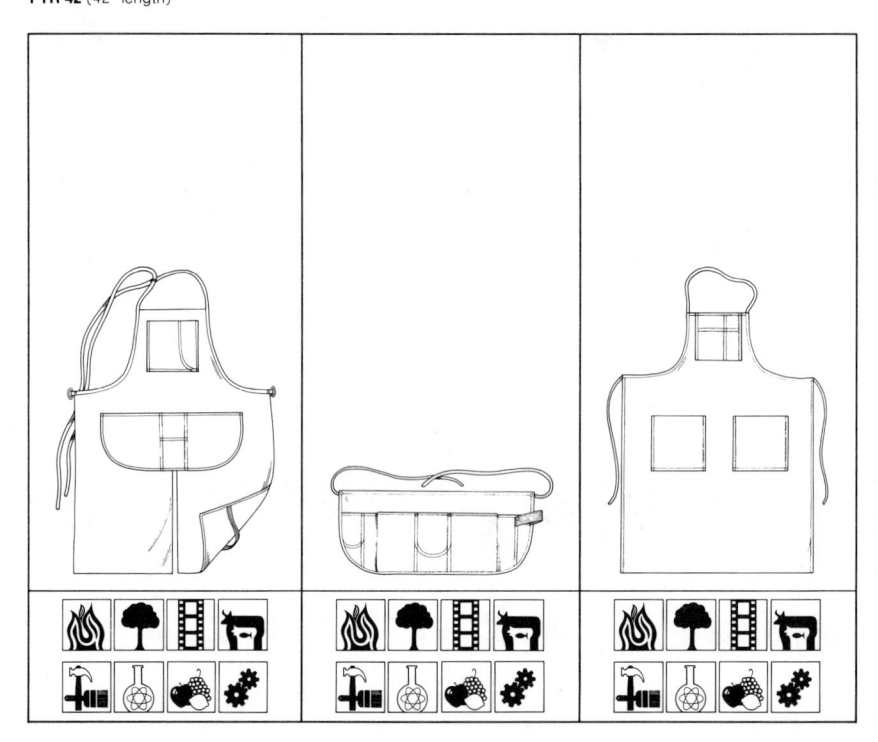

8½ × 11 inch Presentation folder of corporate capabilities. Uses individual insert sheets to give specific information on various aspects of company. Good use of black and white, and excellent copywriting. Note logo and specific nature of marketing done by this firm.

PR/ADE COMMUNICATIONS, INC.

ONE SUTTER ST. SUITE 505 SAN FRANCISCO CALIFORNIA 94104 (415) 982-5448

OUR CLIENTS

MARKETING PLANNING SERVICES

MEDIA RELATIONS & ADVERTISING

ORGANIZATIONS, PRESENTATIONS & ARTICLES

BROCHURES

AUDIO VISUAL PRESENTATIONS

DIRECT MAIL PROMOTION

OUR PEOPLE
Each of our associates has an engineering background and in-depth experience in journalism, technical writing, media relations, advertising, and related fields.

35 years of experience in marketing strategy planning, management, and public relations, leading chemical and engineering firms, served as vice president of marketing and...

PR/ADE COMMUNICATIONS, INC.

ONE SUTTER ST. SUITE 505 SAN FRANCISCO CALIFORNIA 94104 (415) 982-5448

COUNSELING SERVICES
PR/ADE provides consultation on the total spectrum of communications services for architects, designers, and engineers, as well as firms in construction, mining, transportation, and industrial production.

Marketing Communications
The starting point of our marketing communications programs is an examination of present markets and future marketing plans, since this is the foundation upon which all else is built.

Closely related is the matter of how your firm is perceived in the market ... what prospective clients believe about your firm ... whether it is innovative ... cost conscious ... easy to work with traditional ... thus, what image clients and prospective clients have of your firm. Once your present image has been determined, we examine how your firm may need to be altered and what image of your marketing needs to be built in order to achieve your marketing objectives.

community relations will best serve your firm. From dealing with local and state agencies ... to working presentations to local groups ... to establishing a hand-in-hand with clients in establishing the credibility of specific projects with the local media ... to close working relationship with the local causes, PR/ADE can making contributions to local causes, and how to gain both advise you on a course of action and how to help implement these programs and monitor the effect maximum exposure for your efforts. We can help you that they are having on your business.

Client Presentations
Making effective client presentations is one of the most important factors in obtaining new contracts. It is of utmost importance that your presentation team start with the correct information effectively to be able to communicate your proposal options to prospective clients. There are many methodology available to your firm in presentation development and technique. PR/ADE can help you develop formats for effective presentations, and provide answers to such questions as:

How much time and money should be invested...

PR/ADE

provides specialized communications and consulting services to architects, designers, and engineers, as well as firms in related fields for the marketing of their services and products, and the development of their businesses.

We were born in engineering.
Our experience is in technical communications and business development. Each of our associates has an engineering background and in-depth experience in journalism, technical writing, media relations, and related fields of communications. We speak your language: we understand your problems, and we can provide the specialized communications and consulting services that you need for the success of your business.

We can help you communicate effectively with the various publics that are vital to the conduct of your business:

- Prospective clients
- The business and financial community
- Public agencies
- Communities in which you work
- Your own staff

Also, we can provide the written and visual materials required for

- Your business development program
- Client presentations
- Technical presentations
- Communicating with special groups
- Employee communications

PR/ADE will first analyze

- Your markets
- Your competition
- How you are perceived by others
- The image you would like to build
- Your marketing objectives

Then, we can provide the communications and consulting services needed to achieve your objectives.

Our services can be provided in any combination desired, from a specific project to an overall program; they include

- Working with the media to provide exposure for your firm and its activities
- Developing direct mail programs to transmit written materials to potential clients, community leaders, and others
- Working with your clients' public relations staffs to develop recognition for your project input
- Establishing a graphic identity program with a distinctive logo and a unified graphic appearance of all printed materials
- Writing and producing brochures, technical articles, feature articles, press releases, newsletters, etc.
- Preparing presentations for potential clients, professional societies, or business groups
- Producing audio-visual slide shows
- Handling special events such as project ground breakings and dedications
- Organizing community relations programs by working with local leaders, organizations, and the media
- Developing an advertising program to meet your specific needs
- Providing public relations consulting services

To round out our services, we can provide the services of some of the best graphic designers and photographers, as well as consultants in marketing and specialized fields of public relations ... all in one package, with a single point of responsibility.

Over the past five years, we have provided services to a wide range of architectural, engineering, construction, industrial, high-technology, and transportation firms, large and small. We would welcome the opportunity of serving you.

Please call or write:
PR/ADE Communications, Inc.
One Sutter St., Suite 505
San Francisco, Calif. 94104
Phone 415/982-5448

8½ × 11 inch Full color flyer/brochure. Useful for mail-out or inclusion in proposals.

8½ × 11 inch full color flyer/brochure (continued).

C.P.I. performs general machining, specializing in production quantities and short runs. Housed in a large, modern facility in Anaheim, this clean, air-conditioned shop works with all types of metals in a wide range of sizes.

Customers include industrial and aerospace organizations in the Orange County, Los Angeles, and all over the United States.

Highly skilled machinist draw on a comprehensive collection of new machines to produce parts from small to large, simple to complex. Fine craftsmanship is assured through quality control that conforms to MIL-I-45208A standards and to special customer requirements.

Major investments in equipment, including advanced C.N.C. machines, means C.P.I. has the right tools for your job.

Pyong Cha
President

C.P.I. Machining Co., Inc.
1270 La Loma Circle
Anaheim, California 92806
(714) 630-0254

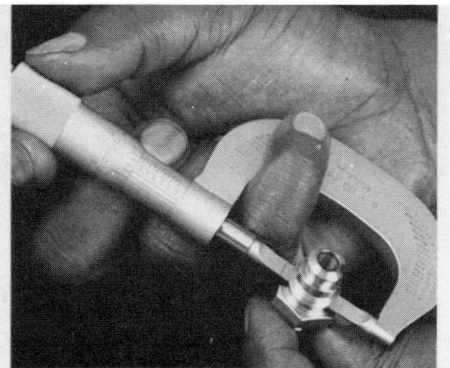

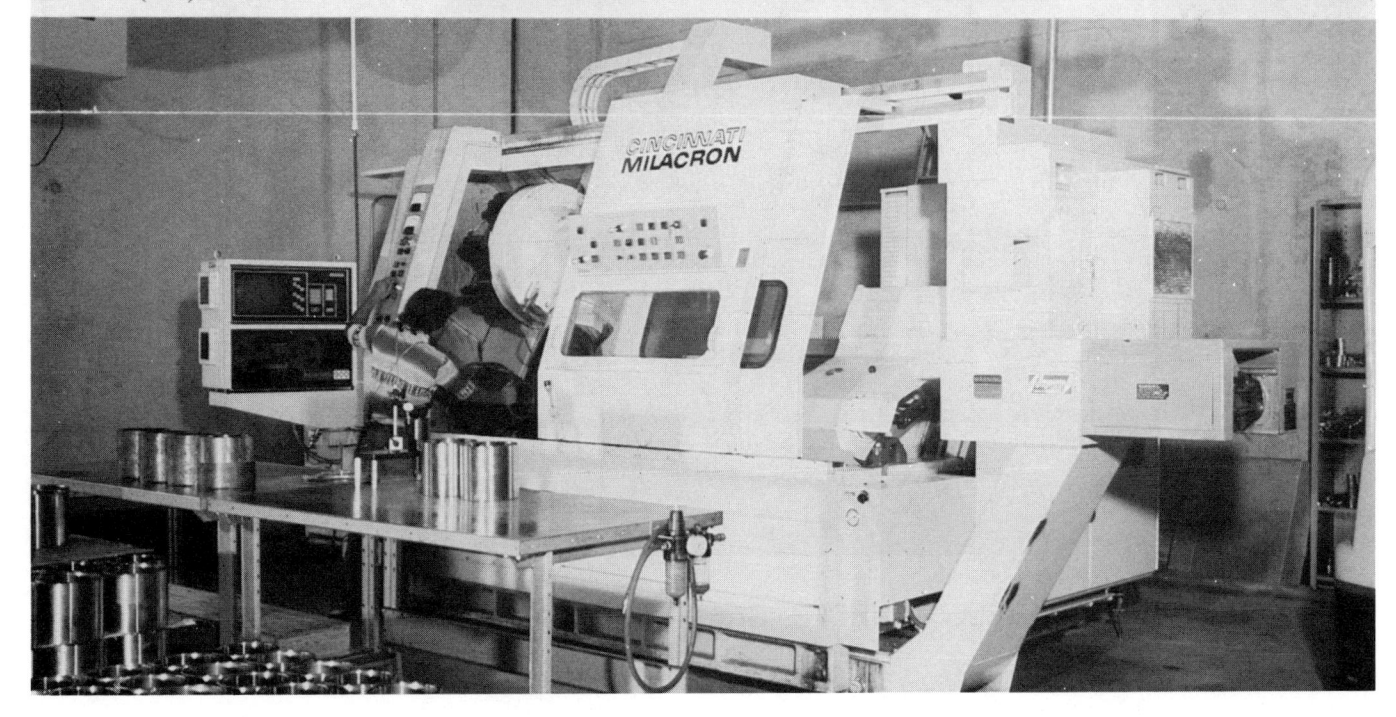

8½ × 11 inch Presentation folder using reproduction of an industry-related blueprint for effective eye-catching exterior. Interior includes insert pages for various corporate segments, as well as flap with slits for business card insertion.

LEE ENGINEERING CORP.
NAVAL ARCHITECTS & MARINE ENGINEERS

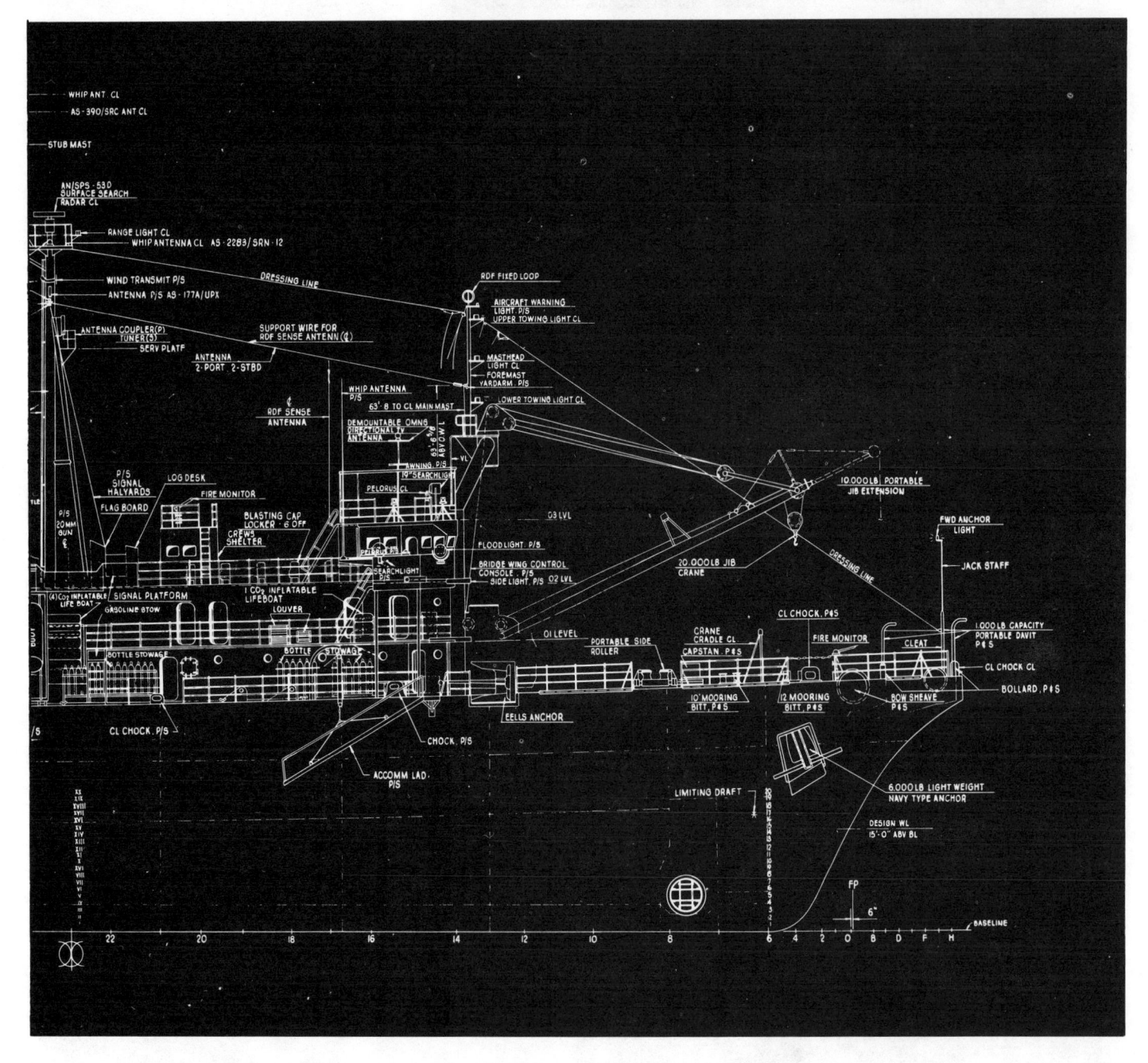

5 THOMAS MELLON CIRCLE • SAN FRANCISCO, CA 94134 • 415 467-0100

8½ × 11 inch Presentation folder (continued).

LEE ENGINEERING CORP
NAVAL ARCHITECTS & MARINE ENGINEERS

Corporate Headquarters:

5 Thomas Mellon Circle
San Francisco, CA 94134
415 467-0100

Lee Engineering Corp., incorporated in 1974, is actively engaged in naval architecture and marine engineering. We have been providing complete quality cost effective design and engineering services in naval and marine technology.

Our extensive range of technical services and capabilities have successfully performed and completed many projects, solutions, and assignments for government, commercial, and private agencies large and small.

Our staff includes many highly qualified licensed professionals in numerous disciplines providing extensive expertise and experience in all aspects of naval and marine technology.

Lee Engineering is technically qualified and accepted by the U.S. Government for naval architectural and marine engineering. This qualification, combined with our technical capabilities and qualified personnel, has led to the presentation of many awards for the recognition of outstanding service.

With a vast range of technical services and capabilities, a large force of highly specialized professionals, and an outstanding record of achievements, Lee Engineering Corp. is well equipped and ready to meet the complex challenges of naval and marine technology.

Overview

Personnel

Clients

Technical Services

Baseline Conceptual Design and Studies
Conceptual Design
Contract Design
Detail Design
Feasibility Study
Planning Study
Preliminary Design

Electrical and Electronics
I.C. Systems
Lighting Systems
Power Generation, Distribution and Storage
Propulsion Control Systems
Radio, Sonar, and Radar Installations
Weapons Control Systems

Hull Design and Naval Architecture
Habitability and General Space Arrangements
Hull Structure
Machinery and Equipment Foundation Design
Ship Trials
Stability Studies
Weapon Stowage
Weight Control Programs

Mechanical
Aircraft Launch, Recovery, and Handling Systems
Automatic Combustion and Feed Water Control Systems
Auxiliary and Deck Machinery Layout
Fire Fighting Systems
Heating, Ventilation and Air Conditioning Systems
Piping Systems
Propulsion Systems and Machinery Layouts
Replenishment-at-Sea Systems
Sewage, Collection, Holding and Transfer Systems
Warping, Towing, Mooring, and Anchor Handling Systems

LEE ENGINEERING CORP
NAVAL ARCHITECTS & MARINE ENGINEERS

FRANK LEE
President

5 Thomas Mellon Circle, San Francisco, CA 94134   415 467-0100
100 Old County Road, Brisbane, CA 94005   415 467-0104
244 N. Wolfe Road, Sunnyvale, CA 94086   408 733-2121
901 Jefferson Davis Hwy #705, Arlington, VA 22202 703 979-4360

7

ADVERTISING CHANNELS

Most people must be motivated to want before they will buy, and advertising is our mass motivator.

The most valuable form of advertising is also the most inexpensive and effective. The most effective sale is a sale as a result of word of mouth referral, the direct contact of a salesperson with the customer, or a sale as the result of a customer responding to a point-of-sale advertisement. But these types of advertising are slow and unpredictable. The kinds of mass advertising to be explored in this chapter are the types that can accelerate the motivation of the customer.

Advertising, as described by the American Marketing Association, is mass, paid communication whose purpose is to "impart information, develop attitudes, and induce favorable action for the advertiser." This favorable action is not necessarily buying. It may just be listening to a sales presentation, asking for an estimate, or coming into a store to examine merchandise firsthand. As we mentioned earlier in the book, advertising is not expected to close the sale. It is important to recognize what advertising can and cannot do.

Advertising has three functions: to inform, to persuade, and to remind. The *inform* function is most important when the product or service is scarce or relatively new to the marketplace. As the marketplace becomes more saturated, the persuasion function gains in importance. Finally, advertising must continually remind those who have been persuaded why they are satisfied with what they bought and where they bought it.

Here are some characteristics of advertising that the small business person should keep in mind:

1. Advertising talks to groups rather than individuals.
2. It is faster.
3. It is directional: it tells people where to buy.
4. It is intrusive: it tells people what to buy.
5. Advertising has drawing power.
6. Advertising must have holding power. This holding power must grow or it will diminish.

Just what can advertising do?

1. It can identify a business with the goods or services it offers.
2. It can build confidence in a business.
3. It can create goodwill.
4. It can increase sales and speed up turnover.
5. It can reduce your expenses by spreading them over a larger volume.

At the same time advertising cannot do some things. It cannot:

1. Make a business prosper if the business offers a poor or inferior product/service.
2. Lead to sales if the prospects that are brought in are ignored or treated poorly.
3. Create traffic overnight or increase sales with a single ad. (Unfortunately, most small businesses use this hit-and-miss type of advertising.)
4. Build confidence as a result of untruthful or misleading advertising.

PLANNING YOUR ADVERTISING

This chapter, in addition to giving the highlights of various advertising media, will also give you the basics to development of your media plan. The media plan is a written document that states where and when you will spend your money on advertising time and/or space. The where and when will relate directly to the marketing objectives you will formulate in Chapter 8. The media plan is an auxiliary plan to the overall company marketing plan.

During the process of planning your media usage, keep in mind:

What you want to advertise.
Where you want to advertise.
How much you can spend.
All the customer benefits you have to offer (gleaned from ad copy).
Dollar expenditures versus results.

Use Form 7.1 to serve as a questionnaire for gathering the information for your media planning.

Your responses to the media planning questionnaire (Form 7.1) will provide a guide for you to use in the decision-making process that will formulate the media plan for a small business. The money spent on the *where* of advertising (up to 80% of an ad budget) never seemed as important as the *what* (the creative concept). In the future it will become increasingly important to exercise "where" judgments and to know that a simple premise supports all media decisions. With limited funds, a

FORM 7.1   Media Planning Questionnaire

1. Why do you want to advertise?
   _____
   _____
   _____

2. What specific goal(s) do you want to achieve?
   _____
   _____
   _____

3. During what period of time?
   _____
   _____
   _____

4. What strategy are you going to use to reach your goal(s)?
   _____
   _____
   _____

5. How much money can be budgeted for media for the time indicated?
   _____
   _____
   _____

6. Where do your major competitors advertise?
   _____
   _____
   _____

7. When do they advertise? (Attach copies of ads if available.)
   _____
   _____
   _____

8. Plot your company sales by month for at least the last year.
   Jan. _____   Jul. _____
   Feb. _____   Aug. _____
   Mar. _____   Sep. _____
   Apr. _____   Oct. _____
   May _____   Nov. _____
   Jun. _____   Dec. _____

9. Plot your advertising expenditures for the period in Question 8.
   Jan. _____   Jul. _____
   Feb. _____   Aug. _____
   Mar. _____   Sep. _____
   Apr. _____   Oct. _____
   May _____   Nov. _____
   Jun. _____   Dec. _____

10. In the past, which media were used?
    _____
    _____
    _____

11. Which media gave the best results?
    _____
    _____
    _____

FORM 7.1 Continued

12. Which vendors can provide a source for cooperative advertising?

13. What makes your business/company unique or outstanding?

14. What are your company's strengths?

15. What do you have to offer that the competition can't or doesn't?

16. List your company products/services and the differences/benefits from your competitor(s).

17. Describe your products/services in a seasonal respect.

18. What targets or segments do you want to reach? Why?

19. How large do you estimate the answer to Question 18 to be?

20. Which of these appeals do you feel your product/service should address? Why?
Thrift (bargain appeal) _____

Service (convenience appeal) _____

Quality (snob appeal) _____

Love-of-family appeal _____

Status appeal _____

Economic appeal _____

Sex appeal _____

Form 7.1 Continued

Natural appeal _____
_____

Youth appeal _____
_____

Nostalgia appeal _____
_____

Health appeal _____
_____

Usage appeal _____
_____

New appeal _____
_____

Humor appeal _____
_____

Statistics appeal _____
_____

typical problem of smaller businesses, you must choose the medium (or media) that reaches your target market most effectively.

Using the information on the media planning questionnaire, fill out the following comparison chart (Form 7.2) to see the impact of the *product*.

Use this form to list all the areas where your product and its benefits differ from your competitors' products/services. The type of media to use may be more product oriented. A product/service may signal certain media. A good example would be an architect or designer whose work is best represented using the proper visuals.

Place plays its important role in media decisions, too. The price of media may dictate the area of coverage. Look at the market segmentation information that you gathered in another part of this workbook.

Price can affect media decisions rather extensively. Low profit margins put a restriction on the amount that can be spent to promote a product. Take time to compile the necessary profit margin information.

What is your *positioning*? It will influence some media choices. A product with a media that can't address it properly will be sure to waste your money and maybe more. . . .

At this time it is wise to begin to put all of your media and marketing plans together. Try to integrate them. The market mix is very influential when you have to make the media decisions. Actually, you won't complete the marketing plan until Chapter 8.

Be prepared to make changes. Media advertising requires continual rethinking and reevaluation. This information will help make the changes seem less traumatic. This may be softened if you have decided to use a media agency or free-lance consultant. Sometimes you can even be lucky enough to find a college student studying communications or art to work part-time with you.

Proper media selection is a difficult task for most small business

FORM 7.2 Product Benefit Comparison Chart

Benefits	Product A	Product B	Product C	Product D
_____	_____	_____	_____	_____
_____	_____	_____	_____	_____
_____	_____	_____	_____	_____
_____	_____	_____	_____	_____
_____	_____	_____	_____	_____
_____	_____	_____	_____	_____
_____	_____	_____	_____	_____
_____	_____	_____	_____	_____
_____	_____	_____	_____	_____
_____	_____	_____	_____	_____
_____	_____	_____	_____	_____
_____	_____	_____	_____	_____
_____	_____	_____	_____	_____
_____	_____	_____	_____	_____
_____	_____	_____	_____	_____
_____	_____	_____	_____	_____
_____	_____	_____	_____	_____
_____	_____	_____	_____	_____
_____	_____	_____	_____	_____
_____	_____	_____	_____	_____
_____	_____	_____	_____	_____
_____	_____	_____	_____	_____
_____	_____	_____	_____	_____
_____	_____	_____	_____	_____
_____	_____	_____	_____	_____
_____	_____	_____	_____	_____

people. For the optimum return, a specialized knowledge is a must. Some organizations offer varying degrees of assistance. These are listed in Appendix 3. The trade associations are also valuable resources. They have the latest information on your industry.

Illustration 7.1 lists other sources of advertising assistance.

YELLOW PAGES AND DIRECTORIES

There are well over 5000 cities with a published telephone Yellow Pages directory. To broaden the concept, telephone directories are published all over the world. Advertising in them is a specific territorial choice. It allows your business to reach many outlying areas. Yellow Pages can be separate volumes or remain a part of the standard residential listings.

Its directory is standardized in its format and widely used by telephone merchants and service organizations. Many manufacturers use the Yellow Pages as a part of their cooperative ad program. It can serve effectively as a "where to buy it" listing. When other forms of national advertising are done, the link is seen when they say "See the Yellow Pages for dealer nearest you. . . ."

ILLUSTRATION 7.1 Sources of Advertising Assistance

1. *Ad Agencies.* These range from one-person shops to operations with more than 7000 employees. There's one that will fit your budget and your business.
2. *Media Agencies.* These do not do creative work, but they choose media according to your market needs and make multiple purchases that save you time and money.
3. *Art Services.* These will supply prepared art and designs for your ads. Drawings that can be cut out and pasted onto your ad also can be purchased and are of suitable quality for reproduction.
4. *Free-lancers.* These persons are willing to cater to your special needs, deal with you on a one-to-one basis, with no job too small. You won't have to know advertising jargon to deal with them, but you should be able to evaluate quality advertising.
5. *Manufacturer's Advertising Kits.* These include copy and art for print media ads. Sometimes radio scripts are also included. Normally these kits contain quality material, and the price is right.
6. *Printers.* If you or someone on your staff has a flair for writing, printers will often do basic layouts. You may be fortunate enough to find a printer with a talented artist on the staff who will draw sketches of your product and illustrate the key benefits.
7. *Radio.* Local stations may offer the service of continuity writing. You can also provide them with a fact sheet about your business, product, or sales event, and the announcer will ad lib the commercial for you.
8. *Magazines.* These sometimes provide basic layout services, particularly for classified or buyer's guide sections.
9. *Cable TV.* To secure your business some cable companies offer writing and production services for your messages.
10. *Mailing Houses.* These specialize in everything from simple addressing of your direct mail envelopes to complete production and mailing procedures.

Bruce Bradukey, Robert Pritchard, Mary Anne Frenzel, *Strategic Marketing*. Copyright © 1982, Addison-Wesley, Reading, MA.

One of the major disadvantages is price. The small business may find the rates for a modest display ad high. The rates are quoted by the month and billed annually. Some offices can make arrangements for you to be billed monthly.

Yellow Pages advertising is a simple means of obtaining good coverage to people who are ready to buy when they pick it up. Everyone has experienced the use of this directory. If you are looking and do not have any knowledge of the advertisers, one important thing to remember is that people will go to the display ads *first*. They are easier to read and tell more about the business being called.

For display advertisements in the Yellow Pages, copy and layout service is furnished without charge in many cities. Stock illustrations are available. You can choose between a variety of advertising (from a one-line to a full-page display ad). Since ad content, format, and size restrictions are set, the competition for a small business is trimmed down to size.

There are other published directories that serve as resource guides for many industries. Purchasing agents are heavy users of directories. More product information is provided in this type of publication. If you choose to use these tools, be sure to monitor the responses you receive. The publishers will have individual standards for assistance, format, and pricing.

NEWSPAPERS

Newspapers, overall, give a good mass coverage in a localized area. Make sure the type of advertisement fits the style of the newspaper. This medium is timely and has a good pass-on value. Also, it can be read at any time. Newspapers are good for coupons and co-op advertising.

Copy and layout assistance should be available with newspapers. You have the choice of sections for your ad, but the placement is up to them. Poor reproduction of photographs can limit some visuals. Some larger metropolitan papers are costly.

Newspapers do not allow much audience segmentation. Their cost per thousand is very high.

$$\text{cost per thousand (CPM)} = \frac{\text{cost of advertising (time/space)}}{\text{no. people reached (in thousands)}}$$

Contact the newspaper for a rate card and discount information. They will also be able to provide you with other market and readership data. This should include basic statistics of the market, consumer sales and brand-purchase analysis, and product/brand distribution analysis.

TRADE PUBLICATIONS AND MAGAZINES

Keep up on your industry through the publications of the trade associations related to your product or service. They all provide an excellent source for specialized advertising as well as a place to get news releases printed. You are familiar with the process from Chapter 5, so use it.

Trade publications provide several merchandising tools that can be utilized by the small business, including merchandising allowances for regular advertisers. Explore this with the publication's representatives. Other things that a trade association can provide are ad reprints for sales tools, consumer response cards, and reprints of articles about your company or product(s).

Most national consumer magazines and business papers usually work with agencies. You can expect about the same amount of help from consumer publications as from newspapers.

Magazine advertising is not directed at the advertisers' segments directly. The magazine may happen to be read by some of the same people. Magazines have early closing dates, some as much as 90 days in advance. Each publisher will have a different rate scale. Request the rate cards and talk to an account representative about your needs. Magazines, like newspapers, have good pass-along value and a longer useful life (usually a month rather than a day).

Consumer-oriented magazines have a different audience and purpose than business or trade publications. Be sure to answer the following questions before choosing a consumer magazine over a trade or business publication:

1. Does the magazine reach the type of reader that we are trying to sell our product or service?
2. How does the distribution of the publication compare to that of the product?
3. What is the cost of reaching a thousand prospects? How does this compare to the cost of advertising?
4. How do readers regard the publication?
5. How thoroughly is it read?

OUTDOOR ADVERTISING

The most common type of outdoor advertising is the billboard. With as much driving as the average person does, there is a lot of visual opportunity on the road. It is used in connection with other media.

The chief categories used by national advertisers are:

Posters.
Painted bulletins.
Spectaculars.

Posters are the billboards that are covered with panels of a larger poster printed at a lithography plant attached . . . blowing in the wind. For 24- and 30-sheet poster advertising, there are two possibilities for outside help. If you are advertising a brand-name product, many manufacturers will supply the poster without charge, usually with your name identification.

Painted bulletins are a larger and more elaborate form of outdoor sign. The most common size is 14 feet × 48 feet. Lighting can enhance the visual appeal.

Spectaculars are events that even we can't suggest a limit for, such as Sunset Boulevard, or Las Vegas. Need one go further? They are the costliest outdoor "signs."

Use Illustration 7.2 to compare outdoor advertising.

TRANSIT ADVERTISING

Transit advertising includes advertisements at bus stops, inside and outside vehicles, and in the transit corridors (e.g., the NYC subway system). The passenger traffic patterns will dictate how localized you can be. It is used as a supplement to other major media in a campaign.

ILLUSTRATION 7.2 Comparison of Standardized Outdoor Advertising. (Source. Otto Kleppner, Advertising Procedure, 6th ed., p.225. Copyright © 1973. Reprinted by permission of Prentice-Hall, Englewood Cliffs, NJ.)

	Description	Chief Characteristics	How Bought	Special Features	Other Comments
Posters	Permanent structure (generally 12' x 25') on which pre-printed advertisements are mounted.	1. The least costly form of outdoor advertising, per unit. Standard size nationwide.	1. By *showings*—a ready-made assortment, bought as a unit. Can be bought on monthly basis.	1. Illuminated in better night traffic locations.	1. Most popular standard sizes, 24-sheet, 30 sheet. Other sizes 3-sheet, 9-sheet. 2. Showing sold as #50 showing, #100 showing, depending upon number of boards. Number of boards in showing differs by markets. 3. Copy changeable monthly.
Painted Bulletins	Permanent structure (usually 14' x 48') on which the message is painted.	1. Placed in higher traffic locations. 2. No uniform size.	1. Individually. 2. Price individually negotiated. Bought on one- to three-year basis.	1. Illuminated. 2. Many extra construction features: clocks, oversize bottles; neonlit trademarks, etc.	1. Some uniformity in frame appearance; otherwise quite individualistic in treatment. 2. Costlier per unit than posters. 3. Usually repainted every four or six months.
Spectaculars	Special steel construction, built to order.	1. Placed in the busiest night urban locations. 2. The most costly form. 3. Each one specially fabricated. 4. The most conspicuous of all forms of outdoor advertising.	1. Individually. 2. Price of construction, rental, and maintenance individually negotiated.	1. Everything is built to order.	1. The costliest form of outdoor advertising. 2. Usually bought on a three- to five-year basis because of high cost of construction. 3. Change of copy costly.

Rates depend on passenger usage on a monthly basis. The transit company controlling the advertising space can be expected to help with the designing and printing. Color is of utmost importance.

RADIO

Radio is a personal medium. You can select any station, and, more than likely, you are going to hear a voice. Most people have a rapport with a particular station and its personalities. You are able to pick the market you wish to penetrate. The demographics play an important part of the selection process since most radio advertising is geared locally. The station format will also help you target the listener/customer.

Radio advertising is used mostly by retail and service businesses and national consumer-product advertisers. It offers a flexible means by which advertising can be spread over a period of time at a selected time or strategic moment. Suppose you wanted to advertise an air-conditioning repair service. You may want your ads on the air only when the weather is above a certain temperature. These aspects can be negotiated with individual stations.

Rates vary according to time classifications and are relevant to the type of programming. The larger the potential audience, the higher the rates will be. Usually professional help is needed to produce a spot, but the stations will be able to assist in production. If they cannot, they will be able to refer you to someone who can. Copywriting is of utmost importance due to the length of a spot. The station will be able to help with this.

Arbitron reports (an independent organization that surveys and publishes statistical information on the size and demographics of stations' audiences) should be used to help identify the appropriate times, target audiences, and station formats for your business. Your identification of market segments will aid in this step.

TELEVISION

Television as an advertising medium is still used mainly by national advertisers and some large local advertisers. It seems likely, however, that the small business advertiser will begin to use it more. It is the closest of all advertising to personal selling. This medium can combine sight, sound, colors, motion, and any other visuals necessary. You can demonstrate the product and make every second count. The realism that can be achieved in TV advertising is very appealing.

TV reaches a large, general-interest audience. You can position it commercially around a program that your potential customers will view. The use of TV advertising is often very prestige oriented.

Professional help is mandatory for development of a commercial. It is also costly. Be sure that you have budgeted the TV production costs before you proceed. Again as with radio, stations are equipped to give whatever help is needed. They can also arrange to get help from outside specialists.

Broadcast time is negotiable, but make sure that you have a media service or a communications consultant assist you. The person must have experience in reading and interpreting the TV statistics. Rates can be obtained by requesting the rate cards from individual stations or consulting the Standard Rate & Data Service listing.

DISPLAYS

Retail businesses rely heavily on the display window to attract attention and, hopefully, traffic. Once put up, the job of the display window is done. Interior displays, as well as the windows, should be kept neat and clean. Don't crowd the display. Windows should change as many as 15 times a year. This depends a lot on the volume of foot traffic. Special times of the year provide excellent chances to draw attention to your place. Plan the window activities well in advance. Include the cost of this in your budget each year. Again, color plays an important part.

POINT OF PURCHASE

The creativity of a good graphic designer will give the best results for you here. Try to maintain the image of the company, even though your assistance may come from a manufacturer. You may be lucky enough to have a manufacturer want to do cooperative advertising. With cooperative advertising, the manufacturer may contribute more than $1 of every $5 you spend. Each manufacturer will have a different plan. Cooperative advertising will almost always include point-of-purchase material. It can also provide a variety of media sources. This type of advertising is covered by the FTC, so be sure you understand the complexity of any legal agreement before you commit yourself. Administration of the plan can sometimes involve excess reporting and record keeping.

ADVERTISING SPECIALTIES

Small business is not alone in the use of special advertising articles. Most offer limited ad space, but people like to get a gift, especially if it's something useful and in good taste. It doesn't take much. Something unusual that can set you up for more use than the gift a competitor gave. Here are a few examples grouped according to place of use. Contact a promotional gift sales company to review the spectrum of these novelties. Remember, you have good control over both the selection and the distribution. For example:

Wall	Calendars, thermometers, artwork, photographs
Desk	Ashtrays, rulers, paperweights
Pocket	Book matches, pens, combs, memo books
Home	Bottle openers, kitchen gadgets, pot holders

SPECIAL PROMOTIONS

Let us begin by cautioning that special promotions are *not* just sales. A special promotion (SP) can only happen three to four times a year. Otherwise it isn't special. The idea behind SPs is to get the customers into your location rather than your competitors'. Once you've got customers there, you must be sure that they have a reason to feel that the situation is special, the product and/or services offered are special, and, most important, that the people there to help them are doing just that. You do not want them to be customers only at the time of the SP, you want future sales and referrals.

The SP must be planned and executed with precision and completeness, including:

Personal contact with media (for coverage).
Paid support advertising.
All the free publicity you can get.
Mail-outs to customers or other acquired lists.
Store signs—inside and out.
Staff involvement and enthusiasm.
A unique theme that involves fun or excitement.
A time limit.
Appeal to more than one member of the family.
Special giveaways.
Product or service specials (not like a normal sale).
Products and prices that are attractive and not misleading.
Manufacturer participation, if possible.

Plan the SP well in advance. This will permit a lot of anticipation for all. Give people something to look forward to and even more crucial, something to come into your facility for. If you are going to want media and press coverage, you must come up with the story or novel idea worth writing about.

Any mailings and promotional pieces should break about a month before the SP begins. Make your mailing convincing. The message should be simple, interest grabbing, and may even offer a special if they bring it in with them. Remember, these are your customers already. Help them realize that you are really doing something special just for them.

The last major issue regarding the SP is the task of you, the manager, and your staff. All employees must be informed. It's more than just knowing about the SP. Everyone must show enthusiasm, be knowledgeable and helpful. Even if you don't make the sale, the potential customers should realize the genuine image of customer service and product knowledge, not to mention good prices!

Some people may want to speak to the boss: you should be available. Your presence will also serve as an example for the rest of the staff. And make sure there are enough staff people on. Special promotions often create a lot of customer traffic. There is nothing worse than being interested or in need of a question answered only to find no one able to help.

In conclusion, a special promotion won't be special unless you make it so. It's a time-consuming project, so be ready to spend that time, use your imagination, and go for it!

TRADE SHOWS

For many businesses, the trade show is the best place to win new customers. The main advantage of trade shows is that your customers attend. A trade show gives you a chance to keep in touch with not only your customers, but your competitors. It has been said that a salesperson should know more about the competitors' products or services than his own. The trade show is where the newest and best is shown.

Participating profitably in a trade show requires three things:

A plan and preshow preparation.
A booth and displays.
Salespeople to talk to the prospective customers.

Not only do most of the trade associations sponsor trade shows, but there are several trade show promotion companies that put on regional trade shows. A list of possible trade shows is available from your industry association. Promoters will probably advertise in trade magazines to get businesses in your industry interested in participating.

A very important characteristic of a trade show is that the buyer's resistance is low. In contrast, a salesperson calling on a prospect expects a high level of resistance. Buyers attending a trade show are there of their own free will and can vote with their feet and leave anytime.

Trade shows have five major advantages:

1. Selling is one-on-one communication at minimal cost.
2. You can see directly what the competition is up to.
3. A trade show is excellent training for sales and sales-support employees.
4. Trade shows provide a means of demonstrating the benefits, applications, and advantages of your product or service.
5. They attract customers' attention, arouse their interest, create desires, and allow them to act on their buying impulses.

However, trade shows also have certain disadvantages:

1. They take a lot of your and the company's time.
2. Trade shows cost money.
3. Problems at the show such as equipment that doesn't work or poor literature and booth arrangement can damage the company image.

Trade shows provide a unique testing ground for new products and services. By demonstrating new items, a company can get immediate responses. Trade shows add information to field market studies.

Plan and Preshow Preparation

One of the best ways to choose the right show is to ask your customers. Call some customers—potential or actual—and ask them what trade shows are the best. If you have several shows to pick from, have the customer rate them from 1 to 10.

In general, you should consider national trade shows first. Unlike smaller regional shows, national shows commit most of their promotional dollars to attracting buyers. They generate a large amount of publicity. At national shows, contacts can be made with most major retailers, distributors, and manufacturers within the industry from across the country.

Regional shows, however, might be better if you have a geographically limited market or a lot of tough national competition or if your product requires high transportation costs.

Plan ahead. Last-minute attempts to get a booth at a trade show generally are very frustrating. You could get last choice of a location or no booth at all because frequently the booths are sold out months before the show.

Even a small increase in the percentage of visitors that enter a company's booth can mean additional leads and sales. Therefore, it is a good idea to organize publicity and advertising to create awareness in advance of the show, perhaps by:

Mailing trade show announcements (and special tickets) to current and prospective customers.

Putting "see us at the show" on your regular advertising, brochures, or catalogs.

Issuing a press release about the company's participation in the show.

Planning for the show means reserving the booth way in advance, planning for the design and layout of the booth, making reservations for hotel space, and preparing literature for the show. As the show time gets nearer, you need to plan what personnel will be involved, what equipment must be transported, and what advertising is to be done.

Booth Location, Design, and Displays

As important as choosing the right show is choosing the right booth location, booth design, and displays for the show.

In the planning phase you should obtain a copy of the diagram of booth locations. Act quickly, because the best locations go first.

Good locations are:

By the main entrance.
By food.
By the bar.
On the corner of two or more aisles.
The booths to the right of the main entrance.

A good thing about being by the entrance is that traffic is heavy and you are assured that everyone who comes to the show will see your booth. A disadvantage of being by the entrance is that when people first walk into a trade show they are in a frenzy to see everything in the show and may not spend much time at your booth. If you are located near food or drinks, people stand near your booth in a relaxed, open frame of mind.

Two or more aisles coming together means that you have more traffic than booths that must depend on one aisle for their traffic. The right half of the exhibit is good because people have a tendency when they walk into a large gathering to move in a counterclockwise fashion after they come into the entrance. They tend to turn to the right, move counterclockwise around the gathering, and exit.

Bad locations are by rest rooms, near an exit, in the middle of aisles, on the left side of the show, and near hot dog stands (unless you like mustard on your equipment and displays).

A professional booth design may cost from $5,000 to $100,000. If you have an exciting new product or service, the quality of the booth is not so important. If, however, your product or service has a lot of competition and there is not much difference between brands, then the image your booth creates is very important.

A good way to determine booth ideas and designs is to walk around a big trade show. If you want to have your booth designed, it is even a better idea to walk around looking at the booths with a professional booth designer. You can get comments on the costs and trade-offs.

The main consideration for booth design is the visual impact that the booth makes as a person approaches it. The components of good visual impact are:

The backdrop.
The way salespeople are dressed.
The furniture in the booth.
The products on display.
Movement in the displays.

Keep the backdrop as light and sturdy as possible because it must not only look good but take a lot of abuse in moving and setting up. A typical backdrop will have: (1) the company logo, (2) folding panels, and (3) visuals. Visuals may include color to get attention, mirrors hung on the backdrop, a back-lighted logo, or spotlights trained on the logo. A visual that is most effective is a closed-circuit TV with the camera trained on your product or showing your service. Moving images attract more attention than static pictures. Videotapes with sound are at a disadvantage because their sounds conflict with what salespeople are saying.

If you don't have special furniture or backdrops, you can rent almost everything you need from the trade-show promoters. Trade shows rent: carpets, backdrops, furniture and accessories, waste baskets, temporary labor, and utilities for the booth for lights and equipment. Rental prices are high. You can buy the stuff for almost as much as they charge to rent it for a few days of the show's run. However, the hassle of getting the stuff in and out of the show and shipping and storing it afterward may make the rent price reasonable in comparison. A rule of thumb is that if the trade show is more than 500 miles from your home base, it pays to rent.

You should be careful about how your booth is laid out. The booth should be designed so that prospective customers can see all the merchandise or display and have an area that they can use to talk to a salesperson. Prospects should have walking access to your booth from every aisle on the booth borders.

Remember, the thing that gets a person's attention fastest is something in your booth that moves, such as a printer printing, a video, or moving lights.

Salespeople and Followup

No amount of money spent on a booth's design will make up for poorly trained, unqualified personnel. Booth staffers will make more contacts in a single day than they do in a week in the field. As a guideline, each salesperson can handle 15 to 20 visitors per hour.

The salespeople must reflect the company's image. Normally, this means dressing conservatively, wearing an ID badge, and acting informed. They must greet and treat each visitor pleasantly and courteously. At a trade show, the salesperson's job is to get leads that will eventually turn in purchase orders and money to the company. They must quickly distinguish customers from browsers. It saves a lot of time and trouble after the show if the sales personnel can qualify their leads to the greatest extent possible during the show.

Each lead obtained is written up formally. Later each is sent a letter and appropriate literature. Sometimes several pieces are mailed out. The lead is then contacted by telephone.

On the average, 72% of the visitors remember a booth after four to eight weeks, but recall begins to drop rapidly after this.

In summary, trade shows offer an opportunity to meet buyers face to face where products can be demonstrated and handled and an opportunity to reach people who are often not otherwise accessible. They also provide an audience of consumers specifically interested in the products or services on display.

SEMINARS

Many times the service or retail business can offer a seminar or self-help conference/workshop that will help to interest potential customers. These activities can be a part of an SP, but most likely will be done independently of the SP agenda. This type of activity can be a good source of community relations or public service.

Some examples include:

Real-estate investment seminars (real-estate agents or brokers).

Computer-use seminars (retail computer stores or computer consultants).

Wine tasting (wine, liquor, or spirit businesses).

Do-it-yourself repairs (hardware store or home improvement center).

The types of businesses that might sponsor these seminars are indicated in parentheses. They can be cost-free or nominally priced to cover the basic materials. Remember, you are doing this to attract attention to your business to win new customers and their referrals.

You can create the interest with the help of publicity in local tabloids, a mail-out to a customer list, or in-store advertising.

TELEPHONE SALES

The telephone is becoming an increasingly valuable selling tool for everything from home improvement and repairs to subscriptions. The newest innovation in telephone marketing is a computerized phoning system where households are dialed automatically and a computerized message is presented.

If your telephone sales program is planned and executed well, you

FORM 7.3

```
TELEPHONE RECORD

Name: _____
Address: _____
_____
Telephone no.: _____
Date of initial call: _____
Talked to: _____
Results: _____
_____
Comments: _____
_____
_____
Call-back date: _____
Results: _____
_____
Comments: _____
_____
_____
```

ILLUSTRATION 7.3 Advertising Media Comparison Chart. (Source. Bank of America, Small Business Reporter—Advertising Small Business, Vol. 13, No. 8. Copyright © 1976, 1978, 1982. Reprinted with permission of Bank of America, N.T. & S.A.)

SMALL BUSINESS REPORTER

ADVERTISING

Medium	Market Coverage	Type of Audience	Sample Time/Space Costs
Daily Newspaper	Single community or entire metro area; zoned editions sometimes available.	General; tends more toward men, older age group, slightly higher income and education.	Per agate line, weekday; open rate: Circ: 7,800: $ .25 16,500: $ .35 21,300: $ .60 219,200: $ 2.10
Weekly Newspaper	Single community usually; sometimes a metro area.	General; usually residents of a smaller community.	Per agate line; open rate: Circ: 5,400: $ .35 20,900: $ .55 40,000: $ 1.20
Shopper	Most households in a single community; chain shoppers can cover a metro area.	Consumer households.	Per one-quarter page, black and white; open rate: Circ: 13,000: $ 45.00 22,500: $ 185.00 183,400: $ 760.00
Telephone Directories	Geographic area or occupational field served by the directory.	Active shoppers for goods or services.	Yellow Pages, per double half column; per month: Pop: 10-49,000: $ 35.00 100-249,000: $ 63.00 500-999,000: $ 152.00
Direct Mail	Controlled by the advertiser.	Controlled by the advertiser through use of demographic lists.	Production and mailing cost of an 8½" × 11" 4-color brochure; 4-page, 2-color letter; order card and reply envelope; label addressed; third-class mail: $.35 each in quantities of 50,000.
Radio	Definable market area surrounding the station's location.	Selected audiences provided by stations with distinct programming formats.	Per 60-second morning drive-time spot; one time: Pop: 400,000: $ 45.00 1,100,000: $ 115.00 3,500,000: $ 200.00 13,000,000: $ 385.00
Television	Definable market area surrounding the station's location.	Varies with the time of day; tends toward younger age group, less print-oriented.	Per 30-second daytime spot; one time; nonpreemptible status: Pop: 400,000: $ 125.00 1,100,000: $ 370.00 3,500,000: $ 615.00 13,000,000: $ 740.00
Transit	Urban or metro community served by transit system; may be limited to a few transit routes.	Transit riders, especially wage earners and shoppers; pedestrians.	Inside 11" × 28" cards; per month 1 bus: $ 5.00 500 buses: $ 2,500.00 Outside 30" × 144" posters; per month: 1 bus: $ 85.00 170 buses: $ 14,110.00
Outdoor	Entire metro area or single neighborhood.	General; especially auto drivers.	12' × 25' posters; 100 GRP per month: Pop: 17,900: $ 650.00 (5 posters) 484,900: $ 9,770.00 (54 posters) 10,529,300: $162,400.00 (500 posters)
Local Magazine	Entire metro area or region; zoned editions sometimes available.	General; tends toward better educated, more affluent.	Per one-sixth page, black and white; open rate: Circ: 30,000: $ 285.00 43,750: $ 435.00 163,460: $ 770.00

ADVERTISING SMALL BUSINESS

MEDIA CHART

Particular Suitability	Major Advantage	Major Disadvantage
All general retailers.	Wide circulation.	Nonselective audience.
Retailers who service a strictly local market.	Local identification.	Limited readership.
Neighborhood retailers and service businesses.	Consumer orientation.	A giveaway and not always read.
Services, retailers of brand-name items, highly specialized retailers.	Users are in the market for goods or services.	Limited to active shoppers.
New and expanding businesses; those using coupon returns or catalogs.	Personalized approach to an audience of good prospects.	High CPM.
Businesses catering to identifiable groups; teens, commuters, housewives.	Market selectivity, wide market coverage.	Must be bought consistently to be of value.
Sellers of products or services with wide appeal.	Dramatic impact, market selectivity, wide market coverage.	High cost of time and production.
Businesses along transit routes, especially those appealing to wage earners.	Repetition and length of exposure.	Limited audience.
Amusements, tourist businesses, brand-name retailers.	Dominant size, frequency of exposure.	Clutter of many signs reduces effectiveness of each one.
Restaurants, entertainments, specialty shops, mail-order businesses.	Delivery of a loyal, special-interest audience.	Limited audience.

have a powerful selling medium at your disposal. Not only does the phone allow you a more cost-effective means of intimate communication to a customer, but it allows you to cover a broader geographic area in less time.

Use the following 12 ideas to improve or help launch a telephone sales program:

1. Plan your calls—calls take time and time is money; calls should express the precise customer impact you have in mind.
2. Prepare a list of prospects.
3. Prepare a brief pitch that has personality and does not exceed 1 minute.
4. Try to gear the style of your calls to any current advertising being used by the your firm.
5. Don't lecture or hard-sell. Give your customer a chance to talk.
6. Keep records of your calls (see Form 7.3).
7. Don't forget to recontact old customers (35% of inactive accounts could be revived in this way).
8. Look for updates and additions to your prospect list.
9. Use followup calls to active customers to maintain good relations and promote goodwill.
10. Take advantage of the new directions and rates of long-distance phone services (e.g., MCI or Sprint).
11. Utilize a positive "you" approach. Show that you are willing to help the prospects.
12. Remember the voice on the phone has to be the image in the mind of the person on the other end of the line.

SUMMARY

The small business that wants to take advantage of the benefits of advertising will not have the budget to go about it in the same way that a large company does. Nevertheless, the plans for an advertising program follow the same procedure whether the budget is $1000 or $100,000.

The exercises in this book allow you to look at the profile of the customer and the customer's surroundings. Answers to the basic profile questions will help to define the advertising media you choose. Use the market planning process to learn and to experiment.

Bank of America publishes an excellent booklet on small business advertising. It is included in their *Small Business Reporter* series and also appears, in part, as Appendix 6 in this book. Of particular interest is the Advertising Media Comparison Chart. The overview it provides is a good review of the media we have used as examples in this chapter. See Illustration 7.3.

8

PUTTING YOUR PROGRAM TOGETHER

What's planning? To most people planning is the art of putting off until tomorrow what you have no intention of doing today. Successful businesses, however, use planning to improve their sales efforts and guide them in the right direction.

For your marketing efforts to work, you must have a plan. The plan should include:

A written plan stating sales objectives, customers, market mix and strategy, and implementation time budget.
An idea of what the plan will cost you.
An idea of how to price your product.
A distribution network.

MAKING A MARKETING PLAN

Making a plan is the process of systematically and consciously thinking about the future of your company as an integrated whole.

When owners or managers systematically think about the future of their company, they will gain certain benefits. The planning process helps you to provide lead time for necessary actions, to make decisions where there are long-term effects, to use resources efficiently, and to improve current operations.

Lead Time. Doing things in business takes time. You must anticipate not only the changes that your business will need but also the time required to make these changes. To develop a new product for the market may take one year or more. Other examples of business activity that require lead time are building a new plant, beefing up a sales force, and putting together a promotional program.

Long-term Effects. Planning helps make decisions where there are long-term effects. Most management decisions involve investments, that is, expenditures of time, effort, or money in the present in order to achieve benefits over a number of years in the future. The marketing objective of developing three more retail franchises may take many years to implement if you have only one outlet now. Market plans help you move in this long-range direction.

Efficient Use of Resources. Planning helps you provide for efficient use of your company's resources. When money, personnel, or facilities are limited, you have to be careful in using them. You must make choices as to *what* will be done as well as *when* it will be done. You should decide which activities are most important, then schedule these activities in a way that produces the best possible results per dollar spent.

Improved Operations. Another benefit of planning is improved current operations. Because planning often involves making periodic evaluations of the company as a whole, it will show present areas of improvement.

A marketing plan defines the goals, principles, procedures, and methods that determine your company's future; it outlines how to successfully penetrate, capture, and maintain desired positions in identified markets. Your marketing plan should be:

Simple—easy to understand.
Clear—precise and detailed to avoid confusion.
Practical—realistic in application and goals attainment.
Flexible—adaptable to change.
Complete—covers all significant marketing factors.
Workable—identifies responsibilities.

The following is an outline of a marketing plan.

MARKETING PLAN OUTLINE

Sales Objectives
    Objectives for next and future years
    Strategies and results to be produced

Customers
    Definition of who your customer is
    Company location in relation to customers
    Customer money available for purchases of your product or service
    Media that reach your customers
    Lists of customers

Market Mix and Strategy
    Product
    Place

Promotion
Price

Market Plan Implementation
    Who does what, where, how, and when
    Time and milestone schedule
    Budget and cost

A sample marketing study is provided in Appendix 1 of this book. If you have any question about what goes in each section of the market study, you should consult Appendix 1.

Sales Objectives

Whenever possible, goals should be defined in quantitative terms so that progress towards them can be measured. Goals should be set high enough to motivate the doers to accomplish them successfully. At the same time, the goals must be attainable. There are dollar goals and nondollar goals.

The only valid dollar goals are those that result in a direct contribution to profit. Dollar goals are specific financial aims overall, by product line, volume and growth of sales, inventory turnover, and backlog of orders. Nondollar goals might be penetration of a certain percentage of a market, getting your product in a new market, or developing a new use for your product.

When determining goals you should answer these questions:

Where am I now and where do I want to be 1 year, 2 years, or 5 years from now?
Why do I want to be there?
What problems must be overcome to get there?

Objectives

Objectives should be result-oriented, measurable, attainable, specific, flexible, and consistent with each other. (Note the following examples of specific workable marketing objectives.)

Sales Productivity—Volume

    Increase the number of customers ___% by December 31, 19___ .

    Increase penetration into a specific market with existing products by ___% by December 31, 19___.

    Increase sales volume of _____(product or service) by ___ % in selected regions, districts, and territories by a specific date.

    Attain sales performance goals on calls per man, orders per call, expense per call, calls per day, etc., by given amounts by specific dates.

Profitability

> Increase profit rate for key regions, districts, and territories by ____ % by a specific date.
>
> Increase overall return on investment by ____% for next fiscal year.

Distribution

> Establish ____ new distributors in specific geographic regions by a specific date.

Advertising/Promotion

> Increase awareness of company products among key purchasers in specific new markets by ____% by December 31, 19____.
>
> Develop high-quality inquiries at $____ per inquiry for company products.

Product Development

> Introduce ____ new products by a specific date.

Use Form 8.1 to help you decide what your specific goals are.

Strategies and Results to Be Produced

The strategy of a market plan must evolve around your objectives. To meet your objectives, you must set overall strategies based on results expected. Here are some examples of results oriented around certain objectives.

Objective	Results
Product development	Distinguish your product from that of competitors.
	Offer one product that attracts several types of buyers.
	Create new uses of existing products.
	Diversify into new markets with new products.
Sales and service	Expand geographical area for sales and/or service.
	Change distribution to better satisfy the market.
	Increase training for sales and service people.
	Determine and increase effort on most profitable products and customers.

(continued)

FORM 8.1 Determining Sales Objectives

Sales Productivity—Volume

Increase:
    The number of customers by _____%
    Penetration into a specific market with existing products by _____%
    Sales volume of _____(product or service) by _____%
    Sales performance goals on calls per man _____, orders per call _____, expense per call _____, calls per day _____
in region _____ districts _____ territory _____
by _____(month)/_____(day)/_____(year)

Profitability

Increase profit rate by _____%
Increase overall return on investment by _____%
in region _____ district _____ territory _____
by _____(month)/_____(day)/_____(year)

Distribution

Establish _____ new distributors in _____(geographic region)
by _____ /_____ /_____ (date)

Advertising/Promotion

Increase awareness of company products to (individuals or companies)
_____
_____
_____
_____

by _____%   by _____ /_____ /_____ (date)
Develop high-quality inquiries at $_____ per inquiry

Product Development

Introduce _____ new products by a _____ /_____ /_____ /.

Other Objectives

_____
_____

by _____%   by_____ /_____ /_____(date)
_____
_____

by _____%   by _____ /_____ /_____ (date)
_____
_____

by _____%   by _____ /_____ /_____ (date)
_____

Objective	Results
Advertising and promotion	Increase margins, bonuses, services, and advertising and promotion subsidies to encourage dealer, company, and distributor sales.
	Increase brand, concept, and product acceptance.
	Address advertising and promotion to key customers.
	Set low prices for new products to increase market penetration and discourage competition.
	Price parts, service, and repairs at cost to gain goodwill.
	Offer quantity discounts to encourage larger unit orders.
Distribution	Have several warehouses at different locations to enable quick delivery.
	Use only one warehouse to minimize inventory control problems

Customers

Remember: Customers are your best source of money, not banks, not investors, but customers. Chapter 4 went to some length to prove this. Consulting that chapter again might help you in your written plan.

The checklist in Form 8.2 may help orient you with respect to your customer.

The questions you want to answer in your written market study are:

1. Who is my customer?
2. How does my company location relate to customers?
3. How much do my customers have to spend on my product or service?
4. What media reach my customers?
5. What mailing lists of my customers exist?

A detailed definition of who your customers are is required before you can proceed with any marketing plan. You should be specific. "My customers are men between the ages of 25 and 45 who live in the area covered by a ½-mile radius from my store" is a specific definition. Another is, "My customers are all the chemical plants, bakeries, canneries, and food processing plants in the Los Angeles, Orange, and Ventura county area."

In retail, as we have discussed, location is everything. Could your

FORM 8.2 Customer Analysis

	Yes	No
Have you estimated the total market you share with the competition?	___	___
Should you try to appeal to this entire market rather than a segment?	___	___
If you concentrate on a segment, is it large enough to be profitable?	___	___
Have you looked into possible changes taking place with your target customers that could significantly affect your business?	___	___
Can you foresee changes in the makeup of your store's neighborhood or clientele?	___	___
Are incomes in your customer base stable?	___	___
Are your customer-base purchases subject to seasonal fluctuation?	___	___
Do you ask your customers for suggestions on ways to improve your operation?	___	___
Do you belong to trade associations (yours and your customers')?	___	___
Do you subscribe to important trade publications?	___	___
Have you considered using a customer jury or customer questionnaires to aid you in determining customer needs?	___	___
Do you visit trade shows and conventions to help anticipate customer wants?	___	___

store be moved to a better location? Is your plant conveniently located near your customers or your source of supply? Could your present location be improved?

How Much Money Do Your Customers Have to Spend?

To find what money is available to purchase your product or service, several techniques are available. First, most associations have information about average expenditures per year per customer. For instance, a florist association might have information that the average per capita expenditure of a California resident is $8.50 per year. By multiplying the population around your florist shop by $8.50, you can obtain the average amount of money available from customers.

For example, the population in a ½-mile area of your florist shop is 8456. If you multiply the population times the average expenditure per person ($8.50), you can expect that you and any competitors in your area will have a market of $71,876 per year. This figure is the total of your customers' average expenditures on floral products per year.

Another technique is to ask your customers how much they expect to spend this year on products and services similar to yours. Then divide that total by what percentage of your sales these companies represent.

Say your company calls 10 of their customers who represent jointly 40% of Yourcompany's last year's sales and finds that next year these customers expect to spend:

Company	Predicted Expenditure
Harkin Company	$ 40,000
Commsep	$ 15,000
S. X. Industries	$ 35,000
Lazlo	$ 10,000
Trump Company	$ 50,000
Tor-Id	$ 10,000
Hayes Company	$ 35,000
Brooks Associates	$ 30,000
Love-Stnkz	$ 60,000
Endco	$ 15,000
Total	$300,000

$$\frac{\text{Sales of group} = \$300,000}{40\% \text{ of last year's } 0.40 \text{ total sales represented by this group}} = \$750,000 \text{ projected total sales}$$

What media do your customers subscribe to, see, or notice? Do they all read a particular trade journal? Do they pass by a certain billboard every day? Do they read flyers put at their door? Do they all listen to a particular radio station? The only way to discover what media your customers consult is to ask them.

If you know who your customers are and where they are, the next natural step is to reach them with your message. A mailing list is required if you want to call or mail to them. Mailing lists are available from list brokers (under Mailing Lists in the telephone Yellow Pages), from trade associations, from magazines, from industrial directories (see Chapter 3), or from the telephone directory.

Form 8.3 will help you determine the *customer* part of your market study.

Market Mix and Strategy

The marketing mix is the interplay of the four basic elements of a marketing program, the four Ps: product, price, promotion, and place.

The best way to define your product is from the point of view of the consumer. The customer's perception (which you control) determines the true nature of your product, and you must be sensitive to this when you define your *product policy*. Your product policy includes the degree of quality you will build into the product, its appearance, and its physical characteristics.

Price is always important in a product. Low price generates more volume, but less status and profit. A high price generates less volume, but more status and more profit. Pricing will be discussed more thoroughly later in this chapter.

FORM 8.3 Customer Market

1. Who is my customer?

2. How does my company location relate to customers?

3. How much do my customers have to spend on my product/service?

4. What media reach my customers?
   Billboards _____   Where? _____
   Magazines _____   Which ones? _____

   Radio _____   Which stations? _____

   Do my customers read flyers?   At home? _____
   On their car windshield? _____
   Dropped on the neighborhood from the air? _____
   At trade shows? _____
   Mailed to their business? _____
   Picked up at a local business? _____

5. What mailing lists of my customers exist?
   Trade associations? _____   List brokers? _____   Telephone book? _____
   Industrial directories? _____   Magazines? _____
   Company files? _____
   Names of sources:

Promotion involves how you will advertise the product. In the broadest sense, promotion is the communication between the producer or distributor and the customer. First you must decide what you want to tell the customer about your product or service. Second, you must decide how to get the message across. Finally, you must have a feedback mechanism to check results of the promotion.

To determine the type of promotion you must ask yourself, Would it be more efficient to "push" or "pull" my product through the distribution channels? *Push* promotion is using a direct marketing method to literally push your product toward the customer. Examples of push promotion are door-to-door salespeople, insurance agents, securities brokers, or manufacturers' representatives. *Pull* advertising pulls the customer to your product. Examples of this would be promotional flyers, television ads, leaflets, and brochures.

Resources for promotion in terms of time and money are limited. Therefore, a major decision for an owner is how to divide these resources among advertising, PR, and direct sales people. (See Chapters 5 to 7.)

Place is where the customer buys the product. Place includes distribution networks and location. We discussed location in Chapter 4. Distribution will be discussed later.

Form 8.4 will help you with your written marketing mix plan.

Plan Implementation

To implement your marketing plan, you must first plan the overall program. The second step is to break each of the programs into component activities and allocate time and personnel for each. For example, see the following sample sales programs.

Sales Programs

    Recruit, select, train, and organize sales force, dealers, distributors, and agents.
    Conduct sales contests and incentives.
    Determine quotas for salespeople.
    Develop slides, flip charts, and other sales presentation aids.
    Develop price lists, product bulletins, and technical literature.

Advertising Programs

    Determine coverage, timing, text, and layout of ads.
    Prepare letters, mailing pieces, and mailing lists.
    Develop customer education program.
    Produce catalogs.
    Evaluate, select, and participate in trade shows.
    Conduct special promotions.
    Develop packaging, trademark, and branding programs.

Product Programs

    Search for, screen, and appraise new product ideas.
    Market test.
    Determine quantity discounts and price breaks.
    Select transportation means and channels for distributing products.

FORM 8.4 Marketing Mix Plan

A. Product

Appearance: How is it distinguished from competitive products?
_____
_____
_____
_____

Quality: Moderate _____ High _____ Very high _____

New Products: Do you plan to introduce new products? yes ___ no ___
What advantage do they have over the competition?
_____
_____
_____

New Uses for Existing Products: Do you plan to establish a new market for a present product? yes ___ no ___
How will that be accomplished?
_____
_____
_____
_____

B. Place

Location: Is your present location generating enough customer traffic? yes ___ no ___
If not, why not?
_____
_____
_____
_____

Distribution: What percentages of sales are from: Direct sales _____%
                                                      Manufacturers' agents _____%
                                                      Distributors _____%
How would you change your distribution network?
_____
_____
_____

C. Promotion

What type is your advertising? Push _____ Pull _____

Public Relations: How will you promote your company through public relations and news releases?
_____
_____
_____
_____
_____
_____

FORM 8.4 Continued

Salespeople: How many salespeople will you have and how will you employ them?
_____
_____
_____
_____
_____
_____

Media Advertising: In what media will you advertise?
Magazines _____ Newspapers _____ Flyers _____ Mailers _____
Yellow Pages _____ Billboard _____ Radio _____ Other _____
How will you do it?
_____
_____
_____
_____
_____
_____
_____
_____

D. Pricing

Price: Low _____ Moderate _____ High _____
Reasons for price range?
_____
_____
_____

Competition: Light _____ Moderate _____ Heavy _____
How is pricing affected by this competition?
_____
_____
_____
_____

Product Profit: What is your most profitable product or service? _____
_____

What is your least profitable product or service? _____
_____

Discounts: Do you offer discounts for high unit sales? Early payment?
How does the discount work?
_____
_____
_____
_____

After you have a general program or programs, break down each program into component activities. For example, producing a brochure involves writing copy, developing illustrations, designing format, picking typeface, preparing camera-ready art, printing, folding, assembling, mailing, and so forth.

When the programs are in component parts, estimate the man-days required for each component. For example, if a given activity will take 3 people 10 days, then it takes 30 working days.

This information is best translated into graphic form. Each activity can be scheduled in a bar chart along a time axis. During the early 1900s, Henry T. Gantt developed the familiar bar chart or Gantt chart. This is a simple bar chart beside each task showing how long in man-hours it will take to complete.

Illustration 8.1 shows a Gantt chart for preparing a customer mailing. Form 8.5, Market Implementation Plan and Schedule, will help you do your own implementation plan.

PAYING FOR THE PLAN

How many dollars should you allot to your advertising and marketing every year?

Review the following five ways to organize your marketing budget, and select the one that fits your needs.

1. *Percentage of Sales.* Many people just allocate a certain percentage of gross sales as the amount of the budget. A retailer decides to spend 5% of last year's sales volume on this year's advertising. If the previous year's volume is $100,000, this year's advertising budget is $5,000 ($100,000 × 0.05).

ILLUSTRATION 8.1 Implementation Schedule to Do a Customer Mailing

Task	Week 1	Week 2	Week 3	Week 4	Week 5	Week 6
Rough draft—text	XXXXXX					
Illustration—rough		XXXXXXX				
Text—final			XXXXXXX			
Illustration—final			XXXXX			
Contact list broker			XXXXX			
Order list				XXXXX		
Typeset				XXXXXXX		
Find printer				XXXXXXXXXXX		
Pick paper and ink					XXXXX	
Read proofs					XXXX	
Receive mail list					XXXXXX	
Assemble mailer						XXXXXXXXX
Mail						XXXXXXXXXX
Followup calls						XXXXXX

FORM 8.5 A. Market Implementation Plan

Major and Component Programs

What are your major market programs?

Sales

_____
_____
_____
_____

    Components of sales program:

    _____
    _____
    _____
    _____
    _____
    _____
    _____

Advertising

_____
_____
_____
_____

    Components of advertising program:

    _____
    _____
    _____
    _____
    _____
    _____
    _____

Product, Distribution, and Pricing

_____
_____
_____

    Components of product, distribution, and pricing program:

    _____
    _____
    _____
    _____
    _____
    _____
    _____
    _____

FORM 8.5 B. Implementation Schedule

	\multicolumn{6}{c}{Bar Chart of Time and Milestones}
	\multicolumn{6}{c}{Time}
Task	Period 1	Period 2	Period 3	Period 4	Period 5	Period 6

2. *Unit of Sales.* This technique bases the budget on the number of *units* of a product sold in the past year and the number expected to be sold this year. For example, a computer store decides to spend $50 for each unit sold for advertising. They hope to sell 500 computers this year, so their advertising budget is $25,000 ($50.00 × 500 units).

3. *Buying Prospect Inquiries.* This method is popular with mail-order companies. The advertising is planned to pay its way as it goes along. The company finds that obtaining an order by mail costs $3. If they aim at $10,000 in sales, their budget would be $30,000.

4. *Following Competitors.* A company may want to keep pace with a competitor by spending whatever the competitor spends.

5. *Combinations.* Almost all of these methods can be combined or varied to meet individual needs. The one rule is this: To be effective, your advertising must be planned carefully and budgeted wisely.

Costing Components of the Market Plan

If you want real control over your market budget, you can use the bar chart (discussed earlier) for implementation and attribute a price to every task. The price should include cost of labor, subcontract, and supplies. Illustration 8.2 shows the mailing implementation chart (Illustration 8.1) with costs added.

You can determine what each task will cost by multiplying the man-hours required for each by what your cost per man-hour is. Costs of subcontract work can be discovered by asking subcontractors (printers

ILLUSTRATION 8.2 Customer Mailing and Costs

Task	Week 1	Week 2	Week 3	Week 4	Week 5	Week 6	Cost
Rough draft—text	XXXXXX						$ 50[a]
Illustration—rough	XXXXXXXX						75[b]
Text—final		XXXXXXX					50[a]
Illustration—final		XXXXX					200[b]
Contact list broker		XXXXXXX					60[a]
Order list			XXXXX				350[b]
Typeset			XXXXXXX				550[b]
Find printer			XXXXXXXXXXX				70[a]
Pick paper and ink				XXXXX			20[a]
Read proofs					XXXX		30[a]
Receive mailing list				XXXXXXXX			10[a]
Assemble mailer					XXXXXXXXXXX		350[a]
Mail						XXXXXXXXXXXX	780[c]
Followup calls						XXXXXX	200[a]

[a]Indicates company labor cost.
[b]Outside contractor cost.
[c]Cost of postage and supplies.

and typesetters in the example) what they will charge for doing your brochure. Cost of postage can be determined by multiplying the total number of brochures you intend to send by the postage cost for one.

It is a good idea to try to determine your costs before you take on a project. (Form 8.6 should help.) This will keep you from being surprised by unexpected checks to write.

For each project you should consider the following costs:

1. Labor of your employees and anyone you might hire to help.
2. Subcontract cost.
3. Art, typesetting, layout, photos, and other media costs.
4. Publication costs such as printing or the fees to run your ad in a newspaper.
5. Telephone and travel cost for salespeople who follow up on leads advertising brings in.
6. Postage and office supplies.

PRODUCT PRICING

One of the Ps of marketing mix is pricing. Price affects how much of your product is sold, to whom it is sold, what services must go with it, and ultimately how much profit you make.

Once you decide that a product is viable, you must still decide how much you are going to charge for it. Chevy automobiles are good products and they have a definite share of the market, but they would not sell at $30,000 each and GM would stop making them at $300 each.

FORM 8.6   A. Budget for Your Market Project

Costs: What are your costs for this project?

Cost	$ Allocated	Tasks	$ Actual
Labor: employees	_____	_____	_____
Labor: outside workers	_____	_____	_____
Subcontractors: _____	_____	_____	_____
	_____	_____	_____
	_____	_____	_____
Art, typesetting, layout	_____	_____	_____
Publication costs	_____	_____	_____
Telephone and travel	_____	_____	_____
Postage and office supplies	_____	_____	_____
	_____	_____	_____
	_____	_____	_____

FORM 8.6   B. Cost Implementation Schedule

Task	Period 1	Period 2	Period 3	Period 4	Period 5	Period 6	Cost

(Time spans Periods 1–6)

Products have predictable life cycles. Demand starts low and goes as high as it will go, then starts tapering off. Prices also go through a life cycle. In a product's introductory stage, the price is usually higher because there is less competition and the consumer is often willing to pay more for a novelty. The first pocket calculators sold for almost $200 each. Later, when the product had reached maturity and many companies were manufacturing them, the prices fell drastically. You should know where a given product is in its life cycle when you determine the price.

Competition obviously affects a pricing strategy. Some products have high profit margins while others have low profit margins. This is a result of *product differentiation*. If the product is nondifferentiated (i.e., all products are similar), the market is highly competitive and profit margins are low. At the other extreme are highly differentiated products such as vitamins, cosmetics, stylish clothing, and drugs. A product that is differentiated (i.e., has something about it that appears unique to the customer) has a higher gross profit margin than the average product.

If you have a product that is difficult to differentiate, try to reposition it away from immediate competition. One solution is to rename the product (Anacin instead of aspirin). Another solution is to emphasize some particular feature (colored toothpaste instead of white). Without differentiation, you dare not raise your price for fear of being abandoned by the consumer.

Before we go further it is a good idea to check your pricing policies against certain questions. Use Form 8.7.

Price Adjustments

The object of raising prices is to increase dollar sales volume and profits by holding unit sales relatively stable at the increased price. But you must avoid a price increase that will drop sales volume below profitable levels. Two examples illustrate this.

The Jive Jewelry company increased retail prices by 20% across the

FORM 8.7 Pricing Questionnaire for Your Company

	Yes	No
Have you determined whether to price below, at, or above the market?	___	___
Do you set specific markups for each product?	___	___
Do you set markups for product categories?	___	___
Do you use a one-price policy rather than bargaining with customers?	___	___
Do you offer discounts for quantity purchases?	___	___
Do you set prices to cover full costs on every sale?	___	___
Have you developed policy regarding when you will take markdowns and how large?	___	___
Do the prices you have established earn planned gross margin?	___	___
Do you clearly understand the market forces affecting your pricing methods?	___	___
Do you know which products are slow movers and which are fast?	___	___
Do you know which products are price-sensitive to your customers (increase in price leads to drop in demand)?	___	___
Do you know which of your products draw people when you have a special sale?	___	___
Do you know the maximum price customers will pay for certain products?	___	___
Do you know what role you want price to play in your overall sales strategy?	___	___
Are you influenced by competitors' price changes?	___	___

board and discovered that unit sales only dropped by 1% as a direct result. This worked because in this instance the market was *inelastic*, that is, the customers were not price-sensitive, and the small loss in unit sales was more than offset by the 99% of stable business paying 20% more for the same items.

Basket Bakery raised bread prices by 5% only to find unit sales dropping by 30%. The market was *elastic*, that is, there was a lot of competition and the consumer was price-sensitive.

When finalizing a price adjustment, you should consider the following points:

How strong is the competition? Would a price hike put you closer to or further away from the competition?

Is your product intended for a luxury, high-price market (not sensitive to price) or intended for a standard commodity market (highly price-sensitive)?

Do you compete primarily on the basis of price or on other areas such as promotion, advertising, location, reputation, innovation, or quality?

Is there anything distinctive or unique about your product that reduces competition of the importance of price competition?

Pricing Strategies

The four basic pricing strategies are:

1. Skim the cream off the market for high short-term profit.
2. Compete at the market price.
3. Charge low prices to create a mass market.
4. Use preemptive pricing at very low levels to keep competitors out.

If there is no comparable product or if the product is newly improved, a high price is warranted. If there are a large number of buyers and little danger of competition, a high price is clearly called for. The disadvantages of high price are that it attracts competition and it discourages some buyers from trying the product. It also requires a broad knowledge of competitive product developments on your part.

When there are several comparable products and a growing market you have to keep your price at the level of your competitor's price.

When there is a product with a long product life span that has a mass market and demand is highly sensitive to price, it is a good idea to charge lower prices. This creates a mass market resulting in cost advantages derived from higher volume. Price should be low enough to attract a large customer base.

If your customers constitute a very large market you must price at low levels. Set prices as close as possible to total unit cost. As increased volume allows lower cost, pass advantages on to buyers via lower prices.

DISTRIBUTORS AND REPRESENTATIVES

A channel of distribution is a link between you and your customer. It is the means by which the sale of your product or service is made to the ultimate consumer. There are three basic ways of distributing a product or service. The three basic channels of distribution are:

1. Direct to the ultimate consumer.
2. Through an independent agent.
3. Through a retailer.

Direct sales are when company employees sell directly to the ultimate consumer of your product or services. Almost all types of businesses use direct to the consumer sales. Some businesses use *only* direct sales. Businesses that use only direct sales include retailers of consumer merchandise, restaurants, personal service companies, mail-order companies, and professional services (e.g., legal, accounting, consulting).

If you are a manufacturer, your product might get to the market through an independent agent such as a broker, wholesaler, or manufacturers' representative. Most businesses that use independent agents also use a direct to consumer sales force and/or retailers. Food manufacturers sell to independent agents (wholesalers), but they also sell to retailers. Most industrial companies use independent agents (manufacturers' representatives) for geographic or market segments where their direct sales force is not effective (e.g., independent agents are used in out of the state or out of the country sales). As a matter of fact, one of the few businesses that use *only* independent agents are exporters.

Even though rarely thought of as such, people who refer someone to you who then buys are independent agents, even though they are not paid. Many personal services such as lawn care businesses, hairdressers, insurance companies, and caterers depend heavily on referrals for sales. Professional services such as commercial lenders, accountants, and office maintenance companies also depend heavily on their customers to act as "independent agents."

Retailing is the most common distribution channel used in the United States today. Retailers range from top-of-the-line specialty shops to mail-order houses. Most manufacturers of consumer items sell directly to the retailer.

Direct-to-the-Consumer Sales

Direct sales is the best option for your company if:

You are a retailer or in personal or professional services.
You have a mass homogeneous market.
The product demands a high level of technical skill or company support.
Sales territories have been established for a long time.

The advantage of direct sales is that the company salespeople sell only the company's products. Another advantage is company control of prices and services. The company also receives good feedback regarding its customers' wants and needs.

The disadvantages of direct sales are the high cost and the time required to build a sales force and train personnel.

Independent Agent

The best time for a company to use an independent agent is when:

The company lacks funds to support a large enough sales force.

The independent agent is selling in an area that the company does not wish to enter themselves.

The company is not well known in that industry.

Customers are accustomed to dealing with independent agents.

The company wishes to open a new territory or market.

Two advantages of using an independent agent are it lowers the cost of sales personnel and decreases the time spent training personnel. Local warehousing of inventory and a good knowledge of the local market provided by the independent agent are also advantages. Usually independent agents already have an established market.

Unfortunately, independent agents may represent other companies as well as yours, restrict your contact with your buyer, and lack enthusiasm for selling your product.

What do independent agents want? They want a profit on the resale of your product. They want you to be reliable and provide them with an easy source of supply.

What should *you* want from independent agents? You need good coverage of their market, assumption of distribution responsibilities, and good consumer service.

Retailers

When you choose a retailer to handle your product, the first question is what type? Do you want a discount house, a department store, or a high-class specialty house to distribute your product? In what locations do you prefer to sell your product? City? Suburb? Office building? Sports arena?

There are three types of retailer distribution: intensive, selective, and exclusive.

Dropping your product in every available store front window is *intensive distribution*. This type of distribution works best for low-priced, high-volume items like razor blades, publications, soda, and cigarettes.

Selective distribution is the process of putting your product only in certain "select" outlets. Selective distribution works best for products of high perceived value or items that the customer perceives as being more than the simple exchange of cash for goods. Products often distributed on a selective basis are music equipment, dresses, and cameras.

High-priced and high-quality products are distributed "exclusively" to one store in an area. Often these products have a small market (Rolls-Royce cars, pianos, or imported crystal), but the buyers will go to considerable trouble to make their purchases.

SUMMARY

Planning is a very important part of the marketing process. A written plan is the culmination of this process. This written plan includes a discussion of your sales objectives; who and where your customers are; what your marketing mix is; and how the plan will be implemented on a time and task basis.

When writing the plan, it is a good idea to plan the costs and what your pricing will be. Also, due consideration should be given to what form of distribution you intend to use.

APPENDIXES

It is not always possible to put all the important material that you think would be of value to the reader in the body of the book. These appendixes include information that will help you better understand marketing.

APPENDIX 1

SAMPLE MARKET PLAN (THE COUNTRY GARDEN)

Following is a market plan for The Country Garden. This gives you a sample market plan to follow when you prepare your own study. Reprinted with permission of Joseph Seals, owner of The Country Garden.

MARKETING PLAN SYNOPSIS

The Country Garden will be a full-service retail nursery (garden center) catering to the local community and a mail-order plant company specializing in garden plants for cutting flowers—distributing nationally.

Future expansion plans include the Country Home, a down-home general store, and the Country Path, a nature store.

The retail nursery and mail-order industries are both actively growing enterprises.

The retail store and growing grounds will be located 10 miles west of the city of Crivitz on a major county road.

The advertising and promotional campaigns will be aggressive ... thorough locally and efficient nationally.

Research will be carried out on fuel-conservation methods, introduction of new plant varieties, and practical studies on cut flowers.

I. PROFILE AND PRODUCTS

A. Profile of Company

1. Full-service retail nursery offering:
   - (a) Ornamental plants (including bedding flowers, potted flowering plants, balled-and-burlapped shrubs and trees, houseplants)
   - (b) Vegetable plants
   - (c) Seeds, bulbs, other packaged dormant plants

(d) Lawn seed
(e) Bulk seed
(f) Pots, containers, baskets
(g) Soil amendments (peat moss, lime)
(h) Fertilizers
(i) Pest-control products
(j) Garden tools, hoses, other hardware
(k) Vases, other simple flower-arranging accessories
(l) Field-grown fresh cut flowers (unarranged, inexpensive)
(m) Dried flowers and other dried natural material
(n) Magazines, books
(o) Birding supplies (seed, feeders, houses)
(p) Firewood
(q) Snowthrowers
(r) Holiday goods

2. Mail-order plant nursery (specializing in garden plants that produce flowers for cutting) offering:
   (a) Perennial plants (2-in. pots in cell-packs)
   (b) Ornamental grasses (2-in. pots in cell-packs)
   (c) Ferns (2-in. pots)
   (d) Perennial seeds (packets)
   (e) Annual seeds (packets)
   (f) Ornamental grass seed (packets)
   (g) Seeds of plants for drying material (packets)
   (h) Wild-flower seed mixes (packets)
   (i) Theme mixtures (plants, bulbs, and/or seeds)
   (j) Bulbs

B. Objectives of Company

1. As a full-service retail nursery, the objective is to become the single popular source of major gardening supplies within the local market. The local market comprises the city of Crivitz and communities within a 30-mile radius (and farther when coming from the west).

2. As a mail-order business, we expect to reach a profitable point in a national market at two years and, in time, to develop an international mailing.

   The two-part profile (above) represents Phase 1 of the company's objectives. Further development will encompass Phases 2, 3, and 4 as follows. The remainder of this business prospectus/market plan is based on Phase 1 only.

3. Phase 2: the Country Home—to be started at the beginning of the fifth year after the plant business shows a worthwhile profit—a

store offering "homemade"-style and actual homemade articles related to nature or the garden with emphasis on the "old-fashioned" feel.
- (a) Canned fruits, preserves
- (b) Ciders, juices
- (c) Dried fruits
- (d) Honey
- (e) Expanded offering of dried flowers
- (f) Dried herbs, spices
- (g) Candles
- (h) Fireplace accessories
- (i) Christmas ornaments, cards (a la nature)
- (j) Holiday wreaths (in addition to traditional Christmas wreaths) of natural material
- (k) Books, magazines
- (l) Exclusive produce (fruits and vegetables not competitive with local grocery markets)
- (m) Coffees, teas
- (n) Sachets, potpourris

4. Phase 2A: a mail-order catalog from the Country Garden offering gourmet and "old-fashioned" vegetable seeds—also to be started at the beginning of the fifth year, after the plant business shows a worthwhile profit.

5. Phase 3: the Country Path—to be started at the beginning of the sixth year—a store offering items from nature and for the appreciation of nature.
   - (a) Books, magazines
   - (b) Expanded birding supplies
   - (c) Art, posters, cards, stationery
   - (d) Crafts of simple natural materials
   - (e) Woodcrafted toys, gifts (a la nature)

6. Phase 4: an orchard and perennial food garden—to be developed during Phases 2 through 3—to supply produce for fresh sales and processing into salable items; emphasis will be on items not easily obtained locally (regionally).

In addition to local advertising, Phases 2 through 4 shall be promoted on a scale that will cultivate an *annual* tourist market from throughout the state and region.

C. Product Description

1. As a full-service nursery, the majority of the items sold will be bought in wholesale quantities for direct resale.

   Bedding plants (including vegetable plants), however, will be grown on-site in pony packs (3½ in. × 5¼ in.), large packs (5¼ in. × 7 in.), and 4-in. square pots. Larger sizes of flowering specialties also will be offered.

2. For the mail-order business, many of the items sold will be bought in wholesale quantities for direct resale.

The majority of the perennial plants (2-in. pots) and ornamental grasses (2-in. pots) shall be propagated on site. Some perennial seed, annual seed, ornamental grass seed, and seed of plants for drying shall be produced on site.

D. Advantages over Competition

1. A *full-service* nursery in this location will be the only one of its kind within 45 minutes of the city of Crivitz and nearby cities and even closer for cities to the west. Two other bedding plant nurseries exist, as well as hardware and feed stores that offer seeds and garden supplies, but there is no "one-stop-shopping" place for all nursery items and knowledgeable nursery service. The product mix, size of inventory, services, and aggressive advertising will give us the competitive edge.

Emphasis will not be on large "specimen" plant material nor other expensive material for basic landscaping, but rather on color material that will appeal to the local citizenry who want to "dress up" their existing gardens, as well as the tourists summering at the resort areas that are near the nursery.

2. The mail-order business will be specialized. In a sense, it too will be a "one-stop-shopping" place for those mail-order buyers who want a few extra cut flowers from their gardens or an entire garden of cutting flowers. Existing mail-order plant businesses offer no comprehensive selection or clearly defined selection of flowers for cutting. And, with the exception of a handful of major mail-order businesses, no companies offer all the necessary "parts" of a complete garden: seeds, bulbs, and perennial plants. There are those that offer seeds, and those that offer bulbs, and those that offer plants, but never the 'twain shall meet.

II. INDUSTRY AND COMPETITION

A. Historical Growth of Industry

1. Recent historical growth for landscape plants and retail nursery merchandise in general has been outstanding. The present status is similarly good.

Demand for nursery products is gradually changing from primarily that of "necessity" purchases to a larger portion of "discretionary income" purchases.

The Scope IV Survey of the American Association of Nurserymen showed a 29% increase in retail nursery stock (plants) sales from 1971 to 1975. *Home and Garden Supply Merchandiser* (June 1975) gave a grand total of $8,692 million for 1971 sales of all garden and lawn supplies.

2. For the mail-order business, the most current figures available are from the *Statistical Abstract of the United States*, 1978. The *Abstract* shows total dollar sales of "mail-order houses" (defined as only catalog sellers for the most part) for 1958 as $1,986 million and $6.8 billion in 1977. *Direct Marketing* magazine (November 1978) reported $4.1 billion in total mail sales for 1975.

   Maxwell Scroge Co. (honest, I didn't make this up) produced "Estimates of Selected Industry Segments of Mail Order" showing $141,000,000 in consumer mail-order sales for gardening and nursery products in 1971.

B. Government and Industry Interaction

Licenses required and relevant regulations for the nursery business as noted by Kenneth P. Robert, Administrator, Plant Industry Division, Department of Agriculture, Trade and Consumer Protection, State of Wisconsin.

From the Wisconsin Statutes:

Chapter 94 (pertaining to the plant industry); particularly relevant are Sections 94.01 (plant inspection), 94.10 (nursery stock; inspection; licensing), 94.39 (seed labeling requirements), 94.64 (fertilizer), 94.705 (pesticides; certification requirements and standards).

From the Department of Agriculture:

Chapter Ag 21 (nursery stock)
Chapter Ag 23 (plant movements; special inspections)
Chapter Ag 29 (pesticide use and control)

Local regulations require:

Fictitious business name filing
Business license
Resale permit from Department of Revenue

For the mail-order business:

Each state to which we will ship has its own Agricultural Codes pertaining to quarantine and inspection. The Plant Regulatory Officials of each state will be contacted.

C. Technological and Competitive Factors

The greenhouse will incorporate many fuel conservation methods and instruments. We expect to reduce traditional fuel consumption by more than half, passing the savings on to customers.

Our inventory and bookkeeping systems will be computerized for both the retail nursery and mail-order businesses. Management and marketing plans will be developed using computerized information.

The mailing list for the mail-order business also will be computerized. Computerized information shall be used to develop efficient marketing plans.

Our mail-order offering will continually introduce many new plant varieties, with emphasis on those that best exemplify our theme (cutting flowers).

D. List and Description of Five Top Competitors

1. Local retail trade
   (a) Sharkey's Floral (Crivitz—the Village)—florist, bedding plant sales, sometime television repair.
   (b) Zak's Floral (florist and nursery in Crivitz, florist in Wausaukee)—florist, bedding plant sales, some nursery items.
   (c) Eric's (Marinette)—near-full-service nursery (bedding plants, potted plants, shrubs, trees, some fertilizers and other chemicals).
   (d) Crivitz Feed Mill (Crivitz)—farmers' supplies (hardware, seeds, bulk fertilizers, amendments).
   (e) Three or more hardware stores (Crivitz and Wausaukee)—complete hardware stores including garden tools, seeds, fertilizers, garden chemicals; some stores more complete than others.
   (f) Guerney's Seed and Nursery Company (Yankton, SD)—mail-order sales of seed of flowers and vegetables nationally, including those people of Crivitz who buy seed.
2. National mail-order market
   The unique offering of our mail-order business makes it difficult to compare competition.

III. MARKET SIZE

A. Industry Total Market Size in Dollar Volume and Units

1. Retail nursery:
   Total Market Size ($)—$8,692,000 (1975)
   Total units—difficult to determine because of variety of retail stores that offer garden supplies (including true garden centers,

lawn-and-garden supply areas of variety stores, power equipment and service stores, hardware stores, farm stores, building supply and home centers, discount stores, and others)

2. Mail-order:

Total Market Size ($)—$141,000,000 (1977)

Total units—the American Mail-order Association of Nurserymen registers 76 firms; of these, 36 offer perennial plants and/or seeds, another 4 offer seeds, another 7 offer bulbs. These are, of course, minimum figures: there are at least 100 additional, smaller firms that do mail-order plant business; most of these are specialists in a particular group of plants (e.g., iris, roses, daffodils, wild flowers).

B. Specific Segment Market Size in Dollars and Units

1. Retail nursery:

Total Market Size ($)—rough estimate of the two "nurseries" in Crivitz: $75,000

Total units—The two mentioned just above; does not include other retailers that offer gardening items (as discussed in IID).

2. Mail-order:

Figures not relevant to local, "specific segment" market

C. Your Sales as a Percentage of Total Market Segment

1. Retail nursery: 50+%
2. Mail-order: a small fraction of the industry total market

IV. SALES OBJECTIVES

A. Results to Be Produced (First year, March 1, 1984 to February 28, 1985—combined retail and mail-order)

Costs of Goods Sold

Production equipment and supplies	$ 4,000
Hard goods purchased for direct resale	2,000
Green goods purchased for direct resale	3,000
Growing supplies (soil, fertilizers, etc.)	4,000
Bulbs, seeds (some direct resale)	6,000
	$19,000

Expenses

Association fees	$ 600
Insurance	1,000
Advertising (local)	500
Advertising (mail-order)	2,500
Shipping supplies	500
Catalog production	500
Direct mail pieces	2,000
Packets (for seed)	500
Office supplies	200
Utilities	600
Miscellaneous	1,000
	$ 8,900
Income	$47,900
Costs of goods sold	−19,000
Gross profit	28,900
Expenses	−8,900
Net profit	20,000
Draws	−18,000
Taxes	−2,000
Retained earnings	-0- (break even)

B. OBJECTIVES FOR SUBSEQUENT YEARS

The overall expansion plan is to increase purchases and production of material for the retail nursery by 15% each year and to increase purchases and production for the mail-order trade by 50% each year.

1. Year 2 (March 1, 1985 to February 28, 1986)

Costs of Goods Sold

Production equipment and supplies	$ 4,000
Hard goods purchased for direct resale	2,300
Green goods purchased for direct resale	3,450
Growing supplies	6,000
Bulbs, seeds (some direct resale)	9,000
	$24,750

Expenses

Association fees	$ 600
Insurance	1,000
Advertising (local)	500
Advertising (mail-order)	3,000
Shipping supplies	750
Catalog production	750
Direct mail pieces	3,000
Packets (for seed)	750
Office supplies	200
Utilities	600
Miscellaneous	1,000
	$12,150

Income	$56,900
Costs of goods sold	−24,750
Gross profit	32,150
Expenses	−12,150
Net profit	20,000
Draws	−18,000
Taxes	− 2,000
Retained earnings	-0- (break even)

2. Year 3 (March 1, 1986 to February 28, 1987)

Costs of Goods Sold

Production equipment and supplies	$ 4,500
Hard goods purchased for direct resale	2,650
Green goods purchased for direct resale	4,000
Growing supplies	9,000
Bulbs, seeds (some direct resale)	13,500
	$33,650

Expenses

Association fees	$ 700
Insurance	1,500
Advertising (local)	500
Advertising (mail-order)	4,500
Shipping supplies	1,075
Catalog production	1,075
Direct mail pieces	4,500
Packets (for seed)	1,075
Office supplies	300
Utilities	700
Miscellaneous	1,000
	$16,925

Income	$78,075
Costs of goods sold	−33,650
Gross profit	44,425
Expenses	−16,925
Net profit	27,500
Draws	−20,000
Taxes	−2,500
Retained earnings	$ 5,000

3. Year 4 (March 1, 1987 to February 29, 1988)

Costs of Goods Sold

Production equipment and supplies	$ 4,500
Hard goods purchased for direct resale	3,000
Green goods purchased for direct resale	4,600
Growing supplies	13,500
Bulbs, seeds (some direct resale)	20,000
	$ 45,600

Expenses

Association fees	$ 800
Insurance	1,500
Advertising (local)	500
Advertising (mail-order)	6,750
Shipping supplies	1,600
Catalog production	1,600
Direct mail pieces	6,750
Packets (for seeds)	1,600
Office supplies	500
Utilities	800
Miscellaneous	1,200
	$ 23,600

Income	$100,200
Costs of goods sold	−45,600
Gross profit	54,600
Expenses	−23,600
Net profit	31,000
Draws	−20,000
Taxes	−3,000
Retained earnings	$ 8,000

V. CUSTOMERS

A. Definition of Who Our Customer Is

1. For retail nursery:

   Our retail customer can be described as the homeowner who is a gardener interested in beautifying the home with flowers inside and out, raising vegetables, small-scale landscaping, and enjoying nature.

   Also included are those vacationing tourists who are interested in adding quick, temporary color inside and out, and, for those tourists who own summer cabins, permanent plants for regular showy summer color.

   In general, it's the homeowner who already buys garden supplies of any kind from the existing local nurseries, hardware stores, and feed mills.

2. For the mail-order trade:

   Our mail-order customers are those pursuing the gardening hobby, particularly those interested in fresh flowers from the garden.

They buy plants by mail-order because:
(a) They're interested in something new
(b) They want the convenience of selection in one catalog
(c) They would otherwise travel long distances to buy plants if they live far from retail garden centers

These customers already buy from existing garden supply mail-order companies.

B. Company Location and Customers

The retail garden store will be located 10 miles west of Crivitz on a major county road that leads to primary resort communities (at least 22 resort sites within 10 minutes). The road is well paved and is one of the first to be cleared after winter snows. It's not far (2 minutes east and west) from where the road joins with two other major county roads that connect with development and other communities to the south. The road also continues to the neighboring county.

The permanent population within 40 minutes is at least 20,000 and running as high as 40,000 or more when including larger cities with existing garden centers just outside the target market.

Summer resort populaton is undetermined as to its size and its time of temporary residency. However, all indications are that it is increasing steadily.

The actual location bears little, if any, influence on the national market for the mail-order business. However, the address of a rural ("country") location does add credence to an "old-fashioned" philosophy.

C. Customer Money Available for Product Purchases (retail nursery only)

Source: Standard Rate and Data Service, Inc.

Marinette County (The target area includes most of this county.)

Population (1/1/83)—40,200
Households—15,010
Spendable income per household—$19,601
Total for county—$294,213,000
Distribution of families by income:
   8,000 - 9,999   = 14.5%
  10,000 - 14,999 = 20.9%
  15,000 - 24,999 = 29.5%
  25,000 and over = 28.1%
Total retail sales per household—$9,378
Total sales for county—$140,767,000
Total retail sales on home furnishings—$4,183,000

Oconto County (to the west; about one-third of this county is in the market area)

Population (1/1/83)—29,600
Households—11,110
Spendable income per household—$17,563
Total for county—$191,121,000
Distribution of families by income:
   8,000 - 9,999 = 16.0%
   10,000 - 14,999 = 21.9%
   15,000 - 24,999 = 28.8%
   25,000 and over = 25.7%
Total retail sales per household—$6,650
Total sales for county—$73,931,000
Total retail sales on home furnishings—$816,000

D. Media That Reaches Customers

1. Local market (the retail nursery trade)
    (a) Newspapers
    Peshtigo Times (weekly)—circulation figures unavailable
    Marinette Eagle-Star (daily)
       Circulation for all counties = 9561
       Circulation for Marinette County = 6434
    Oconto Reminder (daily)
       Circulation for Oconto County = 8240
    Antigo Journal (daily)—total circulation = 6638
    Green Bay Press-Gazette (daily)
       Metro circulation of Sunday edition = 48,049
    (b) Radio, television
    Although no advertising dollars will be spent on radio or television, the opportunity to develop a local radio gardening feature will be investigated.
    (c) Yellow Pages of the local telephone book

2. National market (mail-order)
    (a) Horticulture and gardening magazines primarily; also home and home service magazines with old-fashioned interests.
    American Horticulturist
    Better Homes and Gardens
    Flower & Garden
    Garden Design
    Horticulture
    Pacific Horticulture
    House & Garden

Los Angeles Times Home Magazine
The Mother Earth News
Organic Gardening
Southern Living
Sunset
Country Journal
Country Living
Early American Life
San Diego Home/Garden Magazine
Victorian Homes

(b) Garden societies' newsletters and bulletins with emphasis on those societies that show interests in plants with cut-flower qualities.

American Rose Society
North American Gladiolus Council
North American Lily Society
American Daffodil Society, Inc.
American Hosta Society
American Peony Society
National Sweet Pea Society
The Delphinium Society

E. LISTS OF CUSTOMERS

1. Local market
   (a) Telephone book
   (b) Credit customers (future)
   (c) Those who have pulled permits for construction of new homes
   (d) Local zipcodes selected for purchased mailing lists
2. Mail-order National Market
   (a) Rental or purchase of lists from mailing-list firms
   (b) Purchase lists from other mail-order companies
   (c) Membership lists from garden societies
   (d) List from American Mailorder Association of Nurserymen (those people who have requested the Association's publication "Gardening by Mail—Where to Buy It")

VI. MARKET STRATEGY

A. Salespersons

Me—a trained, professional nursery salesperson (see bio)

B. Advertising

1. Newspapers
   Display ads in newspapers mentioned in VD1a above.
2. Magazines
   Horticulture (display ad)
   Pacific Horticulture (display ad)
   Organic Gardening (classified ad)
3. Garden societies newsletters and bulletins as in VD2b above.
4. Direct mail pieces sent to people on lists purchased from mailing-list companies emphasizing those people who have purchased from mail-order plant companies previously. Also sent to people who have requested publication from AMAN.
5. Mail-order catalogs sent to customers will act as long-term advertising because of their reference value.

C. Promotion

1. Local market
   (a) Articles, question and answer features on general gardening and landscaping offered to local newspapers
   (b) Local garden club contact
   (c) Local garden contests, exhibits (e.g., biggest sunflower)
   (d) Interior display sign showing Specials of the Day, timely news, etc.
   (e) "Get-acquainted" day
   (f) Tie-in promotions to local events/celebrations (e.g., Harvest Festival, Spring Festival)
   (g) Contribution of plants, materials to worthy community projects.
   (h) Extensive flower color, landscaping display around store.
2. Mail-order
   (a) Articles on "cutting flowers" offered to horticulture and gardening magazines including the above-mentioned magazines
   (b) Press releases to members of the Garden Writers Association of America (GWAA)
   (c) Press releases to horticulture and gardening magazines including those mentioned above
   (d) "Thank yous" sent to first customers
   (e) Catalogs to garden societies, magazines, GWAA members

D. Pricing

Although self-service will be encouraged, professional assistance will be available. The pricing will be somewhere low to moderate to reflect such "hybrid" service. Quality will be maintained as high as possible.

E. Distribution

1. The one retail store will be the sole outlet for retail nursery items. Perennial plants may eventually be sold wholesale to other retailers.
2. The mail-order products will be offered through a nationally distributed catalog.

F. Research and Product Development

1. Extensive studies will be made on fuel-conservation methods for greenhouse operation. The proposed greenhouse will be constructed, accessorized, and maintained using recently available and proposed fuel-conservation instruments and techniques. Experimental instruments and techniques also will be implemented.
2. An important effort of the mail-order plant business will be to search for new plant varieties from botanic gardens throughout temperate United States and Canada; to select improved strains from random seeding; and to conscientiously hybridize and develop new cultivars. Test gardens will be developed on site for such study as well as to act as display gardens.
3. Studies will be made on the "cutting" ability of flowers not yet familiar as cut flowers. Plants will be grown on site to produce such flowers for study.

APPENDIX 2

REFERENCE SOURCES FOR MEDIA PLANNING

The following list of organizations will help you with media planning, helpful subscription sources, directories of publications, information about writing, public relations, and so forth. It also includes a list of media-related associations.

MEDIA PLANNING SOURCES

ARBITRON COMPANY, INC.
1350 Avenue of the Americas
New York, NY 10019

AUDIT BUREAU OF CIRCULATION
123 North Wacker Drive
Chicago, IL 60606

AXIOM MARKET RESEARCH BUREAU, INC.
420 Lexington Ave.
New York, NY 10017

BROADCAST ADVERTISERS REPORTS, INC.
500 Fifth Ave.
New York, NY 10036

BUSINESS PUBLICATIONS AUDIT OF CIRCULATION, INC.
360 Park Avenue, South
New York, NY 10010

GALLUP AND ROBINSON, INC.
44 Nassau St.
Princeton, NJ 08541

A. C. NIELSEN CO.
360 North Michigan Ave.
Chicago, IL 60645

SHWERIN RESEARCH CORPORATION
270 Madison Ave.
New York, NY 10016

W. R. SIMMONS AND ASSOCIATES
235 E. 42nd Street
New York, NY 10017

STANDARD RATE & DATA SERVICE, INC.
5201 Old Orchard Road
Skokie, IL 60076

STARCH, INRA, HOOPER, INC.
E. Boston Post Road
Mamaroneck, NY 10544

Appendixes 2 and 3 are from *Marketing Problem Solver* by Cochrane Chase and Kenneth L. Barasch. Copyright © 1977 by the authors. Reprinted with permission of the publisher, Chilton Book Co., Radnor, PA.

MEDIA AND ADVERTISING PERIODICALS

Advertising Age
740 Rush St.
Chicago, IL 60611

Advertising & Sales Promotion
740 Rush St.
Chicago, IL 60611

Broadcasting
1735 DeSales St. S.W.
Washington, DC 20056

Direct Marketing
224 Seventh Street
Garden City, NY 11534

Journal of Marketing
230 N. Michigan Ave.
Chicago, IL 60601

Media Decisions
342 Madison Ave.
New York, NY 10017

Modern Packaging
1301 Avenue of the Americas
New York, NY 10019

Television/Radio Age
666 Fifth Ave.
New York, NY 10020

DIRECTORIES OF PUBLICATIONS*

Ayer Directory of Publications, available at many libraries, has more than 100 maps detailed to show the location of every publication listed. Especially helpful when you mail releases to distant communities. Newspapers and magazines are listed by city and state of publication; several indexes cross-reference publications by interest and title. Includes college and alumni papers. Order from Ayer Press, 210 W. Washington Square, Philadelphia, PA 19106.

Bacon's Publicity Checker, a two-volume directory with information on both magazines and newspapers, is published annually and is revised three times a year. It includes editors' names and the type of publicity releases used by each publication. Order from Bacon's Publishing Company, 14 E. Jackson Boulevard, Chicago, IL 60604 or call (toll free) (800) 621–0561.

The Design and Building Industry's Publicity Directory, first published in 1980, lists consumer magazines and trade journals that use news and feature stories about development, planning, design, and construction firms. Lists editors' names and indicates how material should be submitted. Sold by The Coxe Letter, c/o MRH Associates, Box 11316, Newington, CT 06111.

Editor & Publisher International Year Book, which is available in libraries or can be ordered each year, lists editorial and advertising information for thousands of daily, weekly, college, and foreign language newspapers. For daily newspapers, the *Year Book* lists editors' names and special editions like the home improvements, parade of homes, and boat-show issues. Includes a list of major clipping bureaus. Order from Editor & Publisher, 850 Third Avenue, New York, NY 10022.

Gebbie Press All-in-One Directory lists trade journals, consumer magazines, newspapers, and radio and television stations. It is less detailed than *Bacon's*. To order, write the Gebbie Press, Box 1000, New Paltz, NY 12561.

National Newspaper Association, 1627 K Street, Northeast, Washington, DC, sells a list of the state and regional newspaper associations. For the current price, call (202) 466–7200. You can write the associations listed for their membership rosters. Sometimes free, these rosters are valuable sources of information about the small town papers that may not be listed in the national directories.

*From *The Publicity and Promotion Handbook*, by Linda Carlson. Copyright © 1982 by CBI Publishing Co., Inc. All rights reserved.

SRDS Business Publication Rates and Data, published by Standard Rate and Data Service, Inc., is one of several volumes of a monthly directory. Every business journal that subscribes to the service is listed here by title and subject matter; each entry includes a comment on the publication's focus, its advertising rates, and a list of its special editions and advertising deadlines. The book includes the names of firms that accept ads for publishers and publications' geographical and demographic editions. Intended for advertisers, this directory is available at libraries and advertising agencies.

Ulrich's International Periodicals Directory provides information on magazines, especially foreign publications. This information includes the language of publication, publishers' and editors' names, the frequency of publication, and circulation. The addresses given for some of the publications are those of the parent companies, not the editorial offices. Check *Ulrich's* at your library or order a copy from R.R. Bowker Company, 1180 Avenue of the Americas, New York, NY 10036.

MEDIA-RELATED ASSOCIATIONS

AMERICAN BUSINESS PRESS
205 East 42nd Street
New York, NY 10017

AMERICAN NEWSPAPER PUBLISHERS
ASSOCIATION
Bureau of Advertising
750 Third Avenue
New York, NY 10017

DIRECT MAIL ADVERTISING
ASSOCIATION
230 Park Avenue
New York, NY 10017

MAGAZINE PUBLISHERS ASSOCIATION
Magazine Advertising Bureau
575 Lexington Avenue
New York, NY 10022

NEWSPAPER ADVERTISING BUREAU
485 Lexington Ave.
New York, NY 10017

OUTDOOR ADVERTISING
ASSOCIATION OF AMERICA
625 Madison Ave.
New York, NY 10022

POINT-OF-PURCHASE ADVERTISING
INSTITUTE
521 Fifth Avenue
New York, NY 10017

RADIO ADVERTISING BUREAU, INC
485 Lexington Avenue
New York, NY 10017

TELEVISION ADVERTISING BUREAU
485 Lexington Avenue
New York, NY 10017

TRAFFIC AUDIT BUREAU
1725 K Street, NW
Washington, DC 20006

TRANSIT ADVERTISING ASSOCIATION
500 Fifth Avenue
New York, NY 10036

TRANSIT ADVERTISING ASSOCIATION
1725 K Street, NW
Washington, DC 20005

APPENDIX 3

MARKETING SOURCES OF INFORMATION

Marketing Sources of Information provides an extensive list of resources, some of which have appeared earlier in this book.

GENERAL REFERENCES

Data Sources for Business and Market Analysis, The Scarecrow Press, Inc., 52 Liberty Street, Box 656, Metuchen, NJ 08840. A guide to marketing information on a variety of business areas. It includes references to periodicals, trade associations, business firms, and other key sources.

Dun & Bradstreet Directories, Dun & Bradstreet, Inc., 99 Church Street, New York, NY 10007. Annual lists of U.S. firms, including information on products, annual sales, number of employees, names, and titles of 75,000 key executives. Listing is cross-referenced by company name and product classification.

Encyclopedia of Business Information Sources, Gale Research Company, 700 Book Tower, Detroit, MI 48226. Lists up-to-date information sources on a variety of business problems. It includes references to encyclopedias, handbooks, bibliographies, periodicals, directories, and other useful sources.

Foreign Commerce Handbook, Chamber of Commerce of the United States, 1615 H Street, NW, Washington, DC 20006. Lists over 100 local Chambers of Commerce in the United States which maintain departments, bureaus, and so forth, of foreign trade, and have compiled lists of importers and exporters in their area.

Fortune Plant and Product Directory of the 1,000 Largest U.S. Industrial Corporations, Fortune, Time & Life Building, New York, NY 10020. An annual list of the 1000 largest U.S. industrial companies, with addresses, sales, assets, profits, employment, and products.

Guide to Reference Books, American Library Assoc., 50 E. Huron Street, Chicago, IL 60611. Lists reference books for all major fields of study, including bibliographies, government documents, dissertations, directories, and so forth.

How to Use the Business Library, H. Webster Johnson, South-Western Publishing Company, 5701 Madison Road, Cincinnati, OH 45227.

Appendixes 2 and 3 are from *Marketing Problem Solver* by Cochrane Chase and Kenneth L. Barasch. Copyright © 1977 by the authors. Reprinted with permission of the publisher, Chilton Book Co., Radnor, PA.

Moody's Industrial Manual, Moody's Investor Service, 99 Church Street, New York, NY 10007. An annual publication, with semiweekly updates describing the operations, plants, subsidiaries, officers, directors, comparative income statements, long-term earnings record, and other financial and operating data on domestic and foreign industrial companies. Similar publications are also available on banking, utilities, government, and transportation.

Poor's Register of Corporations, Directors & Executives, Standard & Poor's Corporation, 345 Hudson Street, New York, NY 10014. A multivolume service listing information on U.S. and Canadian corporations and key executives. Lists over 30,000 companies with addresses, products, services, sales, number of employees, and standard industrial classification. Lists over 260,000 prospects, including job titles, business addresses, and telephone numbers of 70,000 top-level officers and directors.

Sources of Business Information, University of California Press, 2223 Fulton Street, Berkeley, CA 94720. Contains 300 pages of references to management, foreign trade, marketing, and related categories.

Statistics Sources, Gale Research Company, 700 Book Tower, Detroit, MI 48226. A guide to data on industrial, business, social, financial, and educational institutions. It includes a summary of all statistical sources.

Sweet's Catalog, Sweet's Catalog Service, Division of F.W. Dodge Corporation, 330 W. 42nd Street, New York, NY 10036. An annual file of manufacturer's catalogs, including names, products, trade names, and market data for the following areas: architectural; light construction; industrial construction; plant engineering; metalworking equipment; and product design.

Thomas Register of American Manufacturers, Thomas Register Company, 461 Eighth Avenue, New York, NY 10001. Lists thousands of manufacturers by product line, size, and geographical location.

Yellow Pages Classified Telephone Directory lists local manufacturers and service firms. Available from local telephone companies, or from Leonard Yellow Pages Library, Inc., 207 W. Gregory Boulevard, Kansas City, MO 64114. (Latter company furnishes exact photocopies of Yellow Pages in any city for any product or service category.)

LOCAL AND STATE SOURCES

The Book of the States, The Council of State Governments, Ironworks Pike, Lexington, KY 40505. Authoritative guide to state government structure and functions, including officials and sources of state statistical data.

Directory of Federal Statistics for States, Government Printing Office, Washington, DC 20402. Describes many sources of statistics for counties, metropolitan areas, cities, and other geographic units; arranged by subject matter.

Sources of State Information & State Industrial Directories, Chamber of Commerce of the United States, 1615 H Street, NW, Washington, DC 20006. Lists public and private agencies that supply information about their states; lists manufacturer's directories.

World-Wide Chamber of Commerce Directory, Johnson Publishing Company, Inc., P.O. Box 455, 8th & Van Buren, Loveland, CO 80537. Lists domestic and foreign chambers of commerce, giving executives, addresses, and phone numbers.

TRADE ASSOCIATION SOURCES

Directory of British Associations, Gale Research Company, 2200 Book Tower, Detroit, MI 48226. Has nearly 8000 entries on associations in Britain and Ireland.

Directory of European Associations, Gale Research Company, 2200 Book Tower, Detroit,

MI 48226. Lists over 7000 entries on associations in every nation of Eastern and Western Europe.

Encyclopedia of Associations, Gale Research Company, 2200 Book Tower, Detroit, MI 48226. A biannual list of over 16,000 national and regional associations, their addresses, officials, number of members and staff, services, and materials made available.

National Trade and Professional Associations of the United States, B. Klein Publications, Inc., Box 8503, Coral Springs, FL 33065. Annual list of about 4500 national associations, executives, addresses, number of members and staff, and materials made available.

National Trade and Professional Associations of the United States, Columbia Books, Inc., Suite 300, 917 15th Street, NW, Washington, DC 20005. Annual list of about 4300 national associations, addresses, key executives, number of members and staff, and materials made available.

DIRECTORY SOURCES

American Guide to Business Directories, Public Affairs Press, 419 New Jersey Avenue, SE, Washington, DC 20003.

American Guide to Directories, Prentice-Hall, Inc., Englewood Cliffs, NJ 07632. Contains 2200 titles in 400 categories.

Bulletin of the Public Affairs Information Service, Public Affairs Information Service, 11 West 40th Street, New York, NY 10018. Lists all kinds of directories from all over the world giving title, price, publisher, and description of contents.

Guide to American Directories, B. Klein & Co., Box 8503, Coral Springs, FL 33065. Lists virtually every kind of industrial and professional directory in the United States and foreign countries, including 5000 directories in 300 categories.

Sources of State Information and State Industrial Directories, State Chamber of Commerce Department, Chamber of Commerce of the United States, 1615 H Street, NW, Washington, DC 20006. Lists information on state and regional directories published by state agencies and private organizations, including title, date of issue, name of sponsoring organization, price, and types of data contained.

Trade Directories of the World, Croner Publications, 211–03 Jamaica Avenue, Queens Village, NY 11429. Lists business directories covering trades in the United States and foreign countries.

DIRECTORIES OF PUBLISHERS

N.W. Ayer & Son's Directory Of Newspapers & Periodicals, N.W. Ayer & Son, Inc., West Washington Square, Philadelphia, PA 19106.

The Standard Periodical Directory, Oxbridge Publishing Co., Inc., 420 Lexington Avenue, New York, NY 10017.

Standard Rate & Data Service: Business Publication Rates and Data, Standard Rate & Data Service, Inc., 5201 Old Orchard Road, Skokie, IL 60076.

Ulrich's International Periodicals Directory, R. R. Bowker Company, 1180 Avenue of the Americas, New York, NY 10036.

RESEARCH SOURCES

Advertising Research Foundation Directory of Members, Advertising Research Foundation, Inc., 3 East 54th Street, New York, NY 10022.

A Basic Bibliography on Marketing Research, Hugh G. Wales and Robert Ferber, American Marketing Association, 222 S. Riverside Plaza, Chicago, IL 60606.

Basic Methods of Marketing Research, by J.H. Lorie and H.V. Roberts, McGraw-Hill Book Company, Inc., 1221 Avenue of the Americas, New York, NY 10036.

Bradford's Directory of Marketing Research Agencies & Management Consultants in the United States & the World, Bradford's Directory of Marketing Research Agencies, P.O. Box 276, Fairfax, VA 22030.

Design of Research Investigations, American Marketing Association, 222 S. Riverside Plaza, Chicago, IL 60606.

Handbook of Commercial & Financial Information Services, Special Libraries Association, 235 Park Avenue South, New York, NY 10003.

International Directory of Marketing Research Houses & Services, American Marketing Association, Inc., 527 Madison Avenue, New York, NY 10022.

A Manager's Guide to Marketing Research, by Paul E. Green and Donald E. Frank, John Wiley & Sons, Inc., 605 Third Avenue, New York, NY 10016.

Marketing and Business Research, by Myron Heidingsfield et al. Holt, Rinehart and Winston, Inc., 383 Madison Avenue, New York, NY 10017.

Marketing Problem Definition, American Marketing Association, 222 S. Riverside Plaza, Chicago, IL 60606.

Marketing Research, by Robert Buzzell, Donald Cox, and Rex Brown, McGraw-Hill Book Company, Inc., 1221 Avenue of the Americas, New York, NY 10036.

Marketing Research, by Richard D. Crisp, McGraw-Hill Book Company, Inc., 1221 Avenue of the Americas, New York, NY 10036.

Marketing Research: A Management Overview, by Evelyn Konrad and Rod Erickson, American Management Association, Inc., 135 W 50th Street, New York, NY 10020.

Marketing Research Trade Association Directory of Members, P.O. Box 1415, Grand Central Station, New York, NY 10017.

Research for Marketing Decisions, by Paul E. Green and Donald S. Tull, Prentice-Hall, Inc., Englewood Cliffs, NJ 07631.

Research Methods in Economics and Business, by Robert Ferber and P.J. Verdoorn, Macmillan Company, Inc., 60 Fifth Avenue, New York, NY 10011.

Research Your Own Industrial Market, Marketing Guidelines, Inc., Park Tower Building, 5200 South Yale, Tulsa, OK 74135.

STANDARD INDUSTRIAL CLASSIFICATIONS

"Relating Company Markets to SIC," *Journal of Marketing,* April 1963, American Marketing Association, 222 S. Riverside Plaza, Chicago, IL 60606.

Standard Industrial Classification for Effective Marketing Analysis, Marketing Science Institute, 14 Story Street, Cambridge, MA 02138.

MANUFACTURING AND DISTRIBUTION SOURCES

Books and Reports

Building Sound Distributor Organization, Experiences in Marketing Management No. 6, The Conference Board, Inc., 845 Third Avenue, New York, NY 10022.

Distribution Channels for Industrial Goods by William M. Diamond, 1963, Bureau of Business Research, Ohio State University, 1659 N. High, Columbus, OH 43210.

Marketing Through the Wholesaler–Distributor Channel, Marketing for Executives Series No. 11, by John M. Brion, 1966, American Marketing Association, Suite 606, 222 S. Riverside Plaza, Chicago, IL 60606.

Some Observations on 'Structural' Formation and Growth of Marketing Channels, Theory in Marketing, 2nd series, by Reavis Cox, Wroe Alderson, and Stanley Shapiro, 1964, (pp. 163–175), Richard D. Irwin, Inc., Homewood, IL 60430.

Magazines

Agency Sales Magazine, Manufacturer's Agents National Association, P.O. Box 16878, Irvine, CA 92713.

Industrial Distribution, Morgan-Grampian Publishing Co., 205 E. 42nd Street, New York, NY 10017.

Industrial Distributor News, Ames Publishing Co., One West Olney Avenue, Philadelphia, PA 19120.

The Representator, Electronic Representatives Association, 600 S. Michigan Avenue, Chicago, IL 60605.

General Associations and Directories

Manufacturers' Agents National Association, P.O. Box 16878, Irvine, CA 92713.

National Association of Wholesalers–Distributors, 1725 K Street, NW, Washington, DC 20006.

Society of Manufacturers' Agents, 7053 Cathedral Street, Birmingham, MI 48010.

Verified Directory of Manufacturer's Representatives, Manufacturers' Agents Publishing Company, 550 Fifth Avenue, New York, NY 10036.

Magazines

Industrial Marketing, Crain Communications, Inc., 740 Rush Street, Chicago IL 60611.

Journal of Marketing, American Marketing Association, Suite 606, 222 S. Riverside Plaza, Chicago, IL 60606.

Marketing Times, Sales & Marketing Executives International, 630 Third Avenue, New York, NY 10017.

Sales & Marketing Management, Bill Communications, Inc., 633 Third Avenue, New York, NY 10017.

Books and Reports

A Sales/Management Handbook for the Electronics Industry, Schoonmaker Associates, P.O. Box 35, Larchmont, NY 10538. (Series of articles on marketing technical products.)

Allocating Field Sales Resources, The Conference Board, Inc., 845 Third Avenue, New York, NY 10022. (Covers organization, matching field effort and sales potential, distribution, and control.)

Brass Tacks Sales Management, The Dartnell Corporation, 4660 Ravenswood Avenue, Chicago, IL 60640. (How to recruit, train, supervise, and motivate the sales force.)

Dartnell Sales and Marketing Service, The Dartnell Corp., 4660 Ravenswood Avenue, Chicago, IL 60640. (Monthly reports and case histories on methods, plans, and techniques of sales management.)

Developing the Field Sales Manager, Sales Executives Club of New York, Hotel Roosevelt, 45th Street & Madison Avenue, New York, NY 10017.

Field Sales Management, Experiences in Marketing Management No. 1, The Conference Board, Inc., 845 Third Avenue, New York, NY 10022.

The Field Sales Manager: A Manual of Practice, American Management Association, Inc., 1515 Broadway, New York, NY 10036.

Goal Setting and Planning at the District Sales Level, Research Study 61, American Management Association, Inc., 135 West 50th Street, New York, NY 10020.

How Sales Managers Get Things Done (how to overcome inertia), Prentice-Hall, Inc., Englewood Cliffs, NJ 07632.

How to Tailor Your Sales Organization to Your Markets, by Merrill DeVoe, Prentice-Hall, Inc., Englewood Cliffs, NJ 07632.

Management of the Sales Force, by William J. Stanton and Richard H. Buskirk, Richard D. Irwin, Inc., 1818 Ridge Road, Homewood, IL 60430.

Marketing for Sales Executives, The Research Institute of America, Inc., 589 Fifth Avenue, New York, NY 10017. (Monthly report on sales management methods.)

Readings in Sales Management, by Thomas R. Wotruba and Robert M. Olsen, eds., Holt, Rinehart & Winston, Inc., 383 Madison Avenue, New York, NY 10017.

Sales Force Management, by Kenneth R. Davis and Frederick E. Webster, Jr., Ronald Press, John Wiley & Sons, 605 Third Avenue, New York, NY 10158.

Sales Management: Decisions, Policies, and Cases, by R.R. Still and E.W. Cundiff, Prentice-Hall, Inc., Englewood Cliffs, NJ 07632.

Sales Manager's Handbook, The Dartnell Corporation, 4660 Ravenswood Avenue, Chicago, IL 60640.

Setting the Size for the Sales Force, by Zarrel V. Lambert, Center for Research of the College of Business Administration, Pennsylvania State University, University Park, PA 16802.

Supervising Salesmen in a Competitive Market, The Dartnell Corporation, 4660 Ravenswood Ave., Chicago, IL 60640.

Time & Territorial Management for the Salesman, Sales Executives Club of New York, Hotel Roosevelt, 45th Street & Madison Ave., New York, NY 10017. (Methods, checklists, working forms.)

Associations

National Council of Salesmen's Organizations, 347 Fifth Avenue, Room 1004, New York, NY 10016. (Federation of sales organizations representing 40,000 wholly commissioned salesmen in all industries.)

Sales & Marketing Executives–International, 630 Third Avenue, New York, NY 10017. (Studies sales and sales management.)

Sales Manpower Foundation, c/o Sales Executives Club of New York, Hotel Roosevelt, 45th Street & Madison Avenue, New York, NY 10017.

DISTRIBUTION SOURCES

Books, Reports, and Directories

ABC World Airways Guide(Airports), Thomas Skinner & Company, Ltd., 111 Broadway, New York, NY 10006.

Air Shippers' Manual, Reuben H. Donnelley Corporation, 211 East 43rd Street, New York, NY 10017.

Business Logistics: Management of Physical Supply and Distribution, by J. L. Heskett, R. M. Ivie, and N. A. Glaskowsky, Jr., Ronald Press Company, 15 E. 26th Street, New York, NY 10010.

DISTRIBUTION SOURCES

Directory of American Ship Services, National Association of Marine Services, Inc., 11501 Georgia Avenue, Silver Springs, MD 20902.

Directory of Foreign Freight Forwarders, Budd Publications, Inc., 107 South Tyson Avenue, Floral Park, NY 11001.

Distribution Cost Analysis, Small Business Bibliography No. 34, Small Business Administration, Washington, DC 20416 (or from nearest SBA office).

Dun & Bradstreet Reference Book of Transportation, Dun & Bradstreet, Inc., 99 Church Street, New York, NY 10007.

Industrial Logistics: Analysis and Management of Physical Supply and Distribution System, by John F. Magee, McGraw-Hill Book Company, Inc., 1221 Avenue of the Americas, New York, NY 10020.

Inventory Control, Small Business Bibliography, Small Business Administration, Washington, DC 20416 (or from nearest SBA office).

Management of Traffic and Physical Distribution, by Charles A. Taff, Richard D. Irwin, Inc., 1818 Ridge Road, Homewood, IL 60430.

Motor Freight Directory, G. R. Leonard & Company, 2121 Shermer Road, Northbrook, IL 60062.

National Distribution Directory, Local and Short Haul Carriers National Conference, 1621 O Street NW, Washington, DC 20036.

National Highway & Airway Carriers & Routes, National Highway Carriers Directory, 925 W. Jackson Boulevard, Chicago, IL 60607.

Official Airline Guide, Reuben H. Donnelley Publications, 2000 Clearwater Drive, Oak Brook, IL 60521.

Official Guide of the Railways, National Railway Publication Company, 424 West 33rd Street, New York, NY 10001.

Official Motor Carrier Directory, Official Motor Carrier Directory, Inc., 1130 South Canal Steet, Chicago, IL 60607.

Official Motor Freight Guide, Official Motor Freight Guide, Inc., 1130 South Canal Street, Chicago, IL 60607.

Physical Distribution and Marketing Logistics: An Annotated Bibliography, American Marketing Association, Suite 606, 222 South Riverside Plaza, Chicago, IL 60606. (Listing of information sources on service, facility location, information flow, inventory management, handling, storage, and warehousing).

Physical Distribution Management, by Donald J. Bowersox, Edward W. Smykay, and Bernard J. LaLonde, Macmillan Publishing Company, Inc., 60 Fifth Avenue, New York, NY 10011.

Scientific Inventory Management, by Joseph Buchan and Ernest Koenigsberg, Prentice-Hall, Inc., Englewood Cliffs, NJ 07632.

Site Selection Handbook, Conway Research, Inc., 2600 Apple Valley Road NE, Atlanta, GA 30319.

Warehousing, Small Business Bulletin, Small Business Administration, Washington, DC 20416 (or from nearest SBA office).

Magazines

Air Cargo Guide, Travel & Transportation Services Division, Reuben H. Donnelley Corporation, 2000 Clearwater Drive, Oak Brook, IL 60521.

Air Forwarder, Travel & Transportation Services Division, Reuben H. Donnelley Corporation, 200 Clearwater Drive, Oak Brook, IL 60521.

American Import and Export Bulletin, North American Publishing Company, 401 North Broad Street, Philadelphia, PA 19108.

American Motor Carrier Directory, American Trucking Associations, Inc., Box 13446, 351 Monroe Place NE, Atlanta, GA 30324.

Brandon's Shipper & Forwarder, Brandon's Shipper & Forwarder, Inc., 1 World Trade Center, Suite 1927, New York, NY 10048.

Cargo Airlift, Reuben H. Donnelley Corporation, 2000 Clearwater Drive, Oak Brook, IL 60521.

Custom House Guide, North American Publishing Company, 401 North Broad Street, Philadelphia, PA 19108.

Distribution Worldwide, Chilton Company, Chilton Way, Radnor, PA 19089.

Exporters' Encyclopedia, Dun & Bradstreet, International Div., Dun & Bradstreet, Inc., 99 Church Street, New York, NY 10007.

Handling & Shipping, Industrial Publishing Company, 614 Superior Avenue, West, Cleveland, OH 44113.

Material Handling Engineering, Industrial Publishing Company, 614 Superior Avenue, West, Cleveland, OH 44113.

Modern Materials Handling, Cahners Publishing Company, Inc., 221 Columbus Avenue, Boston, MA 02116.

Shipping Digest, Shipping Digest, Inc., Room 551, Cunard Building, 25 Broadway, New York, NY 10004.

Traffic Management, Cahners Publishing Company, Inc., 221 Columbus Avenue, Boston, MA 02116.

Transportation and Distribution Management, Traffic Service Corporation, 815 Washington Boulevard, Washington, DC 20005.

Associations

Air Traffic Conference of America, 1000 Connecticut Avenue NW, Washington, DC 20036.

Air Transport Association of America, 1000 Connecticut Avenue NW, Washington, DC 20036.

American Chain of Warehouses, 250 Park Avenue, New York, NY 10017.

American Society of Traffic & Transportation, 547 West Jackson Boulevard, Chicago, IL 60606.

American Warehousemen's Association, 222 West Adams Street, Chicago, IL 60606.

National Association of Shippers Advisory Boards, c/o American Association of Railroads, Room 320, 1920 L Street NW, Washington, DC 20036.

UNITED STATES TRADE CENTER SOURCES (INTERNATIONAL)

Beirut

U.S. Regional Trade Development Office (temporarily located), c/o Commercial Section, American Embassy, 91 Vasilissis Sophias Boulevard, Athens, Greece.

Cologne

U.S. International Marketing Center, Bahnhofstrasse 1–9 ABC Haus, D 5000 Koeln, Germany.

UNITED STATES TRADE CENTER SOURCES (INTERNATIONAL)

London

U.S. International Marketing Center, American Chancellery, 24/31 Grosvenor Square, London, W1A 1AE, UK.

Mexico City

U.S. Trade Center, 31 Liverpool, Mexico 6 D.F., Mexico.

Milan

U.S. International Marketing Center, Via Gattamelata 5, 20149 Milan, Italy.

Moscow

U.S. Commercial Office, Ulitsa Chaykovskogo 15, Moscow, USSR.

Paris

U.S. International Marketing Center, 123 Avenue Charles de Gaulle, 92200 Neuilly, Paris, France.

São Paulo

U.S. Trade Center, Avenida Paulista 2439, Edificio Eloy Chaves, CEP 01311, São Paulo, Brazil.

Singapore

U.S. International Marketing Center, Ground Floor, Malayan Credit House, 96 Somerset Road, Singapore 9, Singapore.

Sydney

U.S. International Marketing Center, 4 Cliff Street, Milson's Point, Sydney, NSW 2061, Australia.

Taipei

U.S. Trade Center, 261 Nanking East Road, Section 3, Taipei, Taiwan.

Tehran

U.S. Trade Center, 61 Elizabeth Boulevard, P.O. Box 50, Tehran, Iran.

Tokyo

U.S. International Marketing Center, 1-1, Higashi, Ikebukuro, 3-Chome Toshima-ku, Tokyo 170, Japan.

Vienna

U.S. Trade Development Support Office, Friedrich Schmidt Platz 2, Vienna 1, Austria.

Warsaw

U.S. Trade Development Center, Ulica Wiejska 20, Warsaw, Poland.

INTERNATIONAL TRADE SOURCES

Reference Book for World Traders. Croner Publications, 211–05 Jamaica Avenue, Queens Village, NY 11428. A market guide covering every country of the world. A loose-leaf service kept up-to-date by monthly supplements. List of contents includes: Advertising agents, cargo superintendents and warehouses, credit information, customs brokers, freight forwarders, export documentation and consular fees, as well as market research and service organizations. One-year subscription: $45; plus $4.95 postage and handling in the United States and Canada.

Trade Directories of the World. Published by Croner Publications, 211–05 Jamaica Avenue, Queens Village, NY 11428. A loose-leaf service kept up-to-date by monthly supplements. Contains approximately 3500 directories from 175 nations covering 687 categories. Contains cross-referencing, countries index, trade and professions and has a general export and import index. One-year subscription: $35; $3.95 postage and handling in the United States and Canada.

U.S. DEPARTMENT OF COMMERCE SOURCES

(INDUSTRY AND TRADE ADMINISTRATION)

Albuquerque, NM 87102, 505 Marquette NW. #1015 (505) 766–2386.
Anchorage, AK 99501, 632 Sixth Avenue, Hill Building, Suite 412. (907) 265–5307.
Atlanta, GA 30309, Suite 600, 1365 Peachtree Street NE. (404) 881–7000.
Baltimore, MD 21202, 415 U.S. Customhouse, Gay and Lombard Streets. (301) 962–3560.
Birmingham, AL 35205, Suite 200–201. 908 South 20th Street (205) 254–1331.
Boston, MA 02116, 10th Floor, 441 Stuart Street. (617) 223–2312.
Buffalo, NY 14202, Room 1312, Federal Building, 111 W. Huron Street. (716) 842–3208.
Charleston, WV 25301, 3000 New Federal Office Building, 500 Quarrier Street. (304) 343–6181, ext. 375.
Cheyenne, WY 82001, 6022 O'Mahoney Federal Center, 2120 Capital Ave. (307) 778–2151.
Chicago, IL 60603, Room 1406, Mid-Continental Plaza Building, 55 E. Monroe Street. (312) 353–4450.
Cincinnati, IL 45202, 10504 Federal Office Building, 550 Main Street. (513) 684–2944.
Cleveland, OH 44114, Room 600, 666 Euclid Avenue. (216) 522–4750.
Columbia, SC 29204, Forest Center, 2611 Forest Drive. (803) 765–5345.
Dallas, TX 75202, Room 7A5, 1100 Commerce Street. (214) 749–1515.
Denver, CO 80202, Room 165, New Custom House, 19th and Stout Streets. (303) 327–3246.
Des Moines, IA 50309, 609 Federal Building, 210 Walnut Street. (515) 284–4222.
Detroit, MI 48226, 445 Federal Building, 231 W. Lafayette (313) 226–3650.
Greensboro, NC 27402, 203 Federal Building, West Market Street, P.O. Box 1950. (919) 378–5345.

U.S. DEPARTMENT OF COMMERCE SOURCES

Hartford, CT 06103, Room 610, B, Federal Office Building, 450 Main Street. (203) 244–3530.

Honolulu, HI 96850, 4106 Federal Building, 300 Ala Moana Boulevard, P.O. Box 50026. (808) 546–8694.

Houston, TX 77002, 2625 Federal Building Courthouse, 515 Rusk Street. (713) 226–4231.

Indianapolis, IN 46204, 357 U.S. Courthouse & Federal Office Building, 46 E. Ohio Street. (317) 269–6214.

Los Angeles, CA 90049, Room 800, 11777 San Vicente Boulevard. (213) 824–7591.

Memphis, TN 38103, Room 710, 147 Jefferson Ave. (901) 521–3213.

Miami, FL 33130, Room 821, City National Bank Building, 25 West Flagler Street. (305) 350–5267.

Milwaukee, WI 53202, Federal Building/U.S. Courthouse, 517 East Wisconsin Avenue. (414) 224–3473.

Minneapolis, MN 55401, 218 Federal Building, 110 South Fourth Street. (612) 725–2133.

Newark, NJ 07102, Gateway Building 4th floor, Market St. & Penn Plaza, (201) 645–6214.

New Orleans, LA 70130, Room 432, International Trade Mart, 2 Canal Street. (504) 589–6546.

New York, NY 10007, Federal Office Building, Thirty-seventh floor, 26 Federal Plaza, Foley Square. (212) 264–0634.

Omaha, NB 68102, 1815 Capitol Avenue, Capitol Plaza, Suite 703A. (402) 221–3665.

Philadelphia, PA 19106, 9448 Federal Building, 600 Arch Street. (215) 597–2850.

Phoenix, AR 85073, 2950 Valley Bank Center, 201 North Central Avenue. (602) 261–3285.

Pittsburgh, PA 15222, 2002 Federal Building, 1000 Liberty Avenue. (412) 644–2850.

Portland, OR 97204, Room 618, 1220 S.W. Third Avenue (503) 221–3001.

Reno, NV 89503, 777 West 2nd Street, Room 120. (702) 784–5203.

Richmond, VA 23240, 8010 Federal Building, 400 N. 8th Street. (804) 782–2246.

St. Louis, MO 63105, 120 South Central Avenue. (314) 425–3302.

Salt Lake City, UT 84138, 1203 Federal Building, 125 South State Street. (801) 524–5116.

San Francisco, CA 94102, Federal Building, Box 36013, 450 Golden Gate Avenue. (415) 556–5860.

San Juan, PR, 00918, 659 Federal Building. (809) 753–4555.

Savannah, GA 31402, 235 U.S. Courthouse and Post Office Building, 125–29 Bull Street. (912) 232–4321, ext. 204.

Seattle, WA 98109, 706 Lake Union Building, 1700 Westlake Avenue North (206) 442–5615.

APPENDIX 4

PRESS RELEASE INFORMATION FORMS

The following press release information forms should help you compile information on the subject of your press release.

Case History Report. (From *Marketing Problem Solver* by Cochrane Chase and Kenneth L. Barasch. Copyright © 1977 by the authors. Reprinted with permission of the publisher, Chilton Book Co., Radnor, PA.)

Information from this form helps us prepare accurate case histories and magazine articles for media use. When you've answered all questions please return this sheet to _____(your address.)_____
The details you provide will answer the five journalistic "W"'s: who, what, where, when, why, plus how. PLEASE PRINT OR TYPE. DO NOT WRITE.
Fill in each blank. Use "N/A" (not applicable) only if logical comment is impossible. Please provide as much information as you can. Elaborate. Give specific sizes, weights, lengths, etc. As you fill this out, think, "What would a reader be most interested in knowing about this application." Thank you for your help.

WHO?

Your company: _____
Division or branch office: _____ Main product/service _____
Your name: _____ Phone number _____
Title: _____
Name of company you served in this application: _____
Address: _____
Person there you worked with: _____ His title _____
Mailing address: _____ Phone number: _____
List companies, individuals, etc. who must approve a completed case history or feature article prior to publication: _____

WHAT?

In simple, declarative sentences state briefly what product/service you provided. Be specific: _____
_____
_____
_____
_____

What exact customer need did you fill? This information is essential. Pinpoint your answer: _____
_____
_____
_____
_____

Describe the way the customer's product/system operated prior to this application: _____
_____
_____
_____
_____

How did you improve this condition? Elaborate _____
_____
_____

WHERE?

Name specific city, location, address, proximity to well-known landmarks, etc. relevant to this application: _____
Give name of particular unit or system in which your product/service was applied (i.e. valve, boiler, electronic or fluid-handling system, pier, etc): _____

Describe your product's exact location in the unit or system. Use specifics: _____
_____
_____

Define the main function(s) of the customer's unit and/or entire system. Give a complete narrative description: _____
_____
_____
_____
_____

Give a summary of what your product/service contributed to the unit or system's end result. This is vital information. Answer fully: _____
_____
_____
_____
_____

242

Now, describe this whole case history completely, in the simplest and easiest-to-understand way you can: _____

WHEN?
(1) Give the date this application of your product/service was completed: _____ (2) Is it still in operation? _____ (3) How long will it last? _____ (4) How long before it becomes obsolete? _____ (5) Give any significant or interesting details regarding the above: _____

WHY?
(1) What caused the consumer to choose your product/services? Was it price? Availability? What, then? Be frank in your answer. (2) Was it uniquely suited to his needs? (3) Could he have used a competitor's product as well? If not, why? Please number and answer each of these questions here: _____

Approximately how many firms could have provided similar products/services? Name all that you know of: _____

Name your direct competitors: _____

HOW?
(1) In this application, did designing, production, installation, etc. pose any unique problems to you that might be of interest to designers, engineers, your other customers, or the general public? (2) Was a custom design necessary? If so, discuss it. (3) If this product/service application was part of a larger project, explain its function as a component of the end result. (4) Was this a new market for your company? Number and answer each of these questions in detail: _____

Draw your own diagram of the completed installation. Attach the drawing to this sheet. Be sure to show your product/service's relationship to other parts of the system. Display it in a way that clearly illustrates its value to the customer. Do not merely attach a blueprint, unless you can provide explicit collateral explanation.

Attach pertinent photographs, diagrams, additional explanations, descriptions, etc., so that a detailed article, ready for publication, could be developed directly from the information provided here. Please carefully review your finished report.

Thank you for taking the extra care to write a good case history.

Your signature: _____

243

Personal History Questionnaire. (From *The Publicity and Promotion Handbook*, by Linda Carlson. Copyright © 1982 by CBI Publishing Co., Inc. All rights reserved.)

```
Complete and return to the Public Relations Department.

Full name _____ Nickname _____

Home address _____

Business address _____

_____ Phone _____

Present job title _____

Brief summary of responsibilities _____
_____

To whom do you report? _____

Operation/Division _____

Location _____

Date of original employment with us _____

Other positions you've held with us:

       Position             Operation              Dates

    _____     _____        _____
    _____     _____        _____
    _____     _____        _____
    _____     _____        _____


Positions you've held with other employers:

       Position              Company               Dates

    _____     _____        _____
    _____     _____        _____
    _____     _____        _____
    _____     _____        _____

Professional associations to which you belong:
_____
_____
_____
_____
```

Personal History Questionnaire   Continued

Education:

Institution	Degree Conferred	Graduation Date
_____	_____	_____
_____	_____	_____
_____	_____	_____

Date of birth _____ Birthplace _____

If married, spouse's name _____

Names of children _____

_____

I'd like press releases written about me sent to these publications
(include alumni paper and hometown paper if desired):

Name	Address
_____	_____
_____	_____
_____	_____
_____	_____

I authorize the Public Relations staff to use this information in producing press releases.

_____
Signature

_____
Date

APPENDIX 5

MARKETING GLOSSARY

The following glossary represents excerpts from *Dictionary of Marketing Terms*, by Irving J. Shapiro, 4th ed., 1981, published by Littlefield, Adams & Company, Totowa, NJ.

ADDED SELLING The attempt to sell additional products and/or services to a customer who has just made a purchase. A valid aspect of salesmanship.

ADDITIONAL MARKUPS In the retail accounting method, increases that raise the prices of merchandise above original retail.

ADD-ONS In retailing, the additional purchases added to the account of a charge account CUSTOMER before the previous balance in the account has been fully paid.

ADVERTISING A nonpersonal, paid message of commercial significance about a product, service, or company made to a MARKET by an identified sponsor. It is the aspect of the selling function that can pave the way for the salesman's activity. It has recently become common to include messages promoting ideas and causes. Contrary to popular belief, advertising can cause people to act only in a manner to which they were predisposed. Advertising *can* cause the realization and recognition of wants not previously known to the market, and it can lead directly to the sale where personal contacts are not involved.

ADVERTISING AGENCY A specialist organization which prepares COPY and LAYOUT, studies MARKET, selects media, works on advertising strategy and campaigns, and performs the physical production aspects of the advertisement in preparation of the medium's requirements.

ADVERTISING MEDIUM The class of vehicle by means of which the advertiser's message is carried to its audience. Commonly considered to the advertising media are: newspapers, billboards, car-cards, magazines, radio, point-of-purchase displays, television, direct mail, advertising specialties, house organs, and TRADE SHOWS. This list is intended to be illustrative rather than inclusive. Advertising media are often classified into (1) print media, (2) broadcast media, and (3) position media.

ADVERTISING NETWORK A group of ADVERTISING AGENCIES, noncompeting and independently owned, who agree to exchange ideas and services in the interests of their clients.

ADVERTISING NOVELTY A small, interesting, sometimes personally useful item with the name and the advertising message of the issuing company printed on it.

ADVERTISING SUBSTANTIATION The documentation advertisers must be able to supply to the FTC in support of their claims made in their ADVERTISING, and must also be able to show that this formed the base on which the advertising was constructed.

ADVERTISING THEME A central thought of an advertising campaign conveyed to the audience in a way to prove the superiority of the benefits of the product or service or idea offered. May be applied to a single advertisement.

AFFILIATE An independent broadcast station that agrees to carry programs provided by a network.

AFFILIATED STORE (1) A retail store that is part of a voluntary chain or a franchise. (2) A retail store operated under a name other than that of the controlling store.

AFTER-MARKET The potential sales associated with the requirements of owners after they have bought a piece of equipment (e.g., repair and replacement parts).

ALLOWANCE A grant made by a manufacturer to a wholesaler or by a wholesaler to a retailer for rendering services usually linked to some form of ADVERTISING or other promotion. May be accomplished by a reduction in the purchase price on a percent basis.

ANTICIPATION DISCOUNT An extra amount in addition to the cash discount allowed if the bill is paid before the expiration of the cash discount period. Usually the extra amount is calculated on the basis of an annual rate of percent agreed upon in advance, just as in the instance of an interest rate. Either the total bill amount or the net amount after cash discount may be specified as the base for an anticipation discount.

APPEAL Direction of a sales effort toward a motive, designed to activate that motive, and to stir a potential buyer toward the goal of purchase of the product or acceptance of an idea.

AUDIENCE PROFILE A DEMOGRAPHIC description of the people exposed to an advertising medium or vehicle.

AUDIENCE RATING The percent of all listeners in the MARKET that a particular radio station gets at a given time. See AUDIENCE SHARE.

AUDIENCE SHARE The number of listeners a radio station has at any time compared to the total potential listening audience. See AUDIENCE RATING.

AUTHORIZED DEALER A retailer accepted by a manufacturer to be permitted to sell a particular item or group of items under a plan of exclusive distribution or selective distribution. This arrangement may be similar to franchising, and in fact such dealers are said to have a "franchise to sell the manufacturer's products."

BANDWAGON EFFECT People are buying a product because others are buying it. Demand is increased by the desire to conform or to be fashionable. The slope of the demand curve may be positive if this effect continues through a situation of rising price of the product. *See* LAW OF DEMAND.

BLEED (1) Extending an illustration to one or more edges of a printed page, leaving no margin. Designated as one-, two-, three-, and four-side bleed. (2) Running the design on a poster panel right to the molding without any blanking at top or sides. (3) Unwanted wandering of camera image into wrong areas.

BLISTER PACK A way of packaging in which a preformed hollow of plastic holds merchandise to a card. Used mainly for relatively small items.

BOILER PLATE Pages in stereotype, sometimes including news and advertisements, supplied to small weeklies by news syndicates to help cut the cost of composition.

BOLDFACE TYPE A typeface which prints so that it stands out prominently. Generally has thicker lines than that usually found in the body of copy. In contrast to lightface type.

BOUNCE-BACK An additional offer sent with a self-liquidator. Sometimes several related items are offered. May be effective for increasing total sales.

BUYING POWER (1) The ability of a CONSUMER to acquire goods and services. (2) The capacity of a firm to purchase in large quantities and thereby obtain concessions in price, deliveries, packaging, and other marketing-related advantages.

BUYING POWER INDEX A relative measure of the effective buying power of a segment of the MARKET, published annually by *Sales & Marketing Management* magazine. It provides an approximate value of the ability of an area to purchase CONSUMER GOODS. For example, if area A has a BPI of 0.012, its market potential is double that of area B which as a BPI of 0.006. Most applicable to mass products sold at popular prices. Other products need more discriminating factors, the farther they are from the mass market.

CAMERA-READY COPY that is prepared so that without further processing it can be used to create plates needed for offset printing.

CAVEAT EMPTOR The Latin phrase which means "let the buyer beware." It denotes the philosophy that the buyer had better take care what he is getting because once the sale is made, the buyer will have no recourse. *See* CAVEAT VENDITOR

CAVEAT VENDITOR The Latin phrase which means "let the seller beware."

CHANNEL OF DISTRIBUTION The course taken by the title to goods as it moves from producer to CONSUMER through middlemen. For some products, the channel has been so shortened that the producer acts himself as a middleman, selling directly to a user.

CIRCULATION (1) The number of copies of a publication distributed. May be counted as paid and unpaid. (2) Used loosely to refer to the number of homes regularly tuned to a certain broadcast station. (3) The number of persons who have an opportunity to observe a TRANSIT ADVERTISING display during a stated period. Reported by rider, measured by the fare box; and by exposure. A rider is one person riding an inside-display-carrying vehicle for one trip. Exposures equal the total number of persons exposed to displays on the outside of the vehicle.

CIRCULATION RATE BASE The CIRCULATION that a magazine guarantees as a minimum. Should the circulation drop below this consistently, the publisher will make pro rata refund.

CLASSIFIED ADVERTISING One of the two broad divisions of ADVERTISING in newspapers and some magazines. It appears in special columns on pages where the advertising is assembled by product or service. Usually the selection of typefaces and sizes is very limited, as is the freedom of LAYOUT. The other broad division is DISPLAY ADVERTISING. See CLASSIFIED DISPLAY ADVERTISING

CLASSIFIED DISPLAY ADVERTISING Some newspapers offer special sections devoted to only one product or service, e.g., Real Estate, in which the LAYOUT and the elements of the advertisement are virtually unlimited, as in other parts of the paper. Advertising in these sections combines the freedom of DISPLAY ADVERTISING with the grouping advantages of CLASSIFIED ADVERTISING.

COLLATERAL MATERIALS Items of an ADVERTISING nature, such as catalogs specification sheets, and the like, not exposed to an audience through the usual advertising media. They are often included in the listing of media as specific, separate types.

COLUMN-INCH A unit of measurement in a print medium of more or less regular issue, one deep and one column wide, whatever the actual width of the column.

COMBINATION RATE (1) A special rate granted in connection with two or more periodicals owned by the same publisher. Usually, the same space and COPY must be used in each. (2) A favorable time rate from two or more associated stations in one geographic area when all those stations are used together.

CONSIGNEE (1) The holder of goods under consignment terms. (2) The one to whom a shipment of goods is addressed.

CONSIGNMENT (1) A stock of merchandise advanced to a dealer and located at his place of business, but with title remaining in the source of supply. (2) A shipment of goods to a CONSIGNEE.

CONSUMER (1) A person who purchases for personal or household use. (2) Anyone who uses up the utilities embodied in goods or services. In MARKETING, one must consider the motives and habits inferred in (1), and at the same time take into account the influence of (2). Industrial and institutional purchasers should be called users.

CONSUMER ANALYSIS The study of the CONSUMER using appropriate marketing research techniques to establish as many psychological, sociological, and DEMOGRAPHIC understandings as possible considering available time and resources.

CONSUMER GOODS (1) Goods bought for personal or household satisfactions. (2) Goods used directly in satisfying human wants. See CONSUMER.

CONSUMER JURY A method of pretesting products or advertisements by getting the reactions of potential purchasers or users.

COOPERATIVE ADVERTISING (1) A way of attempting to induce local advertising by a middleman of a manufacturer's product, in which the manufacturer offers to pay some portion (most commonly 50%) or all of the cost of the middleman's advertisements in local media. The contract usually specifies that any advertisement must have the prior approval of the manufacturer. Frequently used also by wholesalers, especially to promote a private brand. (2) The promotion carried out jointly by firms in an industry through a trade assocation. (3) A joint venture in ADVERTISING by two or more firms.

COPY In a broad sense, all verbal and visual elements which are included in a finished advertisement. Used more narrowly to designate the verbal elements only. The latter is probably more common.

CUSTOMER Someone who has bought a certain product or service from a source. Most often thought of as being a repeater. A customer may be a prospect for a product or service he has never before bought from that source.

CUT (1) The engraving used to reproduce a printed illustration. (2) To delete portions of COPY or program material. (3) An abrupt stop in a broadcast program. (4) An instant switch from one television picture to another without fading.

DEMOGRAPHICS The statistics of an area's population, or a MARKET, with distinguishing characteristics such as age, sex, income, education, marital status, occupation, etc., delineated. Includes all vital statistics.

DIRECT MAIL ADVERTISING That ADVERTISING which asks for the order to be sent by mail. Delivery of the order is by mail. Also the medium which delivers the advertising message by mail. Provides greatest control of direction to a MARKET, flexibility of materials and processes, timeliness of scheduling, and personalization. Its biggest problem is getting the recipient's attention. A part of direct advertising.

DISPLAY ADVERTISING (1) Usually associated with newspapers, this is the advertising which appears in areas other than in classified sections, which have little or no restrictions on LAYOUT or typeface. See CLASSIFIED ADVERTISING, CLASSIFIED DISPLAY ADVERTISING (2) ADVERTISING pieces designed to be self-supporting, such as a window display, or to be mounted on a wall or a background.

EMBOSSING A method of printing using two dyes to raise the printed surface above the rest of the sheet. Sometimes used without ink to raise a name or a TRADEMARK.

FACING (1) A shelf stock one unit wide extending to the top and back of a shelf in a display. Used to determine space allocation for packaged items in a retail store. Example: a facing for canned asparagus might be two cans high and five cans deep for a total of ten cans. (2) Designates the direction of a poster face in relation to the flow of traffic. For example, to be read by westbound traffic, the panel must be facing east.

FAIR CREDIT REPORTING ACT A national law effective April 25, 1971, which is designed to protect people from erroneous credit information exchanged among credit agencies, banks, corporations, and others. The law gives an individual the right to examine the information in his file, to have it deleted if found inaccurate, file a report of his side of the story if reinvestigation does not settle the problem, and to have previous recipients of his file informed of any deletions and additions. In general, any adverse information, except bankruptcy, more than seven years old may not be reported.

FAIR PACKAGING AND LABELING ACT A federal law authorizing the FTC and the FDA to move against, among other things: use of misleading pictorial or verbal matter on labels; omission of ingredients, net quantity and size of serving from labels; misleading package shape and size; and employment of "cents off" deals except on a short-term basis. The FTC has issued a guide defining the permissibility of the use of "cents off" deals.

FLOOR STOCK In general, all merchandise accessible to CUSTOMERS of a store. Sometimes applied more narrowly to merchandise which is displayed by units other than shelves (e.g., suits, dresses, refrigerators).

FOUR-COLOR PROCESS The photoengraving process for reproducing color illustrations by a set of four plates, one each for yellow, blue, red, black. The sequence of printing varies with the subject.

FOUR P'S The major ingredients of a marketing mix as designated in one pattern of analysis. They are: *product*, the right one for the target MARKET; *place*, all the considerations and institutions involved in getting the right product to the target market; *promotion*, communication of all sorts to the target market about the product; and *price*, determination of the price which is the happy balance of maximum attractiveness to the market and capability of enabling the firm to reach its revenue and profit objectives.

GALLEY PROOFS Proofs on sheets printed from the type as it stands in the galley trays before being separated into pages. Errors are correctable most easily at this stage.

GENERIC LABEL An innovation in the food industry in which the product's undecorated package carries a label identifying the contents without brand connection. The label is usually unadorned, with minimum required data.

GENERIC NAME The name by which a certain type of product is identified, as distinguished from its brand name (e.g., petroleum jelly is generic, Vaseline petroleum jelly is a brand name). Unless precautions are taken, brand names may become generic, in which case anyone may use them because they then are considered the identifier of the type of product. In this way the word "aspirin" which was the property of Bayer became generic and may now be used by anyone to describe the basic chemical.

GUARANTY A statement by a seller in which he promises to do certain things should the item bought not perform as specified or prove to be defective in some way within a certain time after being put into use. Now generally used to mean the same as *warranty*. Federal legislation is needed to make consistent among all guarantors the elements to be publicized. Some progress towards this end has been achieved.

HALFTONE A photoengraving plate photographed through a glass screen inserted in the camera to break the picture into dots. Screens vary from 45 to 300 lines to the inch. The more lines in the screen, the finer the reproduction of the subject's pictorial values. Coarse screens, 65- to 85-line, are used on rough paper such as is found in newspapers. The finer screens are used in magazines using smooth papers. The dots, massed in the denser parts of the picture and scattered in the lighter parts, permit the printing of tones such as are found in a photograph. Used for color as well as black-and-white.

IMPULSE ITEM A product which has a high appeal for a customer but which is an unplanned purchase. There is really no such thing as a group of impulse items, but only impulse buying, because any item may be subject to this by some customer at any time. Alert retailers try to arrange their merchandise in such a way as to encourage impulse buying.

INSERT (1) A special page or ADVERTISING unit, often on special paper or cut to a special shape, printed by an advertiser and forwarded to a publisher for binding into a publication. (2) Envelope stuffer. (3) A special advertisement included loose within a newspaper. (4) Promotional material included in a mailing, such as a coupon or a sample of the product. (5) Interchangeable COPY or art signs which fit into a holder.

INSERTION ORDER An authorization from an advertiser or agency for a publisher to print an advertisement of a specified size on a given date at an agreed rate.

LAW OF DEMAND A basic relation in economics which states that the quantity demanded per period is negatively related to price. It is based on these assumptions: a rational CONSUMER with full knowledge of alternative goods, limited purchasing power, and a drive to maximize the utility accruing to him.

LAW OF DIMINISHING RETURNS This states that in most business situations, after a certain point has been reached, successive applications of input factors will add less to total product than each preceding application. If this progresses far enough, total product may decrease absolutely as well as relatively. The point at which total product begins to increase at a decreasing rate is known as the Point of Diminishing Returns. Same as the Law of Diminishing Marginal Productivity.

LAW OF DISUSE One of the laws of learning, it states that if a response to a stimulus is not to be lost, the stimulus must continue to recur. Of real significance to advertisers. See LAW OF EFFECT.

LAW OF EFFECT One of the laws of learning, it states that when a response or series of responses leads to a satisfying state, the connection between the situation and the response is strengthened, while other responses not so satisfying are weakened and made less probable of recurrence. Important to marketers as an insight into how brand loyalty may be built. See LAW OF USE, LAW OF DISUSE.

LAW OF USE One of the laws of learning, it states that as a given situation is frequently followed by a response or group of responses, the bond between the stimulus and the response becomes stronger as it is exercised. Leads to habit formation and the remembering of ideas conveyed. Useful in ADVERTISING and in salesmanship applications. See LAW OF DISUSE, LAW OF EFFECT.

LAYOUT (1) A working drawing showing how an advertisement or a publication is to look. (2) The appearance of the finished advertisement as a whole. (3) The arrangement of fixtures or departments in a store. (4) The arrangements of units in an office. (5) In transit advertising, a line drawing of the COPY scaled to fit the differently proportioned posters being used.

LOGO (1) Musical or sound signature used by an advertiser to identify himself to the audience of a broadcast medium. (2) Brief form for LOGOTYPE.

LOGOTYPE The signature plate or standard name plate of an advertiser. Same as LOGO.

MAIL-ORDER A way of selling goods by receiving and filling orders by mail. This type of MARKETING system owes its stimulus to the origination of the parcel post service.

MAKE-READY The activity involved in mounting and preparing artwork and/or COPY for photographing or reproduction.

MANUFACTURERS' AGENT A functional middleman characterized by his rendering services similar to those of a salesman, by his restriction to a limited territory, by limited authority to make terms, and by offering to finance his principals only under unusual circumstances.

MARKET The totality of those who can benefit from the producer's product or service and who can afford to buy it. More technically: a sphere within which price-making forces operate, and in which exchanges of title tend to be accompanied by the actual movement of the goods affected.

MARKETING All business activities necessary to effect transfers of ownership of goods from producers to CONSUMERs except those normally regarded as manufacturing operations. An examination of the marketing functions will reveal that these activities begin long before the offerings are put into the actual supply mode, and to insure the CUSTOMER's satisfaction they continue long after the actual sale has been closed. In the field of services, all those activities required to make the services desirable and available to those who can benefit from their use and have the purchasing power to acquire them. In recent years the same activities as those used for goods and services have been applied to ideas, political candidates, and social philosophies. Because of the dynamic nature of marketing, all techniques employed are necessarily under continuous development.

MASTHEAD That part of a page in a publication which contains the official heading of the publication, names of key personnel, and in some instances information about the publication's policies.

MAT Short form for: Matrix. An advertisement or a portion of an advertisement in mold form that the medium can use to reproduce the advertisement in a form suitable for printing. It resembles baked cardboard in appearance.

NARRATIVE COPY Usually verbal, but may be a combination of verbal and pictorial elements, this is an imaginative approach to the reader, listener, or viewer which presents a story about how the product or service played an important role in the life of someone with whom a member of the audience can identify. This type of COPY generally consists of four parts: the predicament or problem being faced, the discovery of the solution (provided by the product or service), the happy ending, and the transition, which ends with a direct suggestion to the audience. Once again the product or service has resolved a conflict! This technique is much used in television commercials. Essentially the same as slice-of-life commercial.

OUTDOOR ADVERTISING An advertising medium in which the message is not delivered to the audience as it is with those media which enter the home, but the units are, rather, placed in strategic locations where they can be seen by an audience on the move. Messages in this medium must be brief and easy to read and grasp because the average viewer is exposed to the message for a few seconds only.

PAGE PROOF A rendering of type and plates arranged as they are to appear finally. Usually made after the GALLEY PROOF has been shown and corrected.

PASS-ALONG READERSHIP   While technically this term applies to total people who read a publication through having acquired access to it by means other than as the purchaser, this term is often used to mean essentially the same as pass-along circulation.

PLATE   A term applied in a general way to any unit used to make a printed impression, usually of an illustration with its accompanying captions, by any method of printing.

POINT-OF-PURCHASE (POP) ADVERTISING   Signs and displays at the point of final sale. POP is very flexible as to permanency, format, position, location. Its greatest problem is persuading the dealer to use it. Much of this problem is caused by the advertiser's failure to determine in advance the realistic probability of the dealer's being *able* to use the piece as the advertiser intends.

PRODUCT DEVELOPMENT   A very complex MARKETING activity, not with characteristics common to many companies, but generally encompassing initial development, subsequent change to reflect new ideas, and the determination of new applications.

PRODUCT DIFFERENTIATION   The situation in which two products of similar characteristics and end use, usually made by different producers, acquire divergent images in the minds of segments of the MARKET. Ordinarily comes about through promotional activities by the respective producers.

PRODUCT LIABILITY   Whereas negligence by manufacturers and distributors was formerly held to be the required grounds for damages, recent court cases have introduced the concept of strict liability, which holds manufacturers, sellers, wholesalers, or retailers, equally liable for customer injury without the need by the complainant to prove negligence.

PRODUCT MANAGER   In a firm organized according to the marketing concept, a person charged with planning and coordinating all activities pertinent to the successful introduction and continuous profitable sale of one product, or a series of very closely related products, to the target market. Because this person is not vested with authority, he can discharge his responsibilities only through his powers of persuasion, backed by the implied edict of higher echelons for the necessary interdepartmental cooperation. Essentially the same as Brand Manager, Project Manager.

PRODUCT PLANNING   The company activity which involves the screening and appraisal of an idea, analysis of the MARKET, and the development and testing of a product before production is commmitted. Although specific organization for this effort varies from company to company, it is almost uniformly recognized as belonging in the top management echelons.

PRODUCT POSITIONING   The attempt by marketers to achieve the acceptance by target markets of their products as better fulfilling specific wants, or having specific characteristics superior to competing brands.

PROFESSIONAL PUBLICATION   A periodical addressed to those persons who are able to influence the use of the advertiser's offering in connection with discharging the duties of their callings (e.g., physicians, dentists, teachers, bankers).

PUBLICITY   Unpaid exposure to the MARKET, by an unnamed source, of commercially significant information about a product or company.

PUBLIC RELATIONS   A planned program of policies and conduct designed to build confidence and increase the understanding of one or more of a firm's publics. These publics may be classified as: (1) customers, (2) suppliers, (3) competitors, (4) employees, (5) stockholders, (6) creditors, (7) local community, (8) the government. It should be noted that these are *not* mutually exclusive.

PUSH OR PULL DISTRIBUTION STRATEGY   If *push*, it will have been decided to attempt to convince the wholesaler that it will be advantageous for him to carry the item, then he in turn will attempt to convince the retailer, who in turn will attempt to convince the CONSUMER of the product's merit. If *pull*, it will have been decided to attempt to create DEMAND directly with the consumer through various forms of promotion with the expectation that the consumer will ask the retailer for the item, who in turn will ask the wholesaler, who will order it from the maker. Combination is possible.

RATE CARD   An issue piece of one unit of the advertising media giving the space or time rates, the mechanical requirements data, and other pertinent information specified by the unit.

RATE DIFFERENTIAL   The difference between the higher rate charged by advertising media to national as compared to local advertisers, in some cases as much as double. Because of the controversy which has arisen over the ethics of this practice, many newspapers and other local media have adopted rate schedules that do not discriminate.

REGISTER   Perfect correspondence in printing, as evidenced by correct superimposition of each plate in color printing so that the colors mix properly.

REGISTER MARKS   Cross lines placed in the margin of COPY so that when plates are made for the various colors, REGISTER may be easily achieved by perfect alignment of the printing.

RESIDUAL   An additional fee paid to the talent used in a program or commercial each time the unit is run over a number agreed upon for the first fee. These are generally governed by union agreements. Should be anticipated in developing an ADVERTISING BUDGET because residuals may add up to significant sums.

SEGMENTATION   Division of a MARKET into subgroups with similar motivations. May be a tactic to increase product acceptance by recognizing product appeals, but there is a danger of overconcentration in a particular segment to which selling effort is applied to the extent that the firm is blinded to other possibilities. The most widely used bases for segmenting a market are: DEMOGRAPHICS, geographics, personality, use of product, psychographics, preference, attitudes, values, and benefits. Usually a coarser division than fragmentation.

SHOPPER (1) A publication consisting mainly of advertisements by local merchants, sent free to a controlled list intended to provide saturation coverage of a relevant area. (2) A person engaged in search activity.

SHOPPING GOODS The type of item for which reasonable alternates exist and which the CONSUMER usually wishes to purchase only after comparing price, quality, and style in a number of sources.

SHOTGUN APPROACH A way of trying to accomplish an objective by spraying a large amount of activity over a broad area (e.g., advertising aimed at everyone, which can end up hitting no one).

SHRINK-WRAP A way of covering or packaging something by using a strong, impervious material which shrinks tight around the object when heat is applied. Devices have been developed which can accommodate large items, such as unit loads. An item so covered avoids the need for other weather protection. An item which does not require boxing as a protective device may be shipped so covered, attached to a pair of blocks for fork-lift handling purposes.

SILK SCREEN A method of printing which uses a screen made of a textile of strong fiber. The material is made impervious where ink should not penetrate, thus forming a stencil. When ink is pressed through the screen, the design is printed on the subject. Lends itself well to color operations.

SOCIAL CLASSES Groups of people who are more or less equal to one another in prestige and community status; they readily and regularly interact among themselves formally and informally; and they share the same goals and ways of looking at life. W. Lloyd Warner and Associates have distinguished among six social classes, now widely accepted:

1. *Upper-Upper* or "Social Register" consists of locally prominent families, usually with at least second- or third-generation wealth. Basic values: living graciously, upholding family reputation, reflecting the excellence of one's breeding, and displaying a sense of community responsibility. About ½ of 1% of the population.

2. *Lower-Upper* or "Nouveau Riche" consists of the more recently arrived and never-quite-accepted wealthy families. Goals: blend of Upper-Upper pursuit of gracious living and the Upper-Middle drive for success. About 1½% of the population.

3. *Upper-Middle* are moderately successful professional men and women, owners of medium-sized businesses, young people in their twenties and early thirties who are expected to arrive at the managerial level by their middle or late thirties. Motivations: success at a career, cultivating charm and polish. About 10% of the population.

4. *Lower-Middle* are mostly nonmanagerial office workers, small business owners, highly paid blue-collar families. Goals: respectability and striving to live in well-maintained homes, neatly furnished in more-or-less "right" neighborhoods, and to do a good job at their work. They will save for a college education for their children. Top of the "Average Man World." About 30–35% of the population.
5. *Upper-Lower* or "Ordinary Working Class" consists of semiskilled workers. Although many make high pay, they are not particularly interested in respectability. Goals: enjoying life and living well from day to day, to be at least modern, and to work hard enough to keep safely away from the slum level. About 40% of the population.
6. *Lower-Lower* are unskilled workers, unassimilated ethnics, and the sporadically employed. Outlooks: apathy, fatalism, "get your kicks whenever you can." About 15% of the population, but have less than half of the purchasing power.

Note that these classes are not entirely homogeneous. They include subgroups many of which overlap the class lines as shown due to considerable upward or downward mobility. For a discussion of the marketing significance of these classes see the still fresh: Richard P. Coleman, "The Significance of Social Stratification," in *Marketing and the Behavioral Sciences*, Perry Bliss, ed. (Boston: Allyn and Bacon, Inc., 1962) pp. 156–171.

SPACE CONTRACT An agreement between the advertiser and the publisher on the rate structure for the publication. After agreement on the probable amount of space to be used, billing will be made currently on the rate for the amount as though it had actually been earned, with an accurate accounting to be made at the end of the contract period.

SPECIALTY GOODS The category specifying an item which has such an attraction for a CONSUMER that he will go considerably out of his way to buy it. Applies also to an item for which no reasonable substitute exists and which provides benefits which are in demand.

STORE LAYOUT Actually part of the store design, it is specifically the allocation of space to each selling and nonselling department of a store. Part of this thinking involves aisle width and arrangement. One arrangement is known as a *grid pattern*, in which the aisles are placed at right angles to one another, permitting maximum standardization of fixtures. The other arrangement is known as *free flow layout*, in which there is usually little or no regularity of aisle pattern. Arrangements within departments often use a *wandering aisle* (i.e., an aisle that is formed by the placement of movable fixtures). Such an arrangement may be found quite commonly in women's wear departments' areas in department stores.

STORE TRAFFIC The flow of customers into and throughout a store. Placement of merchandise in various store areas must take into account the natural and the desired pattern of customer movement to and from these areas.

STORY BOARD   A parallel sequence of sketches and COPY of the video and the audio portions of a television program or commercial. It is actually a "LAYOUT" for this medium.

SUBHEADLINE   A restatement of the idea of interest to the reader in a different and more specific way than appears in the headline. Generally placed in the COPY immediately following the headline. Same as subcaption.

SUGGESTED RETAIL PRICE   The list price of an item announced by a producer as the reasonable price to be charged by a retailer. Care must be exercised that the making of such a suggestion does not violate our antitrust laws.

SUPERGRAPHICS   A method of identifying a building by using stripes and rolling balls to move the eye toward wall-size letters on the building's exterior.

SUPERIMPOSE   An effect used in television commercials which allows lettering to appear over the scene. The letters may be still or moving. Very effective in presenting the TRADEMARK and the slogan of the product while the scene is still on.

TAG   The short message presented by a local announcer at the end of a commercial that was recorded. It usually includes the address of the local retailer and other pertinent information.

TAKE-ONES   Coupons, postcards, brochures, and the like, attached to, or placed in pockets attached to, inside TRANSIT ADVERTISING pieces. The passenger who is so inspired by the advertisement tears off or takes out a take-one to request more information or receive a benefit connected with the product or service advertised.

TARGET   (1) The one to whom a selling message is addressed. (2) A MARKET in which a selling effort is made. (3) The MARKETING objective toward which organization resources are directed.

TEAR SHEETS   Copies of advertisements torn from publications, sent to advertisers for checking and as proof that the advertisements were run.

TEST MARKETING   The new product and its marketing program are tried out in a small number or representative customer environments. Validity is subject to various problems, such as competition's activities, total cost of testing, and representativeness of the locale to the rest of the MARKET.

TIE-IN SALE   An additional sale made to a customer who has already been sold another product or service. Usually an item related in use in some way to the other.

TRADEMARK   Any word, name, symbol, device, or any combination of these adopted and used by a manufacturer or merchant to identify his goods and distinguish them from those of others. It is a brand name used on goods *moving in the channels of trade*. Rights in a trademark are acquired only by use, and the use ordinarily must continue if the rights are to be preserved. That provision is made to register a trademark in the Patent Office does not imply that such registration in itself creates or establishes any exclusive rights. However, registration is recognition by the government of the right of the owner to use the mark in commerce to distinguish his goods from those of others. Brand is the everyday term; TRADEMARK is the legal counterpart. Trademarks are registered for twenty years and may be renewed every twenty years thereafter if not abandoned, cancelled, or surrendered.

TRADE NAME A name that applies to a business as a whole. The same name may be used to identify a product, when it will be a TRADEMARK, too.

TRADE PAPER A publication addressed to those who buy for resale, featuring information on how they can do business more effectively in certain lines, thereby increasing profit. ADVERTISING in a trade paper almost invariably is devoted to assuring dealers how profit can be enhanced by handling the advertised products.

TRADE SHOW An event organized in some large, central place which allows a large number of suppliers to convene at one time to show their wares to CUSTOMERs and prospects.

TRANSIT ADVERTISING An advertising medium designed primarily to present the advertiser's message to an audience which is enroute from one point to another in a vehicle of public transportation, or which is exposed to vehicles carrying passengers from one point to another. The top SMSA markets account for over 600 million monthly rides. An advertisement in this medium is often designed much like a full page in a magazine because the average ride is relatively long, 22.5 minutes.

VELOX Trade name for a photographic print incorporating halftone screen dots, and from which a line engraving can be made. Costs less than the regular HALFTONE process, but for some applications may be less sharp.

VERTICAL INTEGRATION Acquisition of a company operating at a different level in the CHANNEL OF DISTRIBUTION than the acquiring company, the CONSUMER considered as the base. It is *backward* if the acquired company is farther away from the consumer, *forward* if nearer to the consumer.

APPENDIX 6

BANK OF AMERICA SMALL BUSINESS REPORTER

Portions of Bank of America, *Small Business Reporter*, Advertising Small Business, Vol. 13, No. 8, 1976, 1978, 1982, reprinted with permission of Bank of America, N.T. & S.A.

Small Business Reporter

Advertising Small Business

BANK OF AMERICA

Advertising Small Business

In 1981, American business spent more than $61 billion on advertising. A good share of those expenditures was made by large firms; the nation's largest single advertiser, Procter & Gamble, spent close to $671 million in 1981 on advertising.

In contrast, the small business owner generally has only a modest sum to invest in advertising. To compete with the larger firms for customers, the small firm must make every advertising dollar go as far as possible. The entrepreneur must learn the mechanics of setting up an advertising program—choosing from among the available media, comparing the costs of each to find the best buy, and, eventually, understanding the workings of the industry and the ways in which advertising can be used to help the small business succeed.

With experience, the business person will come to recognize that advertising is no magical force, one that in some mystic way ensures success for any enterprise. In fact, many experts claim that nothing kills a bad product faster than good advertising. Sometimes, money can even be wasted by advertising good products. If the business is poorly run or if the sales people are rude or uninformed, then money that might be spent on advertising should be used instead to improve these aspects. Once that is done, the business owner can begin to set the goals for the company's progress and to develop an advertising program that will help achieve those goals.

An advertising program needn't be expensive to succeed. The small advertiser can take heart from the knowledge that some of the nation's corporate giants began their advertising ventures with decidedly modest budgets: Procter & Gamble—the king—spent $11,500 the first year; Campbell Soups, $4,000; Borden's, $500; and Wrigley's Gum, $30. With advertising dollars as with any other expenditure, it's not how much is spent, but how well.

COPYRIGHT © BANK OF AMERICA NT&SA 1976, 1978, 1981, 1982
PRODUCED BY MARKETING PUBLICATIONS, DEPARTMENT #3120

What Is Advertising?

Advertising is, according to the American Marketing Association, "mass, paid communication the purpose of which is to impart information, develop attitudes, and induce favorable action for the advertiser." The means of this communication can be as humble as a matchbook, as traditional as a barber's pole, or as elaborate as a celebrity-packed television commercial.

Advertising, strictly speaking, is not a goodwill gesture, though building goodwill can be a valid objective of an advertising effort. Donating money, time, or services to community organizations, for instance, does not come under the heading of advertising in a company's budget, nor do such things as the cost of customer services or remodeling the store. The last, however, can certainly be used as grist for advertising, and it would be the lax business owner who did not take advantage of the opportunity to promote such improvements.

Why Advertise?

The specific purposes of advertising are as many and varied as the products and services promoted, but in general they fall into three categories:
☐ Promoting consumer awareness of the business and its products or services;
☐ Stimulating sales directly; and
☐ Establishing or modifying a firm's image in the public eye.

The first purpose—promoting consumer awareness—applies as much to established vendors as to newcomers. For instance, a store may have stayed in the same place for 30 years, but in that time the store's products and its customers have been changing constantly. New people have moved into the community and probably new competitors have opened. If an established business is to keep or expand its share of the market, an aggressive advertising policy could be one of the best tools at hand.

For the business in the throes of change, advertising can smooth the way. For example, the owner of an independent stationery store had carried used typewriters as a sideline for many years. Then he decided to include new electric typewriters as well as a selection of electronic office machines. By changing his product line, he changed his primary market. Students and letter writers had been his best customers for stationery and used typewriters, but the new machines had as their primary market local businesses.

To prepare for his entrance into the new market, the store owner designed a direct mail campaign aimed at selected companies in the trading area, and he followed up the mailing with personal calls and visits. The result: When the new typewriters and office machines appeared in the store, new customers were already interested in buying them.

Even in times of general economic recession, advertising has its value. In fact, the results of one large survey indicate that advertising in recession periods is especially vital. Of the businesses surveyed since 1958, those that maintained their advertising budgets at prerecession levels, or increased their advertising spending, came out of recessions in better market positions than they had been in before the hard times started.

Creating an Advertising Program

A small business entrepreneur who wants to take advantage of the benefits of advertising won't have the budget to go about it in the same manner as giant companies do; nevertheless, plans for advertising follow the same initial procedure, whether the ad budget is $1,000 or $100,000. The first step in creating an advertising program is to thoroughly assess the business, its products or services, and its competitors. The results can be surprising, says a successful advertising consultant. "One owner of a women's wear shop considered her merchandise to be in the 'moderate' price range. However, because her advertising concentrated on prices and didn't mention quality, it turned out that the public thought of her shop as a cut-rate place," he recalls. "When she started emphasizing quality and stylishness in her ads, she got a whole new group of customers." Most advertising experts recommend that new advertisers start by developing a customer profile. For example, a retailer would ask:
☐ What kinds of people buy from me?
☐ What are their annual incomes?
☐ How far away from the store do they live?
☐ How old are they?
☐ What are their shopping habits?
☐ How do they perceive my product, store, or service?

Answers to these questions can be obtained from the different customer records a business keeps—order slips, charge account files, the lists used to send direct mailings to favorite customers—and simply by observing customers.

One straightforward approach is to develop a questionnaire for distribution directly to customers. As one veteran advertising professional noted, "You wouldn't believe the number of business people I deal with who have no concrete idea who their best customers are. When they start going over their customer questionnaires, frequently they're amazed at the picture that emerges."

Once the firm's customers have been described, the business owner can begin to analyze the company's competitors. Some questions to ask are:
☐ Who are my main competitors in this trading area?
☐ What is my share of the market in relation to the competition?
☐ Why would a customer choose my firm over the competition?
☐ What kind of advertising does the competition do? How much do they spend?

This analysis will help the owner define the company's advertising goals. Specific goals will differ with each enterprise, but some typical objectives might be to:
☐ Increase store traffic;
☐ Acquaint customers with new products;
☐ Promote special events like clearance sales or a new store location;
☐ Change the image of the company;
☐ Keep the business's name before the public;
☐ Tell customers about special services available, such as credit plans, free alterations, or delivery services;
☐ Introduce new employees to the public;
☐ Tie in with manufacturers' national promotions of brand-name merchandise;
☐ Capitalize on the seasonal nature of a product;
☐ Offer incentives to "get acquainted"; and
☐ Give specific data on products and prices.

Over the course of a year, an individual business may have more than one of these goals. However, one goal will usually be the most important to the success of the company. Owners should be as specific as possible when defining goals.

Establishing the Budget

Once advertising goals have been established, the prospective advertiser can begin work on the budget. No matter what the size of the budget or how its distribution is determined, experts offer one universal bit of advice: Consider the advertising budget as a fixed expense, like the rent or utility bills, and not as a luxury to be given up at the first sign of lean times. Professionals all agree that to be effective, advertising must be well conceived, well executed, and consistent.

Budgeting Methods

Using the "all we can afford" approach to budgeting implies that advertising is a luxury and that any difficulty in making ends meet will be solved by borrowing from the advertising budget or cutting it out altogether. The "matching the competition" method of budgeting, by definition, is a defensive rather than aggressive posture, and one that fails to take into account the particular needs of each enterprise. The most practical approaches to budgeting advertising include the percentage of sales method and the objective and task method.

The Percentage of Sales Method. This system involves setting a fixed total amount for annual advertising, then dividing that amount into shares for each advertising medium. This common and often successful approach to budgeting has some drawbacks.
☐ Arriving at a correct percentage for a particular operation is tricky work. Even within a single field, what may be a perfectly adequate advertising budget for one business is woefully small for another.
☐ A percentage figure based on the previous year's sales could be considered regressive, since one of the goals of business is to do better each year—yet a percentage figure based on projected sales for the coming year may be too optimistic.

When using the percentage method, the advertiser must consider all the variables involved, such as the competition, a change in location, or an expansion of the product line.

The Objective and Task Method. Following this procedure, the business owner first determines the company's advertising needs and objectives, then calculates how much it will cost to achieve those goals. Marketing and advertising professionals generally prefer this method because the advertising dollar is spent where it is needed most and has the best chance of making a big impact on sales.

However, a danger exists that the plan will be too ambitious for the money available. In that case, the objectives must be reconsidered and the plan scaled down to fit budget realities or the time frame to meet the objectives must be expanded.

Planning the Advertising Schedule

Firm intentions, closely defined goals, and a coherent marketing approach provide the groundwork for an advertising program. The next step is to develop an advertising schedule with specific media selections and dollar amounts for each.

A rule of thumb for evaluating media costs is to consider that 80 percent of the total amount allotted will be for space or time. Space costs are those paid for running an ad in a newspaper, magazine, or outdoor medium; time costs are those paid to air a commercial on radio or television. The remaining 20 percent will be spent on actual production of the advertisement.

However, actual percentages vary considerably depending on the advertising medium. A television commercial, for instance, may cost at least as much to produce as it does to broadcast once or twice. On the other hand, a newspaper ad may be prepared from mats and copy supplied free from a manufacturer, so the cost of the advertisement would be entirely in its publication.

The calendar is a valuable tool when planning an advertising schedule. Such a calendar should be large enough to accommodate all information about media schedules, costs, and the firm's other activities such as in-house promotions, special events, and sales. Thus, the advertiser can tell at a glance the shape and direction of the advertising program and, if running dollar totals are kept at the bottom of each sheet, the state of the ad budget. (One month from such an advertising calendar appears on page 5.)

To begin a calendar, the advertiser first enters all traditional and anticipated business activities, including community events such as "Dollar Days," seasonal events such as back-to-school and graduation, holidays such as Mother's Day, and important promotional opportunities such as the opening of a new store or the launching of a new product line.

Then peak and slump periods for the particular business must be determined. Trade associations and industry and business publications, as well as the sales records of the firm itself, can supply this information.

The most effective advertising is coordinated with the swings of the business cycle. Advertising expenditures should be higher in the periods when sales are good, enabling the business to capture its full share of the market, and lower when sales are off, so that money will not be wasted on a season with reduced sales potential.

However, the spending reduction in slack times should not be in direct proportion to the drop in sales. The advertiser must still do a relatively strong job of bidding for a share of the tighter market. Whenever the sales and advertising volumes are not fairly close together, the business is missing opportunities to sell.

The overall advertising budget should include a reserve fund, equal to about 10 to 15 percent of the gross budget, for contingencies. This fund allows the business owner to take advantage of unforeseen events such as a special sale or bargain prices. The reserve also might be used in the event of unanticipated media rate increases or a stiffening in the competition.

Selecting Advertising Media

Advertisers use several criteria to select specific media and to determine how much of each is to be used.

Trading Area. The corner delicatessen and the manufacturer of an industrial product will have vastly different trading areas. A medium such as television probably would not be suitable for either, but the delicatessen owner is likely to have success with local media, such as newspapers, shoppers, flyers, window posters, or transit advertising. On the other hand, the manufacturer with a national market may find a business, trade, or special-interest publication effective.

Customer Type. A record store might reach its teenage audience most efficiently through radio, while a building maintenance service can best communicate with property owners and managers through business publications, direct mail, and listings in directories.

Budget Restrictions. If the annual advertising budget is less than several thousand dollars, television would be an unlikely medium for extensive use.

Continuity of Advertising Message. If the product or service is very specialized and the market fairly restricted, advertising at the same level throughout the year in directories or special-interest magazines might be the best approach. If the business owner stresses constant low prices and uses a high-pressure approach, advertising volume and frequency usually are higher than for a lower-keyed operator. For a business as seasonal as a ski resort, advertising will be concentrated in the period preceding the season, continue through its peak, and drop off at the season's end.

The frequency rate that produces the best results is an elusive figure that varies from medium to medium. For instance, one advertising agency executive believes that an ad in a monthly business publication must be run at least six times a year in order to be effective. And it's generally considered that a commercial broadcast on radio or television only once is of virtually no value—unless the offer is extraordinary.

Media Combinations. Many advertisers choose to use more than one medium. This is a valid advertising technique, but it's most effective when the firm's budget is large enough to allow adequate frequency in all media used. In addition, the advertising message must be consistent in all media, so that consumers will recognize the firm's advertising wherever they encounter it.

ADVERTISING SMALL BUSINESS

WINSTON HARDWARE
Advertising Budget

JUNE

SUNDAY	MONDAY	TUESDAY	WEDNESDAY	THURSDAY	FRIDAY	SATURDAY
	Advertising budget for June: 10% of sales = $725.00 Co-op funds = 140.00 Reserve fund = 50.00 Total = $915.00	**1** RADIO: 3 30-sec. spots Flag Sale Cost - $60	**2** NEWSPAPER: 100 lines. Flag Sale Cost - $70 ($50 from reserve)	**3** RADIO: 3 30-sec. spots Flag Sale Cost - $60 Open Tonight	**4** NEWSPAPER: 100 lines Housewares for Brides Cost - $70 Open Tonight	**5**
6	**7**	**8** RADIO: 3 30-sec. spots Flag Sale Cost - $60	**9**	**10** RADIO: 3 30-sec. spots Flag Sale Cost - $60 Open Tonight	**11** NEWSPAPER: 200 lines workbench for Father's Day Cost - $140 ($70 from Co-op) Open Tonight	**12**
13	**14** FLAG DAY	**15** DIRECT MAIL: To all charge account customers: Sprinkler Systems Cost - $45	**16**	**17** Open Tonight	**18** NEWSPAPER: 200 lines Hand tools for Father's Day Cost - $140 ($70 from Co-op) Open Tonight	**19**
20 FATHER'S DAY	**21** FIRST DAY OF SUMMER	**22**	**23** NEWSPAPER: 100 lines. Camping Equipment Cost - $70	**24** Open Tonight	**25** NEWSPAPER: 100 lines Camping and Picnic Equipment Cost - $70 Open Tonight	**26**
27	**28**	**29**	**30** NEWSPAPER: 100 lines 4th of July needs Cost - $70	Advertising expenditures as of 6/30: $3,425.00 Balance of general ad budget: $4,000.00 Balance of reserve ad budget: $700.00		

SMALL BUSINESS REPORTER

Sources of Further Information

Associations

American Advertising Federation
251 Post Street, Suite 302
San Francisco, CA 94108
(415) 421-6867

1225 Connecticut Avenue, N.W.
Washington, DC 20036
(202) 659-1800

American Association of Advertising Agencies, Inc.
8500 Wilshire Boulevard, Suite 502
Beverly Hills, CA 90211
(213) 657-3711

666 3rd Avenue
New York, NY 10017
(212) 682-2500

American Business Press, Inc.
205 East 42nd Street
New York, NY 10017
(212) 661-6360

Direct Mail/Marketing Association
6 East 43rd Street
New York, NY 10017
(212) 689-4977

Institute of Outdoor Advertising
342 Madison Avenue
New York, NY 10173
(212) 986-5920

Magazine Publishers Association, Inc.
Bureau of Advertising
575 Lexington Avenue
New York, NY 10022
(212) 752-0055

National Association of Advertising Publishers
313 Price Place, Suite 12
Madison, WI 53705
(608) 233-5306

National Retail Merchants Association
100 West 31st Street
New York, NY 10001
(212) 244-8780

Newspaper Advertising Bureau
311 California Street, Suite 902
San Francisco, CA 94104
(415) 981-8118

5670 Wilshire Boulevard, Suite 1110
Los Angeles, CA 90036
(213) 933-8526

485 Lexington Avenue
New York, NY 10017
(212) 557-1800

Point-of-Purchase Advertising Institute, Inc.
60 East 42nd Street
New York, NY 10017
(212) 682-7041

Radio Advertising Bureau, Inc.
5900 Wilshire Boulevard, Suite 22060
Los Angeles, CA 90036
(213) 936-5515

485 Lexington Avenue
New York, NY 10017
(212) 599-6666

Specialty Advertising Association, International
1404 Walnut Hill Lane
Irving, TX
(214) 258-0404

Television Bureau of Advertising, Inc.
6380 Wilshire Boulevard, Suite 1711
Los Angeles, CA 90048
(213) 653-8890

485 Lexington Avenue
New York, NY 10017
(212) 661-8440

Standard Rate and Data Service
5201 Old Orchard Road
Skokie, IL 60077
(312) 470-3100

The Transit Advertising Association, Inc.
60 East 42nd Street
New York, NY 10017
(212) 599-2352

Publications

Advertising for Modern Retailers
by Shirley F. Milton
Fairchild Books and Visuals
New York, NY, 1974

How to Get Big Results from a Small Advertising Budget
by Cynthia S. Smith
Dutton Press
New York, NY, 1973

100 Books on Advertising
by Robert Haverfield
University of Missouri
Columbia, MO, 1976

APPENDIX 7

NATIONAL DIRECTORIES FOR USE IN MARKETING

"National Directories for Use in Marketing" by the U.S. Small Business Administration gives a listing of directories arranged by industry. It includes bibliographical and ordering information about each publication.

U.S. Small Business Administration
Management Assistance Office
Support Services Branch

Small Business Bibliography
Number 13

SBA

National Directories for Use in Marketing

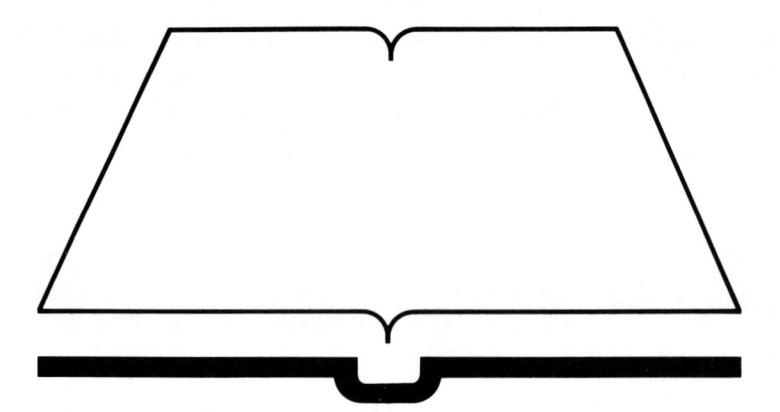

Revised March 1980
Reprinted November 1981

This edition of *National Directories for Use in Marketing* **is a complete revision and replaces all previous editions of** Small Business Bibliography No. 13. **The selected titles are of primary interest to those seeking directories of business firms that buy goods for resale. However, the selected references offer information helpful to those who purchase or sell specific types of merchandise and services. Although only national directories are listed, sources for obtaining local lists are included.**

Space limits the number of listings that can be selected; omission of a publication, therefore, implies no slight to the author. Prices of publications and their availability are subject to change without notice. Publishers and others are invited to notify SBA of relevant publications for possible inclusion in future revisions of this Bibliography.

Dr. Lloyd M. DeBoer, **the author, is Dean, School of Business Administration, George Mason University, Fairfax, Virginia.**

Directories of various kinds offer valuable information for small business owners who need to keep abreast of the variety of services and products in today's complex marketplace. Such directories help the small manufacturers to keep current on the names and addresses of distributors who can reach the markets for their products.

Keeping current is a continuing process because of three key factors:

1. The entry and exit of firms.

2. The shift in importance among different types of outlets—new ones arise, such as mass market merchandisers, while older firms lose their market position.

3. An increase in scrambled merchandising—where stores begin to carry lines of merchandise not customarily carried by them.

While emphasis has been placed on directories of firms who buy goods for resale, other purchasers of goods and services will be interested in some of the directories listed. For instance, persons needing to locate manufacturers of specific kinds of goods in connection with purchasing or in order to sell them directly industrial supplies, components, or materials, should refer to the following major sources: *MacRae's Blue Book* and *Thomas' Register of American Manufactuers*. These two directories are listed under "Manufacturers" in this *Bibliography*. Also included are directories of some professions and organizations that purchase goods for their own use.

Local Listings

Only national directories are listed in this *SBB*. Those who desire mailing lists for specific local areas should consult mailing-list houses, telephone directories, research departments of newspapers, chambers of commerce, and associations situated in the localities for which the directories are desired. Also, many publishers of national directories are able to furnish some local lists.

Locating Sources of National Lists

To find directories and listings not referenced in this *SBB*, check the following sources. Some of the selected directories, as well as the locating guides, are available for reference in public and university libraries.

Mailing lists. A major use of directories is in the compilation of mailing lists. Attention, therefore, is directed to Klein's *Directory of Mailing List Houses*—see listing under "Mailing List Houses."

Trade associations and national organizations. For those trades or industries where directories are not available, membership lists of trade associations, both national and local, are often useful. For names and addresses of trade associations, consult the following directory source—available at most business reference libraries: *Encyclopedia of Associations, Vol. I., National Organizations of the United States*, Gale Research Co., Book Tower, Detroit, Mich. 48226. Published annually, 13th edition, 1979, $80. Lists, trade, business, professional, labor, scientific, educational, fraternal, and social organizations of the United States, includes historical data.

Business periodicals. Many business publications, particularly industrial magazines, develop comprehensive specialized directories of manufacturers in their respective fields. Name and addresses of business periodicals are listed (indexed by name of magazine and by business fields covered) in *Business Publication Rates and Data* published monthly by Standard Rate and Data Service, 5201 Old Orchard Road, Skokie, Ill. 60077. Also, for listings of periodicals by subject index, consult the *Standard Periodical Directory* and for a listing by geographical areas, refer to *Ayer Directory of Publications*. Most libraries have one or more of these directories for reference.

American directories. Another source is *Guide to American Directories,* 10th edition, 1979, $45 a copy. Published by B. Klein Publications, P.O. Box 8503, Coral Springs, Fla. 33065.

F & S Index of Corporations and Industries. It is available in most libraries. Indexes over 750 financial, trade, and business publications by corporate name and by SIC code. Published by Predicasts Inc., 200 University Circle Research Center, 11001 Cedar Ave., Cleveland, Ohio 44106.

The Public Affairs Information Service. Available in many libraries, is published weekly, compiled five times a year and put into an annual edition. This is a selective subject list of the latest books, Government publications, reports, and periodical articles, relating to economic conditions, public conditions, public administration and international relations. Published by Public Affairs Information Service, Inc., 11 West 40th St., New York, N.Y. 10018.

Directories

The following selected national directories are listed under categories of specific business or general marketing areas in an alphabetical subject index. When the type of directory is not easily found under the alphabetical listing of a general marketing category, such as "jewelry," look for a specific type of industry or outlet, for example, "department stores."

Apparel

Fur Source Directory, Classified, 1979-80. Annually in June. 1979. $5. Alphabetical directory of fur manufacturers in New York City area classified by type of fur; name, address, and telephone numbers for each. Also, lists pelt dealers, fur cleaners, fur designers, resident buyers and brokers and those engaged in fur-repairing, processing, and remodeling. Fur Vogue Publishing Co., 127 West 30th St., New York, N.Y. 10001.

Hat Life Year Book (Men's). Annual, 1979. $4. Includes classified list of manufacturers and wholesalers of men's headwear. Hat Life Year Book, 551 Summit Ave., Jersey City, N.J. 07306.

Knit Goods Trade, Davison's. Annual. 88th Edition, July 1979. $35 postage paid. Lists manufacturers of knitted products, manufacturers' agents, New York salesrooms, knit goods wholesalers, chain store organizations, department stores with names of buyers, discount chains, brokers and dealers, and rack jobbers. Davison Publishing Co., P.O. Drawer 477, Ridgewood, N.J. 07451.

Men's & Boys' Wear Buyers, Nation-Wide Directory of (Excludes New York Metropolitan area). Annually in November. 1980. $60. More than 20,000 buyers and merchandise managers for 5,000 top department, family clothing and men's and boys' wear specialty stores. Telephone numbers, buying office, and postal zip code given for each firm. Also available in individual State editions. The Salesman's Guide, Inc., 1140 Broadway, New York, N.Y. 10001. Also publishes *Metropolitan New York Directory of Men's and Boys' Wear Buyers*. Semiannually in May and November. $15 for both. (Lists same information for the metropolitan New York area as the nationwide directory.)

Teens' & Boys' Outfitter Directory. Semiannually in April and October. (Pocket size.) $2-per issue. Lists manufacturers of all types of apparel for boys and students by category, including their New York City addresses and phone numbers; also lists resident buying firms for out-of-town stores, and all trade associations related to boys' wear. The Boys' Outfitter Co., Inc., 71 West 35th St., New York, N.Y. 10001.

Women's & Children's Wear & Accessories Buyers, Nationwide Directory of (Excludes New York Metropolitan Area.) Annually in February. 1980. $60. Lists more than 25,000 buyers and divisional merchandise managers for about 5,000 leading department, family clothing and specialty stores. Telephone number and mail zip code given for each store. Also available in individual State editions. The Salesman's Guide, Inc., 1140 Broadway, New York, N.Y. 10001.

Appliances, Household

National Buyer's Guide 1980. Annual. $25. Lists manufacturers and distributors in home electronics, appliances, kitchens. Gives the products they handle, the territories they cover, and complete addresses for each distributor. Dealerscope, 115 Second Avenue, Waltham, Ma. 02154

Arts and Antiques

American Art and Antique Dealers, Mastai's Classified Directory of. Lists 20,000 art museums, with names of directors and curators; art and antique dealers; art galleries; coin, armor, tapestry and china dealers in the United States and Canada. Mastai Publishing Co., 21 E. 57th St., New York, N.Y. 10022.

Automatic Merchandising (Vending)

NAMA Directory of Members. Annually in July. 1979. $75 non-members. Organized by State and by city, lists vending service companies who are NAMA members. Gives mailing address, telephone number, and products vended. Also includes machine manufacturers and suppliers. National Automatic Merchandising Association, 7 South Dearborn St., Chicago, Ill. 60603.

Automotive

Automotive Affiliated Representatives, Membership Roster. Annual. 1979. Free to firms seeking representation. Alpha-geographical listing of about 400 member firms including name, address, telephone number, territories covered, and lines carried. Automotive Affiliated Representatives, 625 South Michigan Ave., Chicago, Ill. 60611.

Automotive Directory of Manufacturers and Their Sales Representatives, National. Annual. 1980. $15. Alphabetical arrangement of manufacturers serving automotive replacement market. Where available, includes names and addresses of each manufacturers' representative showing territory covered. W. R. C. Smith Publishing Co., 1760 Peachtree Rd. N.W., Atlanta, Ga. 30357.

Automotive Warehouse Distributors Association Membership Directory. Annually. $50. Includes listing of manufacturers, warehouse distributors, their products, personnel and territories. Automotive Warehouse Distributors Association, 1719 W. 91st Place, Kansas City, Mo. 64114.

Auto Trim Resource Directory. Nov. edition; annual issue of *Auto Trim News* (monthly; $7.50 a year; $1.00 a copy; Directory $5.) Alphabetical listing of name, address, and telephone number of auto trim resources and wholesalers who service auto trim shops. Has directory of product sources—listed by product supplied—with name and address of firm. Auto Trim News, 1623 Grand Ave., Baldwin, N.Y. 11510.

Credit and Sales Reference Directory. Three times annually. Available only to supplier-manufacturers on annual fee basis. Contains lisitings of 17,000 automotive distributors in the United States and Canada. Data include name and address of companies, and other pertinent information. Motor and Equipment Manufacturers Assn., NEMA Service Corp., 222 Cedar Lane, Teaneck, N.J. 07666.

Home Center, Hardware, Auto Supply Chains. Annually. 1979. $92. Lists headquarter addresses, telephone numbers, number and type of stores and locations, annual sales volume, names of executives and buyers. Chain Store Guide Publications, 425 Park Ave., New York, N.Y. 10022.

Jobber Topics Automotive Aftermarket Directory. Annual. Lists 7,000 automotive warehouse distributors, automotive rebuilders, manufacturers agents, automotive jobbers, associations, and manufacturers. The Irving-Cloud Publishing Co., 7300 N. Cicero Ave., Lincolnwood, Chicago, Ill. 60646.

Aviation

World Aviation Directory. Published twice a year. Spring and Fall, 79-80 edition. $50 per copy in U.S. and Canada. Other countries $55. Gives administrative and operating personnel of airlines, aircraft, and engine manufacturers and component manufacturers and distributors, organizations, and schools. Indexed by companies, activities, products, and individuals. Ziff-Davis Aviation Division, 1156 15th St., N.W., Washington, D.C. 20005.

Bookstores

Book Trade Directory, American. Annual. Updates bimonthly. 1979. Lists retail and wholesale booksellers in the United States and Canada. Entries alphabatized by State (or province), and then by city and business name. Each listing gives address, telephone numbers, key personnel, types of books sold, subject specialties carried, sidelines and services offered and general characteristics. For wholesale entries gives types of accounts, import-export information and territory limitations. Edited by the Jaques Cattell Press. R. R. Bower Company, 1180 Avenue of the Americas, New York, N.Y. 10036.

Multiple Book Store Owners, Directory of. Annually. $25. Lists over 1,000 chains of book stores by state, city, and alphabetically by store within each city. Oldden Mercantile Corp., 560 Northern Blvd., Great Neck, N.Y. 11021.

Building Supplies

Building Supply News Buyers Guide. Annually. Classified directory of manufacturers of lumber, building materials, equipment, and supplies. Cahners Publishing Co., 5 S. Wabash Ave., Chicago, Ill. 60603.

Business Firms

Dun & Bradstreet Middle Market Directory. Annually in October. 1979. Lists about 31,000 businesses with networth between $500,000 and $1,000,000. Arranged in three sections: alphabetically, geographically, and product classification. Gives business name, state of incorporation, address, telephone number, SIC numbers, function, sales volume, number of employees, and name of officers and directors. Marketing Services Division, Dun & Bradstreet, Inc., 99 Church St., New York, N.Y. 10007.

Dun & Bradstreet Million Dollar Directory. Annually in January. 1979. Lists about 46,000 businesses with a net worth of $1,000,000 or more. Arranged in four sections: alphabetically, geographically, line of business, and officers and directors with the same information as detailed in the preceding entry. Marketing Services Division, Dun & Bradstreet, Inc., 99 Church St., New York, N.Y. 10007.

Buying Offices

Buying Offices and Accounts, Directory of. Annually in March. 1980. $30. Approximately 230 New York, Chicago, Los Angeles, Dallas and Miami Resident Buying Offices, Corporate Offices and Merchandise Brokers together with 11,000 accounts listed under its own Buying Office complete with local address and alphabetically by address and buying office. The Salesman's Guide, Inc., 1140 Broadway, New York, N.Y. 10001.

China and Glassware

American Glass Review. Glass Factory Directory Issue. Annually. Issued as part of subscription (13th issue) to *American Glass Review.* $15 a year. Lists companies manufacturing flat glass, tableware glass and fiber glass, giving corporate and plant addresses, executives, type of equipment used. Ebel-Doctorow Publications, Inc., 1115 Clifton Ave., Clifton, N.J. 07013.

China Glass & Tableware Red Book Directory Issue. Annually. Issued as part of subscription (13th issue) to *China Glass & Tableware.* $12 a year. Lists about 1,000 manufacturers, importers, and national distributors of china, glass, and other table appointments, giving corporate addresses and executives. Ebel-Doctorow Publications, Inc., 1115 Clifton Ave., Clifton, N.J. 07013.

City Directories Catalog

Municipal Year Book. Annual. $29.50. Contains a review of municipal events of the year, analyses of city operations, and a directory of city officials in all the States. International City Management Association, 1140 Connecticut Ave., N.W., Washington, D.C. 20036.

College Stores

College Stores, Directory of, 1980. Published every two years. $35. Lists about 3,500 college stores, geographically with manager's name, kinds of goods sold, college name, number of students, whether men, women or both, whether the store is college owned or privately owned. B. Klein Publications, P.O. Box 8503, Coral Springs, Fla. 33065.

Confectionery

Candy Buyers' Directory. Annually in January. $25. Lists candy manufacturers; importers and United States representatives, and confectionery brokers. The Manufacturing Confectionery Publishing Co., 175 Rock Rd., Glen Rock, N.J. 07452.

Construction Equipment

Construction Equipment Buyer's Guide, AED Edition. Annual. Summer, 1979. $20. Lists U.S. and Canadian construction equipment distributors and manufacturers; includes company names, names of key personnel, addresses, telephone numbers, branch locations, and lines handled or type of equipment produced. Associated Equipment Distributors, 615 West 22d St., Oak Brook, Ill. 60521.

Conventions and Trade Shows

Directory of Conventions. Annually in January. 1980. $60 a year, includes July supplement. Contains about 21,000 cross-indexed listings of annual events, gives dates, locations, names and addresses of executives in charge and type of group two years in advance. Successful Meetings Magazine, Directory Dept., 633 Third Ave., New York, N.Y. 10017.

Exhibits Schedule. Annually in January with supplement in July. 1980. $65 a year. Lists over 10,000 exhibits, trade shows, expositions, and fairs held throughout the world with dates given two years in advance. Listings run according to industrial classification covering all industries and professions; full information on dates, city, sponsoring organization, number of exhibits, attendance, gives title and address of executives in charge. Successful Meetings Magazine, Directory Dept., 633 Third Ave., New York, N.Y. 10017.

Dental Supply

Dental Supply Houses, Hayes Directory of. Annually in August. 1979-80 Edition. $33. Lists wholesalers of dental supplies and equipment with addresses, telephone numbers, financial standing and credit rating. Edward N. Hayes, Publisher, 4229 Birch St., Newport Beach, Calif. 92660.

Department Stores

Department Stores. Annually. 1979. $97. Lists headquarters addresses and branch locations, telephone numbers, number of stores, resident buying office, names of executives and buyers for independent and chain operators. Chain Store Guide Publications, 425 Park Ave., New York, N.Y. 10022.

Sheldon's Retail. Annual. 96th Edition, 1980. $60. Lists 1,700 large independent department stores, 446 large junior department store chains, 190 large independent and chain home-furnishing stores, 694 large independent women's specialty stores, and 270 large women's specialty store chains alphabetically by States and also major Canadian stores. Gives all department buyers with lines bought by each buyer, and addresses and telephone numbers of merchandise executives. Also gives all New York, Chicago, or Los Angeles buying offices, the number and locations of branch stores, and an index of all store/chain headquarters. Phelan, Sheldon & Marsar, Inc., 32 Union Sq., New York, N.Y. 10003.

Discount Stores

Discount Department Stores, Phelon's. 1980-81. $60. Gives buying headquarters for about 2,000 discount stores, chains, drug chains, catalog showrooms, major jobbers and wholesalers; lines of merchandise bought, buyers' names, leased departments, addresses of leasees, executives, number of stores and price range. Includes leased department operators with lines and buyers' names. Phelon, Sheldon & Marsar, Inc. 32 Union Sq., New York, N.Y. 10003.

Discount Department Stores. Annually. 1979. $102. Lists headquarters addresses, telephone number, location, square footage of each store, lines carried, leased operators, names of executives and buyers (includes Canada). Also special section on leased department operators. Chain Store Guide Publications, 425 Park Ave., New York, N.Y. 10022.

Drug Outlets—Retail and Wholesale

Drug Stores, Chain. Annually. 1979. $92. Lists headquarters address, telephone numbers, number and location of units, names of executives and buyers, wholesale drug distributors (includes Canada). Chain Store Guide Publications, 425 Park Ave., New York, N.Y. 10022.

Druggists—Wholesale. Annually in March. $14. Wholesale druggists in United States with full-line wholesalers specially indicated as taken from the *Hayes Druggist Directory*. Edward N. Hayes, Publisher, 4229 Birch St., Newport Beach, Calif. 92660.

Druggist Directory, Hayes. Annually in March. 1979. $80. Lists all the retail druggists in the United States, giving addresses, financial standing, and credit rating. Also publishes regional editions for one or more States. Computerized mailing labels available. Edward N. Hayes, Publisher, 4229 Birch St., Newport Beach, Calif. 92660.

Drug Topics Buyers' Guide. 1979. Gives information on wholesale drug companies, chain drug stores headquarters, department stores maintaining toilet goods or drug departments, manufacturers' sales agents, and discount houses operating toilet goods, cosmetic, proprietary medicine or prescription departments. Drug Topics, Medical Economics Company, Oradell, N.J. 07649.

National Wholesale Druggists' Association Membership and Executive Directory. Annually. Lists 800 American and foreign wholesalers and manufacturers of drugs and allied products. National Wholesale Druggists' Association, 670 White Plains Rd., Scarsdale, N.Y. 10583.

Electrical and Electronics

Electronic Industry Telephone Directory. Annual. 1980. $21.75, with order. Contains over 80,000 listings in White and Yellow Page sections. White Pages: name, address, and telephone number of manufacturers, representatives, distributors, government agencies, contracting agencies, and others. Yellow Pages: alphabetic listings by 600 basic product headings and 3,000 sub-product headings. Harris Publishing Co., 2057-2 Aurora Rd., Twinsburg, Oh. 44087.

Electrical Wholesale Distributors, Directory of. 1978. $265. Detailed information on almost 5,000 listings, including name, address, telephone number, branch and affiliated houses, products handled, etc. Electrical Wholesaling, McGraw-Hill Publications Co., Dept. ECCC Services, 1221 Avenue of the Americas, New York, N.Y. 10020.

Who's Who in Electronics, Including Electronic Representatives Directory. Annual. 1980. $52 postpaid. Detailed information (name, address, telephone number, products handled, territories, etc.) on 7,500 electronic manufacturers, 500 suppliers, 3,500 independent sales representatives, and 2,500 industrial electronic distributors and branch outlets. Purchasing index with 1,600 product breakdowns for buyers and purchasing agents. Harris Publishing Co., 2057-2 Aurora Rd., Twinsburg, Oh. 44087.

Electrical Utilities

Electrical Utilities, Electrical World Directory of. Annually in October. $125. Complete listings of electric utilities (investor-owned, municipal, and government agencies in U.S. and Canada) giving their addresses and personnel, and selected data on operations. McGraw-Hill Publications Co., Inc., 1221 Avenue of the Americas, New York, N.Y. 10020.

Embroidery

Embroidery Directory. Annually in October-November. 1979. $5. Alphabetical listing with addresses and telephone numbers of manufacturers, merchandisers, designers, cutters, bleacheries, yarn dealers, machine suppliers and other suppliers to the Schiffli lace and embroidery industry. Schiffli Lace and Embroidery Manufacturers Assn., Inc., 512 23d St., Union City, N.J. 07080.

Export and Import

American Register of Exporters and Importers. Annually. $50 prepaid. Includes over 30,000 importers and exporters and products handled. Klein Publications, P.O. Box 8503, Coral Springs, FL 33065.

Canadian Trade Directory, Fraser's. June. 1979. Write directly for price. Contains more than 12,000 product classifications with over 40,000 listings from 38,000 Canadian companies. Also lists over 10,000 foreign companies who have Canadian represenatives. Fraser's Trade Directories, 481 University Ave., Toronto, M5W 1A4, Ontario, Canada.

Flooring

Flooring Directory. Annually in November. 1979. $5. Reference to sources of supply giving their products and brand names, leading distributors, manufacturers' representatives and associations. Flooring Directory, Harcourt Brace Jovanovich Publications, 1 East First St., Duluth, Minn. 55802.

Food Dealers—Retail and Wholesale

Co-ops, Voluntary Chains and Wholesale Grocers. Annually. 1979. $86. Lists headquarters address, telephone number, number of accounts served, all branch operations, executives, buyers, annual sales volume (includes Canada and special "rack merchandiser" section). Chain Store Guide Publications, 425 Park Ave., New York, N.Y. 10022.

Food Brokers Association, National Directory of Members. Annually in July. Free to business firms writing on their letterhead. Arranged by States and cities, lists member food brokers in the United States and Europe, giving names and addresses, products they handle, and services they perform. National Food Brokers Association, 1916 M St., N.W., Washington, D.C. 20036.

Food Service Distributors. Annually. 1979. $82. Lists headquarters address, telephone number, number of accounts served, branch operations, executivs and buyers for distributors serving the restaurant and institutional market. Chain Store Guide Publications, 425 Park Ave., New York, N.Y. 10022.

Fresh Fruit and Vegetable Dealers, The Blue Book of. Credit Book and Marketing Guide. Semiannually in April and October. (Kept up to date by Weekly Credit Sheets and Monthly Supplements.) $225 a year. Lists shippers, buyers, jobbers, brokers, wholesale and retail grocers, importers and exporters in the United States and Canada that handle fresh fruits and vegetables in carlot and trucklot quantities. Also lists truckers, truck brokers of exempt perishables with "customs and rules" covering both produce trading and truck transportation. Produce Reporter Co., 315 West Wesley St., Wheaton, Ill. 60187.

Frozen Food Fact Book and Directory. Annual. 1980. $50 to nonmembers, free to Association members. Lists packers, distributors, suppliers, refrigerated warehouses, wholesalers, and brokers; includes names and adresses of each firm and their key officials. Contains statistical marketing data. National Frozen Food Association, Inc., P.O. Box 398, 1 Chocolate Ave., Hershey, Pa. 17033.

Grocery Register, Thomas'. Annual. 1979. 3 vols. $60/set. $45. Vol. 1 & 3 or Vol. 2 & 3. Volume 1: Lists supermarket chains, wholesalers, brokers, frozen food brokers, exporters, warehouses. Volume 2: Contains information on products and services; manufacturers, sources of supplies, importers. Volume 3: A-Z index of 56,000 companies. Also, a brand name/trademark index. Thomas Publishing Co., One Penn Plaza, New York, N.Y. 10001.

Quick Frozen Foods Directory of Wholesale Distributors. Biennually. Lists distributors of frozen foods. Quick Frozen Foods, P.O. Box 6128, Duluth, Minn. 55806.

Supermarket, Grocery & Convenience Store Chains. Annually. 1979. $97. Lists headquarters address, telephone number, location and type of unit, annual sales volume, executives and buyers, cartographic display of 267 Standard Metropolitan Statistical Areas (includes Canada). Chain Store Guide Publications, 425 Park Ave., New York, N.Y. 10022.

Tea and Coffee Buyers' Guide, Ukers' International. Biennial. 1978-1979. Includes revised and updated lists of participants in the tea and coffee and allied trades. The Tea and Coffee Trade Journal, 18-15 Francis Lewis Blvd., Whitestone, N.Y. 11357.

Gas Companies

Gas Companies, Brown's Directory of International. Annually in August. 1979. $95 plus $1.50 handling. Includes information on every known gas utility company and holding company worldwide. Brown's Directory, Harcourt Brace Jovanovich Publications, 1 East First St., Duluth, Minn. 55802.

LP/Gas. Annually in March. $5. Lists suppliers, supplies, and distributors. Harcourt Brace Jovanovich Publications, 1 East First St., Duluth, Minn. 55802.

Gift and Art

Gift and Decorative Accessory Buyers Directory. Annually in August. Included in subscription price of monthly magazine. *Gifts and Decorative Accessories*, $17 a year. Alphabetical listing of manufacturers, importers, jobbers, and representatives in the gift field. Listing of trade names, trademarks, brand names, and trade associations. Geyer-McAllister Publications, 51 Madison Ave., New York, N.Y. 10010.

Gift and Housewares Buyers, Natiowide Directory. Annually with semiannual supplement. $90. 1979-80. For 4,673 different types of retail firms lists store name, address, type of store, number of stores, names of president, merchandise managers, and buyers, etc., for giftwares and housewares. State editions also available. The Salesman's Guide, Inc., 1140 Broadway, New York, N.Y. 10001.

Gift and Tableware Reporter Directory Issue. Annual. August 1979. Alphabetical listing by category of each (manufacturer, representative, importer, distributor, or jobber). Includes identification of trade names and trademarks, and statistics for imports, manufacturing, and retail sales. Gift & Tableware Reporter, 1 Astor Place, New York, N.Y. 10036.

Gift Shop Directory. Biennially. Lists 900 gift shops in the U.S. Resourceful Research, Box 642, F.D.R. Station, New York, N.Y. 10022.

Hardware

Hardware Wholesalers Guide, National. Annual. 1980. $7.50. Alphabetical listing of manufacturers of hardware and building supplies. Where available, includes names and addresses of each manufacturer's representative showing territory covered. W.R.C. Smith Publishing Co., 1760 Peachtree Rd., N.W., Atlanta, Ga. 30357.

Hardware Wholesalers, Verified List of. 1979. Lists distributors (wholesale general hardware houses and hardware chain stores) serving the United States and Canada. Also lists manufacturers' agents handling hardware and allied lines. Chilton Co., Chilton Way, Radnor, Pa. 19089.

Home Furnishings

The Antiques Dealer. Annual Directory Issue. Issued in September as part of subscription. $12 a year. Lists major wholesale souces by geographical section. Includes special listing for show managers, auctioneers, appraisers, reproductions, supplies and services. Ebel-Doctorow Publications, Inc., 1115 Chilton Ave., Clifton, N.J. 07013.

Home Lighting & Accessories Suppliers. Directory issue. Semiannual. Issued in March and October as part of subscription. $12 a year. Lists names and addresses of suppliers to the lamp and lighting industry. Ebel-Doctorow Publications, Inc., 1115 Chilton Ave., Clifton, N.J. 07013.

Interior Decorator's Handbook. Semiannually. To trade only. $12 a year (2 issues). Published expressly for decorators and designers, interior decorating staff of department and furniture stores. Lists firms handling items used in interior decoration. Columbia Communications, Inc., 370 Lexington Ave., New York, N.Y. 10017.

Hospitals

American Hospital Association Guide to the Health Care Field. 1979 edition. Annually in August. $43.75. Lists registered hospitals, with selected data as well as listings of nursing homes, health related organizations, and professional schools. Includes international, national, regional, and state organizations and agencies. American Hospital Association, 840 North Lake Shore Dr., Chicago, Ill. 60611.

Hotels and Motels

Hotel-Motel Guide and Travel Atlas, Leahy's. Annually. 1979. $20. Lists more than 47,000 hotels and motels in the United States, Canada, and Mexico; includes room rates, number of rooms, and plan of operation. Also has extensive maps. American Hotel Register Co., 2775 Shermer Road, Northbrook, Ill. 60062.

Hotel Red Book. Annually in May. 1979. $25. Lists hotels in the United States, Canada, Caribbean, Mexico, Central and South America. Includes a section covering Europe, Asia, and Africa. Gives detailed information for each hotel. American Hotel Association Directory Corporation, 888 Seventh Ave., New York, N.Y. 10019.

Hotel Systems, Directory of. Annually in July. 1979. $15. Lists approximately 300 hotel systems in the Western Hemisphere. American Hotel Association Directory Corporation, 888 Seventh Ave., New York, N.Y. 10019.

Housewares

Housewares Reps Registry. Annually in May. 1979. (Included with subscription to *Housewares*, $8 a year.) Compilation of resources of the housewares trade, includes listing of their products, trade names, and a registry of manufacturers' representatives. Housewares Directory. Harcourt Brace Jovanovich, 1 East First St., Duluth, Minn. 55802.

Jewelry

The Jewelers Board of Trade Confidential Reference Book. Seminannually in March and September. Supplied only to members subscribing to the agency service. Write directly for prices. Lists manufacturers, importers, distributors, and retailers of jewelry; diamonds; precious, semiprecious, and imitation stones; watches; silverware; and kindred articles. Includes credit ratings. The Jewelers Board of Trade, 70 Catamore Blvd., East Providence, R.I. 02914.

Liquor

Wine and Spirits Wholesalers, Blue Book of. Annually in December. 1979. Lists names of member companies; includes parent house and branches, addresses, and names of managers. Also, has register of suppliers, and gives State liquor control administrators, national associations, and trade press directory. Wine and Spirits Wholesalers of America, Inc., 2033 M St., N.W., Suite 400, Washington, D.C. 20036.

Mailing List Houses

Mailing List Houses, Directory of. 1980. $35. Lists more than 3,000 list firms, brokers, compilers, and firms offering their own lists for rent; includes the specialities of each firm. Arranged geographically. B. Klein Publications, P.O. Box 8503, Coral Springs, Fla. 33065.

National Mailing-List Houses. (Small Business Bibliography 29). Free. Lists selected national mailing list houses; includes both general line and limited line houses. Small Business Administration, P.O. Box 15434, Ft. Worth, Tex. 76119.

Mail Order Businesses

Mail Order Business Directory. 1980. $45. Lists more than 6,300 names or mail order firms with buyers' names, and lines carried. Arranged geographically. B. Klein Publications, P.O. Box 8503, Coral Springs, Fla. 33065.

Manufacturers

MacRae's Blue Book. Annual, 1979. $69.25. In five volumes: Volume I—Corporate Index, lists company names and addresses alphabetically, with 60,000 branch and/or sales office telephone numbers. Volumes 2, 3, and 4—companies listed by 40,000 product classifications. Volume 5—company product catalogs. MacRae's Blue Book, 100 Shore Drive, Hinsdale, Ill. 60521.

Manufacturers, Thomas' Register of American. Annual. 1979. $85 post-paid. In 14 volumes. Volumes 1-7—products and services; suppliers of each product category grouped by State and city. Vols. 9-14—manufacturers' catalogs. Thomas Publishing Co., One Penn Plaza, New York, N.Y. 10001.

Manufacturers' Sales Representatives

Manufacturers & Agents National Association Directory of Members. Annually in July. $35 a copy—includes 12 monthly issues of *Agency Sales*. Contains individual listings of manufacturers' agents throughout the United States, Canada and several foreign countries. Listings crosss-referenced by alphabetical, geographical and product classification. Manufacturers' Agents National Association, P.O. Box 16878, Irvine, Calif. 92713.

Mass Merchandisers

Major Mass Market Merchandisers, Nationwide Directory of. (Excludes New York Metropolitan area). Annually. 1980. $55. Lists men's, women's, and children's wear buyers who buy for over 175,000 units—top discount, variety, supermarket and drug chains; factory outlet stores; leased department operators. The Salesman's Guide, Inc., 1140 Broadway, New York, N.Y. 10001.

Mass Retailing Merchandiser Buyers Directory. Annually. Lists 7,000 manufacturers, mass retail chains, manufacturers' representatives, jobbers and wholesalers serving the mass retailing field. Merchandiser Publishing Co., Inc., 222 West Adams, Chicago, Ill. 60606.

Metalworking

Metalworking Directory, Dun & Bradstreet. Annually in May. Published in one national and five sectional editions. 1979. Retail price available upon request. Lists about 44,000 metalworking and metal producing plants with 20 or more production employees. Arranged in four sections: geographically, line of business, alphabetically, and statistical courts summary. Marketing Services Division, Dun & Bradstreet, Inc., 99 Church St., New York, N.Y. 10007.

Military Market

Buyers' Guide. Annually. 1979. $2.50. Lists suppliers names and addresses, military representatives and civilian brokerage firms that specialize in serving military stores. Military Market, 475 School St., S.W., Washington, D.C. 20024.

Non-Food Products

Non-Food Buyers, National Directory of. Annually. Alpha-geographical listing of 9,000 buyers of non-food merchandise for over 336,000 outlets. United Publishing Co., 1372 Peachtree St., N.E., Atlanta, Ga. 30309.

Paper Products

Sources of Supply Buyers' Guide. 1980. $40. Lists mills and converters of paper, film, foil and allied products, and paper merchants in the United States alphabetically with addresses, principal personnel, and products manufactured. Also lists trade associations, brand names, and manufacturers' representatives. Advertisers and Publishers Service, Inc., P.O. Drawer 795, 300 N. Prospect Ave., Park Ridge, Ill. 60068.

Physicians and Medical Supply Houses

Medical Directory, American. 27th Ed. 1979. Price U.S.A., possessions, Canada, and Mexico, $225 for five volumes. Volumes 1-4 gives complete information about all physicians in the United States and possessions—alphabetical and geographical listings. Volume 5—Directory of Women Physicians. American Medical Association, 535 Noth Dearborn St., Chicago, Ill. 60610.

Physician and Hospital Supply Houses, Hayes' Directory of. Annually in August. 1979-80. $44. Listings of 1,850 U.S. wholesalers doing business in physician, hospital and surgical supplies and equipment; includes addresses, telephone numbers, financial standing, and credit ratings. Edward N. Hayes, Publisher, 4229 Birch St., Newport Beach, Calif. 92660.

Plumbing

Manufacturers' Representatives, Directory of. Annually as a special section of the February issue of *The Wholesaler* magazine, currently $20 a copy. . . 1980 will be $25. Write directly for subscription price. Lists representatives of manufacturers selling plumbing, heating and cooling equipment, components, tools, and related products, to this industry through wholesaler channels with detailed information on each. Scott Periodicals Corp., 135 Addison Avenue, Elmhurst, Ill. 60126.

Premium Sources

Premium and Incentive Buyers, Directory of. Annual in September. 1980. $110. Lists over 16,000 executives for 12,000 firms with title, telephone number, address, and merchandise executives desire to buy in the premium, incentive and travel fields. The Salesman's Guide, 1140 Broadway, New York, N.Y. 10001.

Incentive Marketing/Incorporating Incentive Travel: Supply Sources Directory. Annual in January. $2 a copy. Contains classified directory of suppliers, and list of manufacturers' representatives serving the premium field. Also, lists associations and clubs, and trade shows. Incentive Marketing, 633 Third Ave., New York, N.Y. 10017.

Purchasing, Government

U.S. Government Purchasing and Sales Directory. Book by Small Business Administration. Sept. 1977. Designed to help small business receive an equitable share of Government contracts. Lists types of purchases for both military and civilian needs, catalogs procurement officers by State. Lists SBA regional and branch offices. Order from Superintendent of Documents, U.S. Government Printing Office, Washington, D.C. 20402.

Refrigeration and Air-Conditioning

Air Conditioning, Heating & Refrigeration News. Dec. 31, 1979 issue, $10 a copy. Lists alphabetically and by products, the names of refrigeration, heating and air-conditioning manufacturers, trade names, wholesalers, and associations in the United States. Business News Publishing Co., P.O. Box 2600, Troy, Mich. 48084.

Air-Conditioning & Refrigeration Wholesalers Directory. Annually. $5. Lists alphabetically 950 member air-conditioning and refrigeration wholesalers with their addresses, telephone numbers, and official representatives by region, state, and city. Air-conditioning and Refrigeration Wholesalers, 22371 Newman Ave., Dearborn, Mich., 48124.

Restaurants

Restaurant Operators. (Chain). Annually, 1979. $94. Lists headquarters address, telephone number, number and location of units, trade names used, whether unit is company-operated or franchised, executives and buyers, annual sales volume for chains of restaurants, cafeterias, drive-ins, hotel and motel food operators, industrial caterers, etc. Chain Store Guide Publications, 425 Park Ave., New York, N.Y. 10022.

Roofing and Siding

RSI Trade Directory. Annually in April. 1979. $5 a copy or with subscription ($9 a year in U.S.A.) to *Roof Siding and Insulation*, monthly. Has listing guide to products and equipment manufacturers, jobbers and distributors, and associations in the roofing, siding, and home improvement industries. RSI Directory, Harcourt Brace Jovanovich Publications, 1 East First St., Duluth, Minn. 55802.

Selling, Direct

Direct Selling Companies/1979-80, A Supplier's Guide to. $100 ($25 for members). Information supplied by member companies of the Direct Selling Association includes names of contact persons, company product line, method of distribution, etc. Direct Selling Association, 1730 M St., N.W., Washington, D.C. 20036.

Direct Selling Directory. Annually in February issue of *Special Salesman and Business Opportunities Magazine*. 1979. $1 a copy. Alphabetical listing of name and address under product and service classifications of specialty sales firms and their products. Specialty Salesman, 307 North Michigan Ave., Chicago, Ill. 60601.

Who's Who in Direct Selling. Membership roster of the Direct Selling Association. No charge for single copies. Active members classified by type of product or service. Alphabetical listing gives name, address and telephone of firm, along with managing official. Direct Selling Association, 1730 M St., N.W., Washington, D.C. 20036.

Shoes

Chain Shoe Stores Directory. Lists chain shoe stores at their headquarters including officers, buyers, lines carried, trading names of stores, number of operating units. The Rumpf Publishing Co., Division of Nickerson & Collins Co., 1800 Oakton St., Des Plaines, Ill. 60018.

Shopping Centers

Shopping Centers in the United States and Canada, Directory of. Alphabetical listing of 16,000 American and Canadian shopping centers, location, owner/developer, manager, physical plant (number of stores, square feet), and leasing agent. National Research Bureau, Inc., 424 North Third St., Burlington, Iowa 52601.

Specialty Stores

Women's Specialty Stores, Phelon's. 7th Edition, 1980-81. $60. Lists over 18,000 women's apparel and accessory shops with store headquarters name and address, number of shops operated, New York City buying headquarters or representatives, lines of merchandise bought and sold, name of principal and buyers, store size and price range. Phelon, Sheldon, & Marsar, Inc. 32 Union Sq., New York, N.Y. 10003.

Sporting Goods

Sporting Goods Buyers, Nationwide Directory of. 1979-80. $75. Including semi-annual supplements. Lists over 4,500 top retail stores (23 different types) with names of buyers and executives, for all types of sporting goods, athletic apparel, and athletic footwear, hunting and fishing, and outdoor equipment. The Salesman's Guide, Inc., 1140 Broadway, New York, N.Y. 10001.

The Sporting Goods Register. (Including jobbers, manufacturers' representatives and importers). Annual. 1980. $20. Geographical listing of firms (name, address, buyers, type of goods sold, etc.) doing wholesale business in sporting goods merchandise and equipment. Similar data for Canadian firms. Alphabetical grouping of manufacturers' representatives and importers. The Sporting Goods Dealer, 1212 North Lindbergh Blvd., St. Louis, Mo. 63132.

The Sporting Goods Dealer's Directory. Annual. 1980. $5 a copy. Lists about 5,000 manufacturers and suppliers. Also includes names of manufacturers' agents, wholesalers and sporting goods associations and governing bodies of sports. The Sporting Goods Dealer, 1212 North Lindbergh Blvd., St. Louis, Mo. 63132.

Trailering Parks

Campground Directory, Woodall's North American/Canadian Edition. Annually. 1980. $8.95. Lists and star rates public and private campgrounds in North American continent alphabetically by town with location and description of facilities. Also lists more than 1,000 RV service locations. Regional editions available. Woodall Publishing Company, 500 Hyacinth Place, Highland Park, Ill. 60035.

Trucking

Trinc's Blue Book of the Trucking Industry and Trinc's Five Year Red Book. Retail price upon request. Together these two directories furnish comprehensive statistics on the trucking industry and individual truckers represented by about 3,500 Class I and Class II U.S. motor carriers of property. TRINC Transportation Consultants, P.O. Box 23091, Washington, D.C. 20024.

Variety Stores

General Merchandise, Variety and Junior Department Stores. 1979. $86. Lists headquarters address, telephone number, number of units and locations, executives and buyers (includes Canada). Chain Store Guide Publications, 425 Park Ave., New York, N.Y. 10022.

Warehouses

Distribution Services, Guide to. Annually in July. $15. Lists leading public warehouses in U.S. and Canada, as well as major truck lines, airlines, steamship lines, liquid and dry bulk terminals, material handling equipment suppliers, ports of the world and railroad piggyback services and routes. Distribution Magazine, Chilton Way, Radnor, Pa. 19089.

Public Refrigerated Warehouses, Directory of. Annually. Free to concerns in perishable food business. Geographical listing of over 750 public refrigerated warehouse members. International Association of Refrigerated Warehouses, 7315 Wisconsin Ave., N.W., Washington, D.C. 20014.

Stationers

Wholesale Stationers' Association Membership Roster. Annually. $15. Alphabetical listing by company of over 300 wholesaler companies. Wholesale Stationers' Assn., 3166 Des Plaines Ave., Des Plaines, Ill. 60018.

Textiles

Textile Blue Book, Davison's. Annual. 1979. $50 postpaid. Contains over 18,000 separate company listings (name, address, etc.) for U.S. and Canada. Firms included are cotton, wool, synthetic mills, knitting mills, cordage, twine, and duck manufacturers, dry goods, commission merchants, converters, yarn dealers, cordage manufacturers' agents, wool dealers and merchants, cotton merchants, exporters, brokers, and others. Davison Publishing Co., P.O. Drawer 477, Ridgewood, N.J. 07451.

Toys & Novelties

Toys, Hobbies & Crafts Directory. Annually in June. 1979. $5. Lists manufacturers, products, trade names, suppliers to manufacturers, suppliers products, character licensors, manufacturers' representatives, toy trade associations, and trade show managements. Toys Directory, Harcourt Brace Jovanovich Publication, 1 East First St., Duluth, Minn. 55802.

Wholesalers and Manufacturers, Directory of. Contains information on wholesalers, manufacturers, manufacturers' representatives of toys, games, hobby, art, school, party, and office supply products. Toy Wholesalers' Association of America, 1514 Elmwood Ave., Evanston, Ill. 60201.

Single copies of **Small Business Bibliographies** are available free from SBA, P.O. Box 15434, Ft. Worth, TX 76119. Information presented is necessarily selective and no slight is intended toward material not mentioned. **Bibliographies** may be reprinted but not used to indicate approval or disapproval by this Agency of any private organization, product, or service. Credit to the U.S. Small Business Administration will be appreciated if this **Bibliography** is reproduced. **Use of funds for printing this publication has been approved by the Director, Office of Management and Budget, through June 30, 1985.**

☆ U.S. GOVERNMENT PRINTING OFFICE: 1983-380-942:201

INDEX

Accounting Corporation of America, 49
Advertising, 113
   characteristics of, 164
   defined, 164
   functions of, 164
   limitations of, 165
   media comparison, 182
   sources of assistance, 170
Advertising specialties, 175
Almanac of Business & Industrial Fi, 49

Bacon's Publicity Checkers, 49
Brochures, 118
   design of, 123
   samples of, 130
   steps in preparation of, 120
Budget, 197
   for printed material, 122
Bureau of Business Research, 49
Bureau of Census, 46
Business cards, 118
Business Periodicals Index, 48

Census of Population and Housing, 50
Channel of distribution, 204
Color, 126
Company brochure, 118
Competition, 52
Congressional Yellow Book, 47
Consumer information, 51
Consumer magazines, 172
Consumer needs, 29
Consumer perception, 192
Consumer research, 52
Convenience retailer, 67
Copywriting, 108
   rules for, 123
Cost per thousand (CPM), 171
County Business Patterns, 47
County and City Data Book, 51
Customer, 62, 190
   analysis of, 191
   referrals by, 84
   spending patterns of, 191
Customer base, 63, 78

Demographics, 27
Directories, 169
Direct sales, 204
Displays, 174
Dun & Bradstreet, Inc., 49

Encyclopedia of Associations, 44

Federal Statistical Directory, 46
Federal Yellow Book, 47
Four Ps, 34. *See also* Marketing mix

Geography, 27

Image, 4, 87, 97
   creation of, 99
   elements of, 88
   human elements of, 96
   reinforcement of, 100
Independent agent, 205
Interviews, 55
   personal, 59
   telephone, 59

Layout, 126
Location, 63
   buy or lease decision, 66
   factors to consider, 64
   inspection of, 76
   primary and secondary research, 67
   rating of, 66
Logo, 114
   samples of, 115

Mail, 80
Mailing lists, 51
Mailings, 57
Mail survey, 56
Maps, 72
Market, 5
   characteristics of, 25
   flowchart of, 36
   sources of information for, 229
Market area, 68
Marketing, 12

Marketing (*Continued*)
   six basic concepts of, 11
Marketing budget, how to organize, 197
Marketing Information Guide, 51
Marketing mix, 33, 168
   defined, 34
Marketing plan, 185
Market mix, 192
   example of, 35
   planning of, 195
   variables of, 34
Marketplace, 2, 11
Market plan:
   budget form, 201
   cost of, 197
   costing components for, 199
   implementation of, 198
   implementation plan, 194
   objectives of, 188
   sample of, 209
   strategies for, 188
Market planning, 5
Market plan outline, 8, 186
Market research, 51
   analysis and interpretation, 42
   data collection, 40
   guide to, 44
   importance of, 38
   methodology of, 40
   problem definition, 39
   report format, 42
   steps in, 39
   strategic decisions, 38
   strategic information data, 41
   tactical decisions, 38
   tactical information data, 41
Market segment, 2, 5, 11
   by benefits, 27
   characteristic matrix, 30
   dimensions of, 29, 31
   dimension worksheet, 32
   profile of, 30
Market segmentation:
   benefits of, 32
   defined, 27
   how done, 27, 31
   variables of, 28
   how done, 31
   variables of, 28
Market size, 13
Media, 83
   different types, 83
Media planning, 165
   benefit comparison, 169
   reference sources for, 225
Media planning questionnaire, 166

National Technical Information Serv, 47
NCR Corporation, 49
NCR Expenses in Retailing, 49
Networking, 85

Newspapers, 171
News release, 108
   sample format, 108
   see also Press release

Objectives of customers, 26
Objects of market, categories for
      classification, 24
Occasions of market, 24
Occupants of market, 24
Operations of buying, 26
Organization of market, 24
Outdoor advertising, 172
   comparison of types, 173
Outlets of marketing, 26
Outposts of marketing, 26

Package design, 127
   related to communication, 128
Packaging trends, 128
Painted bulletins, 172
Pedestrian traffic count, 75, 78
Persuasion, 4
Place, 168, 194
   related to image, 92
Point of purchase, 175
Population, 69
Position, 168
Posters, 172
Press Information Questionnaire (P.I.Q.), 105, 106
Press kit, 111
Press release, 104
   information forms for, 241
   sample of, 109
   writing of, 106
   see also News release
Price, 168, 192
   adjustments to, 202
   related to image, 94
Pricing questionnaire, 202
Pricing strategies, 203
Primary research, 55
   definition of, 43
Printed material, 122
Printing, 126
Product, 91
Product brochure, 119
Product differentiation, 202
Product life cycle, 201
Product pricing, 200
Profile and products form, 8
Promotion, 193
   push or pull, 194
   related to image, 95
Psychographics, 27
Public Affairs Information Service, 48
Publicity, 102
Public relations, 101

Quantity breaks, 127

INDEX

Questionnaire, 56
    analysis of data, 60
    for customer use, 98
    planning for, 58
    processing and using data, 59
    rules for, 57
    tabulation, 60
    for vendor use, 99

Radio advertising, 173
Referrals, 85
Retailers, 205
    types of, 67
RMA Annual Statement Studies, 49
Robert Morris Associates, 49

Sales, personal meetings, 82
Sales forecasting, use with primary research, 55
Sales objectives, 189
Sampling size, 55
Sampling techniques, 55
Secondary research, 45, 50
    definition of, 43
    information sources, 52
Seminars, 180
Shopping retailer, 67
Site evaluation, 71
Small Business Barometer, 49
Sources of State Information, 48
Special promotions, 175
Specialty retailer, 67
Spectaculars, 172
Standard Rate & Data Service, 51

State Industrial Directories, 48
Superintendent of Documents, 44
Survey of Current Business, 46

Target market, 2, 11, 33
    how to choose, 33
    identification of, 33
    related to image, 90
Taxable Sales in California, 48
Telephone sales, 81, 181, 184
Telephone survey, 56
Television, 174
Terms of payment, 79
Timing, 3
T.I.P. marketing model, 2, 3, 11, 12
Trade magazines, 171. *See also* Trade publications
Trade publications, 111. *See also* Trade magazines
Trade publications, 171
Trade shows, 80, 176
    booths for, 178
    planning for, 177
    sales people for, 180
Trading area, 67
Traffic statistics, 72
Transit advertising, 172
Typesetting, 126

U.S. Industrial Outlook, 13, 46

Word of mouth, 79
Workbook approach, 1

Yellow pages, 72, 169

DUE

DEC 0

HIGHSMITH #45230

Printed in USA